Real Lace

REAL LACE

AMERICA'S IRISH RICH

Stephen Birmingham

HARPER & ROW, PUBLISHERS

*New York, Evanston,
San Francisco, London*

FIRST EDITION

Designed by Patricia Dunbar

Library of Congress Cataloging in Publication Data

Birmingham, Stephen.
   Real lace: America's Irish rich.
     1. Irish in the United States—Biography.
2. United States—Social life and customs. 3. Upper classes—United States.
I. Title.
E184.I6B57   917.3'06'9162 [B]   73-4061
ISBN 0-06-010336-1

For my father,
Thomas J. Birmingham

Codla saimh dhiubh agus slan libh

CONTENTS

A section of photographs follows page 130.

FOREWORD

I grew up in a small New England city where Irish Catholics, or those of "Irish extraction," were not asked to join the country club, and so—being of that extraction myself—I have long been aware of the strong, and at the same time vulnerable, position of the Irish in American life. But more than my own personal experiences and sentiments have gone into the production of this book, and there are a number of people whom I would like to thank for their assistance, insights, impressions, memories, and materials. Most particularly I am grateful to Mr. John Murray Cuddihy of New York for access to his voluminous data on the Murray-Cuddihy-Bradley-McDonnell family complex, as well as for his own considerable researches on the general topic of the Irish in America. I am also indebted to Mr. Cuddihy's wife, Harriet De Haven Cuddihy, for help as well as for hospitality, nor should I overlook the two older Cuddihy children, Heidi and John, who— despite the fact that they have a perfect attendance record at their

Episcopalian Sunday school classes at St. Thomas's—helped make the many hours I spent in the Cuddihy household researching their Irish Catholic antecedents peaceful and productive.

I am also deeply grateful to Mr. Cuddihy's sister, Mary Jane Cuddihy MacGuire of Ste. Agathe, Quebec, for photographs, family recollections, and guidance in both Church and family matters, and I should also thank the Cuddihys' mother, Mrs. H. Lester Cuddihy, for her help and support. Mrs. Charlotte McDonnell Harris of New York was of great assistance with McDonnell family anecdotes, and Mr. John F. Murray, Jr. of Wainscott, New York, was similarly helpful in terms of his family, the Murrays.

Because many of the Irish families were large, the list of people who have helped me with this book is long, but there are certain individuals to whom I owe a special word of thanks. I would like to thank Mr. and Mrs. Donald W. Marshall of Bedford Hills, New York; Mrs. Alison Murray of Weston, Connecticut; Mr. Clendenin J. Ryan III of Far Hills, New Jersey; Father Regis Ryan, S.J., Mr. J. Patrick Lannan, Miss Mary Pritchard, Miss Martha Butler, Miss Margaret Thalken, Mrs. Marianne Strong, and Miss Julia McCarthy, all of New York, and the Hon. John D. J. Moore of Dublin who, from the outset, took a lively interest in, and encouraged, this project. I would also like to thank Mr. Joseph T. P. Sullivan, President-General of the American Irish Historical Society, for his interest and help. I am grateful to Mrs. Carol Buckley Learsy of New York for permission to quote from letters and memoranda of her late father, William F. Buckley, Sr.; to Father Robert J. Gannon, S.J., for permission to quote from the diaries and letters of the late Francis Cardinal Spellman; and to Mr. William G. Post of Rye, New York, for permission to quote a letter from his grandmother, Emily Post.

A number of authors proved important sources for this book, including Father Gannon with his biography of Cardinal Spellman; M. R. Werner and John Starr, whose *Teapot Dome* provided excellent insights into the career of Edward L. Doheny; and L. Clayton Dubois, whose revealing analysis of the Buckley family was published in the *New York Times Magazine*. Cecil Woodham-Smith's *The Great Hunger* offers probably the best account of the Irish potato famine, and John Brooks's *Once in Golconda* presents by far the most thorough and accurate version of the rise and fall of Allan A. Ryan.

At Harper & Row, I am grateful to my editors, Cass Canfield, Sr. and Mrs. Frances Lindley, for their help and encouragement. As always, I am indebted to my literary agent, Carol Brandt, for guiding the project throughout with cool precision.

And yet, while all of the above have contributed greatly to my book, I alone must be held accountable for any shortcomings or inaccuracies which may appear.

S.B.

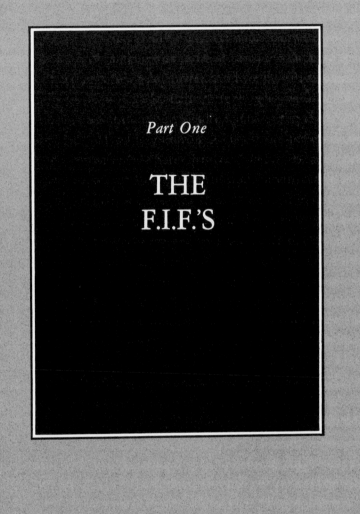

Part One

THE
F.I.F.'S

Chapter 1

"WHAT HAPPENED?"

n an unseasonably warm early spring evening, Thursday, March 12, 1970, strollers past the tall glass windows of McDonnell & Company's main uptown office at 250 Park Avenue were presented with a curious sight. It was as though, someone commented, burglars had rifled the elegantly decorated offices of this, one of New York's oldest and most respected brokerage houses. Drawers of filing cabinets and secretaries' desks hung open, with papers cascading out and strewn about the floor, wastebaskets were overturned disgorging their contents, and lampshades were standing at rakish angles. New Yorkers in the neighborhood had become accustomed, over the years of the firm's tenancy at that prestigious address, to the normally tidy and ordered appearance of the offices behind the big panes of glass. Now, in their dishevelment, the offices looked as if they had been hastily, even angrily, vacated by the entire McDonnell & Company staff. "What's happening here?" one puzzled spectator asked.

The next morning, the *New York Times* provided the ominous answer. The staff had indeed left hurriedly and in some distress the night before because, after sixty-five years in business, McDonnell & Company and its chairman and chief executive officer, T. Murray McDonnell, had, as a result of a spiraling and tangled series of fiscal problems that had at last become insoluble, announced its financial collapse, with over $20 million in debts.

The firm's troubles, it seemed, were the immediate result of the 1969–1970 stock market decline, the so-called Nixon Recession. McDonnell & Company had become the first major Wall Street house to fall victim to this decline (there would soon be a number of other firms to go under). But the firm's woes appeared to extend much further than this. It was soon announced that Murray McDonnell himself was being singlehandedly held responsible for his company's demise, and in a sharply worded statement the New York Stock Exchange accused McDonnell of "failure to provide adequate supervision and control, and . . . violation of capital, bookkeeping and segregation rules." The Exchange noted that, in an offer of settlement, "Mr. McDonnell consented to a suspension as a registered representative for a period of 12 months. . . . In addition, Mr. McDonnell further consented to an imposition of a penalty that he will not make application for, nor be granted, the position of an allied member or member of the Exchange or any supervisory position with any member or members of the Exchange." This latter punishment, a particularly harsh one, in effect permanently barred Murray McDonnell from ever again becoming an officer or partner of a Big Board member firm—for the rest of his natural life.

Reached by telephone at his home in Peapack, New Jersey, Murray McDonnell said that the suspension from working as a registered representative (which is the formal title for a securities salesman) was "the only thing I think is tough." It seemed an oddly lighthearted dismissal of the situation. And yet, a few days later, Murray McDonnell, looking shaken and tired, was seen emerging from the residence of Terence Cardinal Cooke behind St. Patrick's Cathedral on Madison Avenue, after a conference with the Cardinal. Murray McDonnell was also the chief financial adviser for the Archdiocese of New York, and had for a number of years been managing the quite considerable Archdiocesan funds.

The 1970 failure of McDonnell & Company was more than a gloomy bellwether of worse Wall Street days to come, and more than a personal tragedy and fall from grace of the son of the founder of the company. It was also a stunning blow to a vast, and vastly scattered, family—a blow that would set brothers against sisters, mothers against sons. And it seemed like the dismal final chapter to one of the most brilliant business and social success stories in America, which had been the rise to enormous prominence of the huge and intricately interrelated McDonnell-Murray-Cuddihy families, who, in their heyday, helped make Southampton, Long Island, a fashionable summer resort, and who had often set that community on its ear—such as the time pretty Mary Jane Cuddihy dated Errol Flynn. At one point, the McDonnell apartment at 910 Fifth Avenue had been the largest single apartment in New York, a duplex and a simplex thrown together to accommodate the fourteen children of Mr. and Mrs. James Francis McDonnell (the former Anna Murray). When the dining room chandelier in that apartment crashed to the table one day, the Home Insurance Company paid a $100,000 claim. In Southampton, the McDonnell summer house had required a staff of sixteen servants —or exactly one for each member of the family—and, what with all the Murray and Cuddihy cousins in the family compound, there were never less than twenty for Sunday dinner, with four huge turkeys in the oven to feed them. There were yachts, Daimlers, racing stables, a polo field. In happier days in Peapack, Murray McDonnell had had, as his house guests, the likes of Mrs. Jacqueline Kennedy Onassis and her children, in keeping with

5

Mrs. Onassis's policy of camouflaging her own children with hordes of others so that photographers had difficulty telling one child from another.

The Murrays, McDonnells, and Cuddihys had, furthermore, in just three generations' time, not only managed to decorate voluminously the pages of the *Social Register* in various American cities, but they had also managed to ally themselves, through marriage, to a number of other American and international fortunes. Murray McDonnell's sister Anne, for example, had married Henry Ford II in what had been described at the time as "The Wedding of the Century." A first cousin, Jeanne, had eloped with Alfred Gwynne Vanderbilt, and another married a Byers from Pittsburgh, related to Mellons. A niece had been married to the Greek shipping tycoon, Stavros Niarchos, and another to an Italian named Giancarlo Uzielli. The relationships became so mind-boggling that when, not long ago, one of Murray McDonnell's sisters was asked to list her own brothers and sisters in the order of their ages, she could not do so—though her mother, Anna Murray McDonnell, remembers the names and birthdays of all her sixty-five grandchildren and six great-grandchildren. When, in 1957, one of Grandpa Thomas E. Murray's heirs petitioned, through the Kings County Court in Brooklyn, for a change in the trust set up by his grandfather, all the possible recipients of funds from the trust had to be notified. A legal document addressed to a total of 152* different people had to be composed—people with names such as Cooley, Murphy, Hennessy, Conniff, Sullivan, Harris, MacGuire, Cavanagh, Sheridan, as well as Murray, McDonnell, Cuddihy, Ford, Vanderbilt, Niarchos, and Uzielli, and including several Jesuit priests and at least one Sacred Heart nun. Lawyers had to travel to such places as San Francisco and Beirut to track down signatures.

And now, with the liquidation of McDonnell & Company, and

* A later petition, in 1966, named 241 beneficiaries.

6

family affairs in a shambles, it seemed that, in just three generations, a whole segment of this dynasty had fallen by the wayside. One episode in the glittering and complicated saga of the American Catholic rich had ended—or, as one of Murray McDonnell's sisters, Charlotte McDonnell Harris, put it dryly at the time, "The Catholic *ex*-rich—thanks to my brother."

What did happen? It is a story that begins, just a little more than a century ago, in the bogs and narrow country lanes of Ireland.

Chapter 2

IN THE BEGINNING

The little town of Drumlish (population 212), County Longford, some fifty miles northwest of Dublin, is a hamlet which contains, in addition to a cluster of stained and woebegone houses all along a single street, a trim little church, a parish house, a greengrocer's shop, and a pub. A few farms dot the surrounding hills, but that is all. There is only one visible beggar in the town—an aging crone in a black shawl, who wanders up and down the street with hand outstretched to the occasional tourist or passer-by, seeking funds, she says, to send to ailing relatives across the county. But otherwise the atmosphere of Drumlish is one of hard and steady poverty.

There are few people in the town today who remember the McDonnells. One man pauses, scratches his head under his gray cap and says, "Yes, there was a McDonnell who had a farm, years ago, on the hill up there. Decent folk, the McDonnells were. But they're all gone now." Other villagers associate the name with

8

great wealth in America, but look startled when told that, until a few years ago, one American McDonnell was married to a man named Henry Ford. "Gotten very fancy, have they?" they ask. And there is a story told in the local pub—possibly apocryphal, as are so many stories told in this land of dreamers and tellers of tall tales—of a rich McDonnell who came back, a long time ago, to visit relatives and old friends in Ireland. At the pub, this McDonnell encountered an old schoolmate from boyhood days, recognized him, clapped the fellow on the back, and said, "Paddy, I remember in the third grade when you came to school in your first pair of shoes!" Slyly the Drumlisher eyed the American for a moment and said, "Yes, and I remember you asking me what they were."

It is true that in the 1940's the late James Francis McDonnell, at that point a millionaire, who headed the Wall Street firm of McDonnell & Company with assets in the tens of millions, took his wife and tribe of fourteen children back to Ireland to inspect the McDonnell roots in Drumlish. The family and their retinue of servants took over a huge section of First Class on the old *Queen Elizabeth* and, as the children recall it, when the family got to Dublin, they managed to "demolish" a good deal of the fashionable Gresham Hotel. There was a great flurry of interest in the Dublin press about the visitors, and the McDonnell children amused themselves by granting interviews and giving out fanciful accounts to the reporters, with exaggerated descriptions of the family yachts, polo ponies, houses, and motorcars. Then James Francis McDonnell engaged a fleet of Daimlers with chauffeurs to take the family to Drumlish, which none of them had ever seen. The visit was, in many ways, a disappointment, for Drumlish was no more prepossessing then than it is today. But the children visited the grocery store and were treated to lemon squashes, and the villagers sang songs and danced jigs for the assembled family, at the patriarch's request. Outside, in the street, a little boy was playing in the dust and the senior McDonnell stepped across to the lad

9

and asked him his name. "Peter McDonnell, sir!" the boy replied. Delighted that he had found some sort of relative, James Francis McDonnell stepped over to his Daimler, and returned with a sackful of copper pennies, which he presented to the owl-eyed child.

That Peter McDonnell, along with all the others, is gone from Drumlish now. But the first McDonnell of the Drumlish clan was also a Peter, who emigrated to New York at some point between 1845 and 1855—no one is quite sure of the year, for family records were sketchily kept—to escape the great potato famine that ravaged the face of Ireland throughout that decade, and from which the country has never really recovered.

"What hope is there for a nation that lives on potatoes!" a nineteenth-century English official once wrote. And yet, for centuries, potatoes had been Ireland's only hope. One estimate has placed the population of Ireland in 1791 at 4,753,000. In the next fifty years, some 1,750,000 Irishmen departed for America, and yet, despite this emigration, the Irish census of 1841 revealed that the population of the tiny country had jumped to at least 8,175,-000. With more than eight million mouths to feed, in a land that had been condemned by British colonial rule to agriculture, and forbidden to compete in world commerce or industry, the only answer had been to subdivide the landscape into tiny farms, and the only crop that could be raised with any profit at all on these farms was the humble potato. An acre and a half of land, for example, could provide a family of five or six with food for a year, while to grow the equivalent amount of corn or grain would take an acreage four to six times as large. The potato, furthermore, was ideally suited for growth in the moist soil of Ireland. Only a spade was needed to grow potatoes. Trenches were dug and beds were made, and potato sets were laid out, and earthed up from the trenches. When the shoots appeared, they were earthed up again. Potatoes could also be grown on hillsides too steep to be plowed for any other crop, and, as the population grew through the early

1800's, potato fields extended up the mountain slopes. Best of all, the potato was an extraordinarily useful food. It could be cooked in a variety of ways, it could be ground into flour, it produced fat and healthy children, and one did not tire of its taste. Chickens, pigs, and cattle thrived on it. His potato crop, in fact, solved nearly every Irishman's need—provided it did not fail.

And yet the potato is also one of the most unstable of crops. In Ireland, potatoes were packed in barrels which were buried in pits, but still they did not keep well and could not be stored from one potato season to the next. Each year, some two and a half million Irishmen more or less starved during the summer months when the old potatoes were gone and the new ones had yet to come in. June, July, and August were therefore known as "meal months," when there was danger that the potatoes would run out and meal would have to be eaten instead—bought at outrageous prices or on credit from the hated "gombeenman," or the village usurer.

By the early 1840's the Irish had grown used to the possibility of potato-crop failure, and regarded the chances of its occurring as philosophically as one might view a change in the weather. In 1728 there was reported "such a great scarcity that on the 26th of February there was a great rising of the populace of Cork." In 1739 the crop was reported "entirely destroyed," and the following year another "entire failure" was recorded. There had been a failure in 1770, and another "general failure" in 1800. In 1807 half the Irish potato crop was lost through frost, and in 1821, and again in 1822, the potato failed completely in Munster and Connaught and "distress horrible beyond description" was reported in and around Skibbereen. The years 1830 and 1831 were ones of failure in Counties Mayo, Donegal, and Galway, and, with gong-like regularity, the years 1832, 1833, 1834, and 1836 produced failures in a large number of areas from "dry rot and curl." In 1835 the entire potato crop of Ulster was lost, and the two years following brought "extensive" failures throughout the country.

In 1839 there was again "universal failure" from Bantry Bay to Lough Swilly, and 1841 and 1844 were also disastrous years. There was, therefore, no real reason to suppose that 1845 would be any worse or any better. And yet by early July of that year the outlook was exceptionally bright. The weather had been perfect—hot, sunny, and dry, and on July 23 the *Freeman's Journal* was able to say with confidence, "The poor man's property, the potato crop was never before so large and at the same time so abundant." Old potatoes—"even at this advanced season"—were coming into the market and were of excellent quality, and fine new potatoes were being dug. In London, the *Times* reported that "an early and productive harvest was everywhere expected" in Ireland. The first ominous note appeared in August, from the potato fields of the Isle of Wight, where "a blight of unusual character" appeared to have struck the summer crop. It was indeed unusual. Freshly dug potatoes appeared perfectly healthy, but, within a few days, or in some cases a few hours, they turned black and pulpy, emitted a black, oily ooze and a noxious odor like that of rotted meat. The disease appeared to have come, ironically enough, from the United States.

Furthermore, it seemed to be spreading, and on August 23, Dr. John Lindley, professor of botany at the University of London, published an article in the *Gardeners' Chronicle*, which said, "A fearful malady has broken out among the potato crop. On all sides we hear of the destruction. In Belgium the fields are said to be completely desolated. There is hardly a sound sample in the Covent Garden market . . . as for cure for this distemper there is none." And on September 13, in the same journal, Dr. Lindley told his readers, "We stop the press with very great regret to announce that the potato Murrain [as it had been labeled] has unequivocally declared itself in Ireland. The crops about Dublin are suddenly perishing . . . where will Ireland be in the event of a universal potato rot?"

In London, meanwhile, the British Government—in order that its administration appear in as good a light as possible, and that the world might not be unduly reminded of the impoverished state of the Irish populace—took a more sanguine view of the situation, and the first official comment spoke of the "alleged" failure of the Irish potato crop, and called the reports "very greatly exaggerated." And on October 6, to counter reports of widespread starvation and death, Sir James Graham, the British Home Secretary, announced his "belief that the potato crop, tho' damaged, is not so much below the average as some of the exaggerated reports from Ireland have led us to apprehend." The Irish, Sir James implied, were a race of liars anyway. As more and more disastrous news flooded in from across the Irish Sea, the government continued to release bland and comforting news about these "false alarms."

The blight spread like fox-fire across Ireland, and farmers tried to rush their crops to the markets and sell them cheaply before the potatoes turned black and putrid. When diseased potatoes were fed to pigs and other livestock, they sickened and died. When starving people tried to eat the evil-smelling tubers, they, too, became violently ill. In the wake of starvation came, quickly, disease—cholera, typhus, typhoid, or "fever." A parish priest wrote:

I was called in to prepare a poor fellow, whose mother lay beside him dead two days. . . . I was called in two days after to a miserable object, beside whom a child lay dead, for the twenty-four hours previous; two others lay beside her just expiring, and, horrible to relate, a famished cat got upon the bed, and was just about to gnaw the corpse of the deceased infant, until I prevented it . . . a third of the population has been already carried away. Every morning four or five corpses are to be found on the street dead, the victims of famine and disease.

In many Irish hamlets there were no hospitals and no doctors, and the home remedies—herb juices, wild garlic, sheep's blood, milk and water boiled with salt—did no good, and in some cases may have speeded death. Suddenly it was a commonplace sight to see a small band of frightened children pushing a wheelbarrow in which two dead parents lay. Mass burials became a necessity, and bodies were dumped in open pits on top of other bodies that waited there, scattered with lime. By late October, 1845, when more than half the potato crop of Ireland had either been utterly destroyed or soon would be, the Home Secretary was ready to admit that the state of affairs was "very alarming."

No one, furthermore, had any notion of what was causing the blight. Various theories were advanced. It was said that the potatoes had been damaged by "static electricity" from the air, and it was suggested that puffs of steam from passing locomotives—recently introduced in Ireland—might be to blame. One theory held that the disease was caused by "mortiferous vapours" rising from "blind volcanoes" in the interior of the earth, and another school of thought held that the villain was guano manure, made from the droppings of seagulls, that was used as fertilizer in some areas. Did it come from the air, the earth, from the water? From County Clare came a report that one section of a field, where clothes had been laid out to dry, had escaped the blight. "This," said a local expert, "proves that the blow came from the air." Dr. Lindley's own analysis was no more helpful. He declared that the potatoes were suffering from "dropsy"—a human disease had invaded the plant kingdom. And while all this discussion was going on, the disease spread at a rampage, in regions wet and arid, from sheltered valleys to the highest mountainside. "Alarm" became terror.

A scientific commission was dispatched from London to Dublin, and presently the commissioners had drawn up a report: "Advice Concerning the Potato Crop to the Farmers and Peasantry of Ireland." The advice was that the Irish farmer should dry his potatoes in the sun, then "mark out on the ground a space six feet wide and as long as you please. Dig a shallow trench two feet wide all round and throw the mould upon the space, then level it and cover it with a floor of turf sods set on their edges." On top of this was to be sifted "packing stuff," made by "mixing a barrel of freshly burnt unslaked lime, broken into pieces as large as marbles, with two barrels of sand or earth, or by mixing equal parts of burnt turf and dry sawdust." If these preliminaries were not complicated enough, the detailed and lengthy instructions that followed were downright unintelligible—as the commissioners seemed to realize, for their report concluded: "If you do not understand this, ask your landlord or Parish priest to explain its meaning." The landlord to ask, meanwhile, was in most cases an absentee, miles across the sea in England.

And even those farmers who did understand the commissioners' recommendations found the procedure did absolutely no good at all. Next came instructions on how to prepare diseased potatoes for eating. The Irish peasant was to provide himself with a grater, a linen cloth, a hair sieve or cloth strainer, a pail or tub or two of water, and a griddle. Potatoes were then to be finely grated into the tubs, washed, strained; then the process was to be repeated and the resulting black pulp was to be dried in the griddle over a slow fire. The result, the commissioners said, was starch, and good bread could be made out of it. "There will," the report noted, "be of course a good deal of trouble in all we have recommended, and perhaps you will not succeed very well at first." The report closed on a note of chauvinism, urging the Irish to keep a stiff upper lip through it all. "We are confident all true Irishmen will exert themselves, and never let it be said that in Ireland the inhabitants wanted courage to meet difficulties against which other nations are successfully struggling."

As word of Ireland's peril spread, other suggestions poured in from well-meaning, if sometimes wild-eyed, authorities. One suggestion was that rotted potatoes should be baked—in primitive Irish cabins—at a temperature of 180 degrees Fahrenheit for eighteen to twenty minutes, or until "blackish matter" with a foul smell came oozing out in oily gobbets. The potatoes could then, it was claimed, be peeled and would be found sweet and white again. The process did not work. Nothing did, not even a proposal that the potatoes should be sliced and soaked in bog water, spread with lime or salt, or else treated with chlorine gas—"easily" made by cottagers by mixing vitriol, manganese dioxide, and salt. If tried, this method would have had the peasants manufacturing poison gas.

And the disease could not be stopped. The terrible winter of 1845 grew into a worse year in 1846. The potato blight would continue, unstopped and unstoppable, for a full ten years. At the end of this period, the Irish population, with normal growth, should have stood at about 9,000,000. Instead, it had dropped to 6,552,385. With terrible slowness, relief funds trickled in from Britain and across the Atlantic. One of the first groups to help was the Society of Friends, or Quakers. Soup kitchens were set up. But still, over the ten-year period, more than a million Irish died, and more than a million others fled to other lands. In 1845, 50,000 came to America. The following year, it was 68,000. A year later, the figure climbed to 117,000, and continued to climb until the peak year of the famine, 1851, when 216,000 Irish souls made their way, in steerage, into New York Harbor. The immigration continued heavily through 1854, and then dropped to about what it had been in 1845, or 57,000. Peter McDonnell was one of this vast and hungry horde.

The situation that greeted the arriving Irishman in New York—where most immigrants disembarked—was not much better than the one he had left in Ireland. New York was already a city of great wealth, the money capital of the United States, with huge mansions parading up Fifth Avenue and across Murray Hill. But it was also a tough, rough-hewn, and competitive town whose leading men were entrepreneurs and, in many cases, outright scoundrels. For all its fine trappings, New York had a coarse underbelly. Vagrant pigs acted as scavengers, and garbage thrown in the street was dealt with in this manner. On August 20, 1847, the New York *Sun* complained of "pigs dangerous as hyenas." An angry citizen wrote a letter to the editor about the pigs he met "lounging up Broadway." A "Quaker lady" was charged by a pig, knocked down and bitten right on Fifth Avenue, and in another part of the city a pig attacked a child that was sitting on a stoop, and snatched a piece of bread from her hand. Other animals roamed freely about the city, and newspapers of the period carried advertisements for lost cattle and horses, including one for a "large, fat ox, red with a white face," last seen strolling up Third Avenue. Manhattan's side streets were rutted mud tracks, unsafe to walk in, and packs of wild dogs, many of them rabid, patrolled the town at night. New Yorkers today who complain of danger and violence in their city might well be grateful that they are not living in the mid-nineteenth century.

In her book *The Great Hunger*, an account of the Irish migration to America, Cecil Woodham-Smith has said, "The story of the Irish in the New World is not a romantic story of liberty and success, but the history of a bitter struggle, as bitter, as painful, though not as long-drawn-out, as the struggle by which the Irish at last won the right to be a nation." Certainly the arriving Irish in New York found conditions much worse than those of the native New Yorker. There had been, to begin with, the six-to-eight-week journey in steerage across the Atlantic. Steerage passage cost between twelve and twenty-five dollars, depending upon the cupidity of the ship's captain (the fare was sometimes paid by the British landlord, not out of charity but out of eagerness to clear his land of starving and dying people who could no longer pay their rents), and passengers were crowded belowdecks, seldom permitted to go above for fresh air, and the standard food ration was a bowl of pork and beans and a cup of water a day. Steerage was a hotbed of fever, and a report that as many as fifty persons had died during a single crossing was no surprise. The lucky arrivals were the healthy ones. A healthy male could find work as a laborer for seventy-five cents a day, and a healthy girl could work as a house-maid for room and board and a dollar a week. The sick were another matter.

All ships entering the port of New York were inspected by a port physician, and any passenger or crew member found ailing was sent to the hospital at the Quarantine Station on Staten Island. The Station, on the northeastern tip of the island, was located on thirty acres of ground and consisted of two hospitals, built to accommodate four hundred patients, plus a special smallpox hos-pital which could handle fifty cases at a time, and a workhouse for the destitute. By 1847, with as many as a hundred sick persons per arriving shipload, the hospitals were hopelessly overcrowded, and shanty outbuildings were thrown together to house the overflow. Inside, conditions were, at best, deplorable. Patients were placed on iron beds upon which a thin layer of straw was spread. The hospitals were understaffed, and doctors were cruel or indifferent; male nurses abused and beat patients for minor infractions. The kitchens were filthy, the food uneatable, and the sanitary arrange-ments hopelessly primitive. Even the officials of the hospital ad-mitted that things were in "a bad state," that the roofs leaked and that the patients' beds were often soaking wet. A reporter from the New York *Tribune* visited the hospital, was shocked by what he saw, and wrote that there was not a single patient in the place who was not Irish.

A few patients who were strong enough to do so managed to escape from the hospital by stealing small rowboats and rowing the five and a half miles to Manhattan. And so it was inevitable that "ship fever" made its way quickly to the city. In the spring of 1847 an epidemic of typhus and typhoid fever broke out in New York, and 1,396 deaths were reported. The actual figure was unquestionably higher because, although one was supposed to report all such deaths, there was no penalty for not doing so.

Meanwhile, Staten Island had become a wealthy summer resort for rich New Yorkers, and a number of fine Greek Revival mansions lined its shores. Staten Islanders were soon complaining about the hordes of "diseased Irish" in their midst, and one property owner, Robert Hazard, claimed that the stench from the hospital was so unbearable that he had to close the windows of his house, Nautilus Hall, whenever the wind was blowing from that direction. Local indignation finally came to a head in 1858 when a group of Staten Islanders rioted, stormed the hospital, and burned it to the ground. Many patients perished in the blaze.

Manhattan for the Irish had, in the meantime, become a city of cave- and cellar-dwellers, with families crowded into downtown basements and dug-out hollows beneath the floors of buildings. One cellar, beneath 50 Pike Street, measured ten feet square and eleven feet high with a single tiny window. In this room lived two Irish families, ten persons in all. In another cellar below 78 James Street an investigator found, lying on some straw, the corpse of a woman who had died of exposure and starvation. The single room contained no furniture, the floor was wet, and the woman's husband and five children sat "moaning" in a corner. All were Irish immigrants who had landed in New York three weeks earlier. In the 1840's the problem of Irish beggars in the streets—including old women and small children—had reached such proportions that the *Tribune* demanded sternly, "Cannot this be stopped?"

For many of the Irish poor, drink—"the curse of the Irish"— became the quickest path to forgetfulness of suffering and poverty. It wasn't long before "Irish" became synonymous with drunkenness, rowdyism, bar fights, destruction, and crime. Because so many Irishmen bore the name of Paddy—for Padraic, the Gaelic form of Patrick, the patron saint—the term "Paddy" became generic for all Irishmen. Phrases such as "poor as Paddy Murphy's pig" entered the language. And the paddy wagon became the name of the vehicle that carried the drunken Irishman, shouting and cursing, off to jail.

For the Irishman who escaped fever and starvation, the greatest peril awaiting him in the New World was the professional bondsman. New York law required that shipowners guarantee that each immigrant passenger would not, upon arrival, become a candidate for public welfare. Shipowners would not or could not provide such guarantees for the Irish, and so the job fell to the bondsman, or passenger broker. The bondsman met the new arrival at the pier, and sold him a guaranteeing bond at anywhere from ten cents to a dollar, or as much as he could extract. If the immigrant did indeed become destitute, as thousands did, and turn to the state for aid, he was referred back to the man, or firm, that had bonded him. As a rule, the bondsman offered no help at all or, if he did, gave it in the cheapest possible way. The bondsmen had deals with cheap rooming houses, and in some cases operated "private workhouses" of their own. They also served as recruiting agents for American companies looking for cheap Irish labor, and had emissaries abroad who scouted Irish villages lining up young men willing to come to America and work at hard labor for little money. These men arrived in New York wearing identifying colored tags on their caps to indicate which railroad or construction firm had contracted to ship them off to work gangs across the country.

Bonding was extremely profitable. There were commissions to be collected at every angle—from railroad and steamship lines, from boardinghouses, from employers, and from the immigrants themselves. One firm collected eighty thousand dollars in a single year, and paid out only thirty dollars in "benefits." The bondsmen were considered "irresponsible from every point of view," and carried on their trade with the connivance of city and state officials, who took their cut of the profits. One Emigration Commissioner wrote: "The entire business became a private traffic between a set of low and subordinate city officials, on the one hand, and a band of greedy unscrupulous brokers on the other." And yet some of the luckiest Irish immigrants of all were those clever enough to get employment in this line of work.

Peter McDonnell of Drumlish, County Longford, was described in an early Manhattan business directory of the period as a "Railroad and Steamship agent." But he was, in actuality, a bondsman.

Not much else is known about Peter McDonnell except that he prospered, and that he prospered sufficiently to send his son, James Francis McDonnell, to Fordham University, from which the young man graduated in the class of 1900. James Francis McDonnell was a short, compact, somewhat strait-laced man—hardworking, ambitious, with a deep longing for respectability and social acceptability. Within five years of his graduation from college he was able to ally himself with a partner named Byrne, and the firm of Byrne & McDonnell set itself up as stockbrokers in a small booth on the floor of the New York Stock Exchange. The future father-in-law of Henry Ford II used to like to remind his grown children, as they sat around one or another of their heated swimming pools in the family compound at Southampton, that, in his youth, he had had to swim in the East River—neglecting to add that in those days the East River was clean and sparkling, delightful for swimming. He also liked to say that, as a young man, he had determined to make a million dollars before marrying and that, after that, his goal had been to make another million for each of his fourteen children. Whether he actually made the full million before choosing his bride is uncertain, yet when he chose her ten years after opening his brokerage firm, he chose not only an Irish beauty, but the daughter of a multimillionaire—Miss Anna Murray of Brooklyn.

The McDonnell-Murray wedding, on May 24, 1916, was given nearly an entire page of society-section coverage in the Brooklyn

21

Eagle. The Bishop of Brooklyn officiated at the ceremony, at the Church of Our Lady of Victory, and over forty priests were in the chancel. The bride wore white with touches of pink, and the church was "gorgeous with flowers," as the *Eagle* noted, and "distinguished by the large number of Manhattanites who attended." There were more than nine hundred people at the wedding and the reception and breakfast that followed, at the Murray mansion at 783 St. Marks Avenue, described as "the most spacious residence in Brooklyn." With this union, the McDonnell name entered the ranks of those who had already begun to call themselves the First Irish Families of America, or, for short, "the F.I.F.'s."

The same issue of the *Eagle* carried the announcement of the forthcoming marriage, in June, of the bride's brother, Joseph Bradley Murray, to Miss Mary Theresa Farrell, daughter of the "Steel King," James A. Farrell, who headed both the United States Steel Company and the Farrell Steamship Line, another member of the F.I.F. The newspaper carefully traced the lineage of Anna Murray and her brother. They were children of Mr. and Mrs. Thomas E. Murray, the former Catherine A. Bradley; they were the grandchildren of John and Anastatia McGrath Murray, and of Daniel and Julia Duane Bradley.

None of the bridegroom's antecedents was mentioned.

Chapter 3

"EVERYTHING BUT THE LIGHT BULB"

The success story of Thomas E. Murray in America is, in slight contradiction to Mrs. Woodham-Smith's thesis, a genuinely romantic one. A second-generation Irishman, Grandpa Murray—as he is still known in the family—was born in Albany, New York, on October 21, 1860, a carpenter's son and one of twelve children. He was in the fourth grade at public school when his father died, and, at the age of nine, he was forced to leave school and go to work to help support his mother and her brood. He went to work as a lamplighter for the city of Albany, lighting the gas lamps that lit the city's streets. With this little money, he put himself through two more years of night school, attending classes after his evening chores were done. He then worked for a while in the drafting rooms of local architects and engineers, and, for four more years, worked as an apprentice machinist for various shops in Albany. In 1881, at the age of twenty-one, he was made operating engineer of the pumping plant of the Albany Waterworks.

23

It was in this capacity that he came to the attention of Mr. Anthony N. Brady, an Irish-American who had made a fortune in railroads and electric light companies in and around Albany, and in Brooklyn. As a youth, walking the streets of Albany, Tom Murray had passed the window of a pastry shop and had become fascinated by the electrical mixing apparatus he saw inside, mixing cake dough. Through the glass, he studied the machine, made sketches of it, and, in his spare time—for his own amusement as much as for anything else—constructed a similar mixer with an electric motor. It operated perfectly, and Murray even added a few improvements and innovations of his own. Anthony Brady was impressed that a man so young could create a machine from simply looking at another machine through a window, and, in 1887, Brady hired Murray to take charge of the power station of the Albany Municipal Gas Company. From there on, under the wing of Mr. Brady, Thomas E. Murray's rise was rapid.

He was soon placed in complete charge of the gas company's entire operations, and was made a consultant on other Brady companies, including the Troy City Railway, the Troy Electric Light Company, the Kings County Electric Light & Power Company, and the Albany Railway Company. He was also called in to help consolidate the Brady electric companies in Brooklyn, and helped form the Edison Illuminating Company, later known as the Brooklyn Edison Company, and now a part of Consolidated Edison. During these years, he traveled busily back and forth between Brooklyn and Albany, and also managed to launch himself as an inventor. Most of his inventions were in the electrical field— condensers, switches, electrical protection devices—but they also included copper radiators, pulverized-fuel equipment, water-wall furnaces for steam boilers, and automatic welding. The list of Murray patents lengthened. Once, in a railroad car, a cinder landed in his eye. He noticed the way his own tears were able to wash the cinder out, and this immediately gave him the idea of a

24

water-screen filter to reduce the amount of smoke and soot that belched into the air from the Edison Company's big smokestacks. With this invention, he became one of America's earliest environmentalists. His copper-radiator system still heats the occupants of New York's Chrysler Building.

He loved music, and he loved to sing and, at an operetta in Albany, he met a young Irish girl named Catherine Bradley. For the hierarchy of First Irish Families in America, it was an auspicious encounter.

Catherine Bradley was one of four children of Daniel Bradley, another Irishman who had risen from relative poverty to considerable prominence. Born in Londonderry on Saint Patrick's Day, 1833, Dan Bradley had made the stormy two months' crossing of the Atlantic with his parents in the famine year of 1849. He was sixteen years old, and was fortunate enough, when he landed at Castle Harbor, to be met by family friends and escorted to Brooklyn, which in those days was a separate, independent city with its own mayor and its own municipal government, physically and emotionally far removed from Manhattan across the river. His first mail from the old country was addressed to:

> Daniel Bradley
> Fornenst the Catholic Church
> Brooklyn, U.S.A.

"Fornenst" means "nearby," a clear indication that his relatives in Ireland knew that wherever the young man settled a Catholic church would not be far away.

For a while, Dan Bradley worked in a small tobacconist's shop, not far from where the massive footings of the Brooklyn Bridge now stand. But it was not long before he was making his way inexorably into local politics.

Why did so many immigrant Irish—even those from the tiniest villages and hamlets—find themselves so readily adaptable to the politics of large American cities and, in particular, to the activities of the Democratic Party? There are several good reasons. To begin with, there is the traditional Irish feisty, scrappy nature—a nature that loves a good fight, particularly when the Irishman believes without a shadow of a doubt that right is on his side. Freedom and justice have for centuries been the goals of the Irishman's fighting nature. Sean O'Faolain has written, "I do not myself believe that anything will ever completely kill that ancient, almost wild passion for personal freedom that is the very marrow of the Irishman's nature." "No people," William Butler Yeats wrote, "have undergone greater persecution. . . . No people hate as we do in whom that past is always alive; there are moments when hatred poisons my life and I accuse myself of effeminacy because I have not given it adequate expression. . . . This is Irish hatred and solitude, the hatred of human life that made Swift write *Gulliver* and the epitaph upon his tomb, that can still make us wag between extremes and doubt our sanity." Of this curiously Irish passion, Yeats also wrote, "The Irish mind has still, in County Rapscallion or in Bernard Shaw, an ancient cold, explosive, detonating impartiality. . . . The English mind . . . has turned into a bed-hot harlot." In a poem, Yeats wrote, "I carry from my mother's womb/A fanatic heart."

Jews arriving in the New World from reactionary Germany at about the same time had also, for generations, endured the same sort of persecution, and had been politically repressed. But the Jews, though proud and independent—refusing, among other things, to take the menial jobs the Irish took in America, as ditch-diggers and housemaids, and preferring instead to take off with packs of dry goods on their backs and roam the countryside as foot peddlers—simply lacked this inner Irish fire. It was a fire, of course, that for centuries had been fed and nourished by the Church in Ireland. In Europe, rabbis had counseled moderation in the Jews' relations with the outside world, a more subtle way of

26

dealing, perhaps, with the pressures of persecution. "Live as best you can within the strictures of the system," had been the rabbis' advice; "don't be too conspicuous in your demands; stay out of fights, which only call attention to your presence; be ready to pack up and go when the enemy threatens; don't rock the boat, for you might rock yourself right out of it."

Then, too, there was the Irish gift for talk, for poetry and oratory—all useful tools for the clever politician.* Just as nineteenth-century New York had few Jewish maids and gardeners and footmen, there were even fewer Jewish orators and firebrands. The Jews were not great talkers. A European visitor in the 1870's, calling on both Jewish and Christian banking firms in New York, commented that all Wall Street firms did business in much the same way, "But the Jews appear to do it quicker because they do it with less talk." In all this, of course, the Irish were assisted by an enormously important single fact: they spoke the language. It did not take, as it did with other Europeans, a full generation before an immigrant family became fully English-speaking. While a German Jew could make money peddling—displaying the wares from his cart or pack before a rural housewife, using gestures and symbols when he did not know the words—he shied away from politics and other forms of endeavor that required direct and precise communication with an English-speaking people. The Irish, on the other hand, leaped into politics with gusto.

There is also the fact that the Irish have always been a highly social people—again unlike the Jews, who have been traditionally timid and reluctant to mix with "outsiders." The Irish love company and, in Ireland, have become famous for the relish and charm with which they invite passing strangers into their houses.

* No one personified Irish oratory better than Boston's Mayor "Honey Fitz," who once told an audience, "Having been wined and dined by all the high potentates of Europe, I return to the old North End, where every cobblestone beneath my feet seems to say, 'Welcome home, John F. Fitzgerald, welcome home. . . .'"

Cecil Woodham-Smith has pointed out that the Irish "depend to an exaggerated extent on human intercourse," and when, in County Donegal, Lord George Hill in the nineteenth century tried to move some of his tenants into better houses, he found the farmers unwilling to move because it meant separation from their neighbors. In America, Irish pride and ferocity and what Yeats labeled "fanaticism" caused the Irish to maintain, and even exaggerate, their national characteristics. Through all this, of course, they were supported by their priests, who constantly reassured them that, because they were truer to the letter of their faith than other Catholics—the German, the French, the Italian, the Spanish —the Irish Catholics were the noblest and best Catholics in the world.

In nineteenth-century American politics, the Irish also had the strength of sheer numbers. In 1850 the Irish constituted 42.8 percent of the entire foreign-born population of the United States, which represented a goodly share of voters. The Catholic Irish loyalty to the Democratic Party, meanwhile, extended back to pre-famine days into the earliest years of the Republic, and to the famous schism between Thomas Jefferson and Alexander Hamilton. Hamilton had advocated that only the propertied classes be allowed to vote, and his sympathies lay with England. Jefferson despised the monarchy and the whole social system of Britain, Ireland's ancient enemy. The trickle of Irish immigrants which had arrived before the famine sided with Jefferson's Republican Party (as the present Democratic Party was then called), and later arrivals followed the example of their countrymen. Allegiance to the Democrats was buoyed in the 1850's when the Know-Nothing Party came very close to overthrowing the Democrats on a platform dedicated to "checking the stride of the foreigner and alien, of thwarting the machinations and subverting the deadly plans of the Jesuit and the Papist," and which stated publicly that "Americans must rule America; and to this end native-born citizens should be selected for all state, federal, and municipal offices of government employment, in preference to all others." At the time, only five years' residence was required for an immigrant to become a United States citizen—and there was not even, then, a literacy-test requirement. The Know-Nothings, however, wanted to deny citizenship, and therefore political franchise, to anyone who had not lived in America for a full twenty-one years—nearly a whole generation's worth of voters—and to exclude "all paupers and persons convicted of crime from landing on our shores," which would have been another heavy blow to the incoming Irish. There were celebrations in every American Irish household when Buchanan won the election, and the Know-Nothings ran a very poor third—and eventually collapsed into extinction.

As a result of all these factors compelling the Irish logically toward politics, Edward F. Roberts, in *Irish in America*, has said, "It is probably true that the political machine was not invented by the Irish or conspicuously by anyone, but it is certain that it was developed to its greatest extent and has reached its highest degree of efficiency through the peculiar genius of the Irish for political organization."

New York's Tammany Hall, despite its long association with Irish Democratic politics—and, more recently, with Italian-American politicians—was originally the creation of Old Guard WASP aristocrats, and was as bigoted against the Irish as, if not more so than, the Know-Nothings. Before the American Revolution, a number of groups who were opposed to the revolutionary cause and who proclaimed their loyalty to George III organized under such names as the societies of St. George, St. Andrew, and St. David. As a countermove, a group of revolutionary loyalists formed the Sons of Liberty, or the Sons of St. Tammany—the latter named after a Delaware Indian chief called Tammanend, a man celebrated for his wisdom, benevolence, and love of freedom. The "Saint" was thrown in just to mock the other saintly groups.

Though the Sons of St. Tammany proclaimed themselves "democratic," their democracy did not at all extend to the lower economic groups, or to immigrants, and membership in what became the executive committee of the Democratic Party of New York County—or Tammany Hall—was carefully restricted to the landed gentry and "native-born patriots." As early as 1806, revelations of widespread political corruption among Tammany Hall's sachems —as, Indian-fashion, its leaders were called—resulted in the dismissal of a number of city officials, including the comptroller, the superintendent of the almshouse, the inspector of bread, and the society's founder himself. But in spite of these proven charges, these men remained powerful Tammany figures. On April 24, 1817, in protest against Tammany bigotry and its anti-immigrant stance, a noisy horde of hundreds of Irish immigrants stormed Tammany Hall, breaking into a general committee meeting, swinging sticks and hurling brickbats. It was really fear for their lives in the face of the fighting Irish that finally forced Tammany to take in the Irish, to help them become naturalized, and to join in the fight for manhood suffrage. Through sheer numbers, the Irish began taking over Tammany Hall, and by the time of the great wave of immigration in the 1840's the Irish were running the organization, so that the arriving Irishman found his staunchest political allies in Tammany's ranks.

Dan Bradley, on the other hand, was a vociferous opponent of bossism and machine politics—McLaughlin in Brooklyn and Tammany in New York. To him, Tammany was anathema, and he worked assiduously to avoid its "taint." In this respect, he was the polar opposite of such political bosses as his contemporary, Mayor "Honey Fitz" Fitzgerald of Boston, and, later, Jim Curley. He considered machine politics morally dangerous (on his deathbed he warned his children to stay out of politics: it was too corrupting). Taking a political stance of righteous indignation, and charging out against graft and corruption with blackthorn stick in hand, in his rough-hewn, blunt, and moralistic way, he rose rapidly in Brooklyn's political world.

In 1874, Bradley was elected to the New York State Assembly on a combined Democratic and Independent ticket. It had been a fierce fight and, in the process, a split had developed in the Kings County Democratic Party on the old slavery issue, between the "Hards" and the "Softs." The Hards, or Hard-shells, were the more conservative faction, the Softs the more liberal, and Dan Bradley was a Soft. In Albany, Dan Bradley was placed on one of two rival Democratic committees, the other being presided over by Hard Judge John J. Vanderbilt, known as "Kings County's Favorite Son." At the time, the Brooklyn *Eagle* commented that "The contrast between the two men could hardly have been more manifest. Bradley was a mechanic [meaning he had worked with his hands], a plain unlettered man and an uncompromising Democrat. Judge Vanderbilt was . . . one of the finest looking men in the State of New York, a man of high culture, of commanding presence, well known throughout the State, having once run for Lieutenant Governor." The *Eagle* refrained from pointing out that Dan Bradley was an immigrant Irish Catholic, and that Vanderbilt was a member of an old-established Dutch Protestant family, though the implication of anti-Catholic snobbishness is clear.

In the Assembly, to which he was twice re-elected, Dan Bradley became known as a fighter against graft and corruption in the state government. Once, walking into an office building in Albany, and seeing large checks from building contractors lying blatantly about on the desks of other Assemblymen, he strode from desk to desk, seized the checks, and tore them up. He became quickly known for his personal incorruptibility, earning the nickname of "Honest Dan," and, as his grandchildren proudly point out, "In those days honest *meant* honest." As his reputation grew, he was also called affectionately "Uncle Dan."

In 1893 he ran for the New York State Senate as a "Reform"

Democrat, and this was another bitter fight. His opponent in this contest, William Van Slooten, was also a member of New York's Dutch Protestant Establishment. Though Van Slooten was a part of the powerful Hugh McLaughlin machine, he was otherwise relatively unknown, and Dan Bradley took the phrase "Who *is* Van Slooten?" as his campaign slogan. Shortly after Uncle Dan's resounding victory, which, though he was then almost sixty, made him the youngest man in the Senate ("Still on the sunny side of seventy," as he declared in his acceptance speech), the question of who was Van Slooten was answered in spectacular fashion. Whether or not as a result of his defeat, William Van Slooten took a revolver and "blew his head off" in his house at 52 Sidney Place. The suicide filled the newspapers, and the weapon appeared to have mystified the authorities, who had never seen a revolver quite like it. The detectives couldn't operate the gun or even take the cartridges out and, when they tried to dismantle it in the coroner's office, the gun suddenly went off and a bullet pierced a desk and several thick books, and narrowly missed a man standing nearby. In the newspaper stories that followed, it turned out that Van Slooten had worked as a mining engineer for Hamilton McKeon Twombly, who was married to a granddaughter of the old Commodore Vanderbilt— "My mortal enemies!" as Dan Bradley used to declare. If the dead do turn in their graves, something of this sort must have happened, many years later, when one of Uncle Dan Bradley's Murray great-granddaughters eloped with a Vanderbilt.

A tall, arresting figure who stood "straight as an arrow," with abundant white hair, according to contemporary reports, Dan Bradley wore tall silk hats, affected semiclerical garb with reversed collar, and was frequently mistaken for a priest. Like his Irish ancestors before him, he was a devout and dedicated Catholic. He was a member of the Church of the Assumption at York and Jay streets in Brooklyn, was active in the Catholic Benevolent

Legion, helped establish new branches of the Legion, and was a member of the board of managers of the Catholic Orphan Society. Devotion to Catholic charities, particularly to orphans, would become a persistent theme in the lives of the F.I.F.'s. In this latter capacity, Dan Bradley made frequent visits to the orphanage, and lectured his children on the importance of maintaining this visiting schedule. At one meeting of the Society, Dan Bradley and his friend Bernard McCaffrey were both presented with gold-headed canes for their services. The souvenir menu on this occasion stated that Don Bradley's age was seventy-seven. In his acceptance speech, Dan Bradley announced that he intended to christen his cane by breaking it over the head of the person who had inserted that figure. He was, he insisted, only seventy-four. (The menu, meanwhile, may have been correct; there is a possibility that he was born in 1830, and not 1833, and, since he enjoyed being known as the youngest man in the Senate, "Honest Dan" may have indulged in the not-uncommon politician's practice of lying about his age.)

One of Bradley's first bills in the Senate, in 1894, had been a proposal to establish fixed salaries for Senators. Theretofore, state Senators had been paid in a casual manner that consisted mostly of whatever graft they could collect from contractors and other constituents with special interests in mind. Bradley decided to stop all that. "My bill proposes," he announced, "to pay the men elected under it one thousand dollars, but I'm willing to make it fifteen hundred, which is a nice salary. The man who takes more pay than he agreed to accept office for is something more than a salary grabber—he is a thief! I represent all shades of politics. I am a whole party in myself. Those who had the best interests of the city at heart voted for your humble servant. I know a little about politics. I know what it is to bring out the vote!"

Pronouncements of this sort did not, perhaps, endear the humble servant to his fellow legislators. One newspaper report of the period said, in commenting on his legendary honesty, that "He was so honest that those perhaps a little less scrupulously so than he thought that his honesty was 'overdone.' " On the other hand, no one really questioned his integrity—nor his devoutness—and he had become indeed the darling of the voters of Kings County, particularly those of Irish descent. Though he could proclaim himself "a whole party," he could also be humble, and the day after he defeated Van Slooten, Dan Bradley appeared at the office of the editor of the Brooklyn *Eagle* and announced, "Mr. Editor, if tonight after I said my prayers, the Lord should come into my room and ask me, 'Dan Bradley, what else do you want?' I would say to him, 'Nothing, Lord, but more of Thy Grace.' "

In 1894, Daniel Bradley took an active part in the investigations of the "notorious" Lexow Committee of the State Senate, which uncovered scandal after scandal in the New York City Police Department—voting frauds, policy and prostitution protection, sale of liquor licenses by the Excise Board, and cases of police brutality which make recent charges against New York's "finest" seem tame by comparison. It made no difference to Bradley that much of the New York police force was Irish, though, in his questioning of witnesses, he tended to make a distinction between a "good" Irishman—one who didn't drink—and a less-good Irishman, who had succumbed to the Irish weakness. As the investigation wore on, powerful forces were set in motion to call the hearings off. Tammany Hall was beginning to show up in a much less than favorable light. Bradley would have none of it, and told a reporter from the *Eagle*, "No power on earth can call the Committee off" (implying his recognition of a distinction between "power on earth" and "power in heaven"). He went on to declare in his flamboyant style that "We will not only finish investigating the police but we will fully investigate the police justices, the Excise Board, and other departments. Not one of the big officers will be allowed to escape the probe. Before the end of next week we will have Byrnes

34

and Williams and the other bigwigs of the police force on the rack." True to his word, the hearings continued until some 57,666 pages of "shocking and revealing" testimony had been heard, and over 3,000 subpoenas had been served.

Dan Bradley and his wife, the former Julia Duane, had had four children—three girls and a boy. Because of Bradley's preoccupation with the evils of the Demon Rum, his daughter Catherine mixed whiskey with her children's castor oil when they were sick, so they would always associate it with a vile taste. It worked. They always did. When, therefore, the enterprising young Tom Murray, already busily amassing a tidy fortune with his inventions, became engaged to Uncle Dan Bradley's youngest daughter, it was considered an imposing match. It was an alliance of both political and money power. The announcement of their marriage, in 1885, did not fail to note Thomas Murray's "poor, hard-working origins." But it also called him a "master inventor" and a "millionaire." The wedding write-up also commented on the bride's "handsome and useful presents . . . from her friends and associates in the local Sodality of the Church of the Assumption." Theirs was said to have been the first Nuptial Mass ever performed in Brooklyn. They went to Niagara Falls for their honeymoon.

Thomas and Catherine Murray had, over a spate of years, eight children. And, as the number of Thomas E. Murray's patents increased, so did the inventor's fortune. He was also proving himself to be a bold and assertive businessman. Once, when he and his partner, Mr. Edison, needed some power lines strung up in a hurry, Mr. Murray went to the telephone company and asked whether he could use their poles. The telephone company said no. Thomas Murray and his crew went out in the dead of night and put the lines along the telephone poles anyway. When someone suggested that the telephone company might object, and rip the power lines down in the morning, Murray shook his head and said, "No, the telephone company is so scared of power that they'll never touch us." He was right, and to this day in certain outlying areas Consolidated Edison and the telephone company still share their poles, in a state of uneasy coexistence.

The great Murray house was built at 783 St. Marks Avenue—he felt comfortable living on a street named after a saint. Although it did not contain its own private chapel, where Mass could be celebrated for the family, Murray was given the privilege, unusual even for rich Catholics, of keeping the Holy Sacrament in his own house and could thus live in the continuous presence of the Host. The children were dutifully enrolled, one by one, in Catholic schools. Thomas E. Murray was made a Knight of St. Gregory and a Knight of Malta, two of the most prestigious Papal orders. During World War I, meanwhile, his invention for welding shells was found to be the only one that could be used in the production of the 240-millimeter mortar shell, which earned him, in addition to another fortune in government contracts, a special commendation from the War Department. For the dozens of safety appliances he had invented, he received in 1913 the gold medal of the American Museum of Safety in New York. He became president of the Association of Edison Illuminating Companies, the Murray Manufacturing Company and, eventually, headed five different corporations. At night, he kept sheets of copperplate by his bedside. Whenever an idea for a new invention struck him, he would get up and carefully sketch it out on a copper sheet with a metal stylus. He also installed an alarm in his bedroom, and whenever anything went wrong in one of his power plants, the alarm would go off and Grandpa Murray would leap from his bed and head for the trouble.

His father-in-law, Dan Bradley, remained a powerful figure in Brooklyn politics. Once, when two of his Murray grandsons were arrested for throwing a baseball through a neighbor's window, Dan Bradley marched down to the station house, pounded on the sergeant's desk, and said, "Do you realize that if these two boys are booked on this they'll never be able to hold political office?" The boys were released, and the arresting officer—who happened to be an Irish Protestant—was chastised.

Thomas E. Murray was a stern, strict, and pious parent. Whenever one of his children had a date with a non-Catholic, that young person was required to wait for his escort in a special anteroom, kept just for Protestants, at 783 St. Marks. "Grandpa Murray was sort of the conscience of the family," one of his grandchildren says. Another says, "The Murray brand of Catholicism was all hellfire and damnation—but we paid attention to him." He could also be kind and generous. As the family grew, he established the practice of giving each child, on its birthday, a little sack containing five twenty-dollar gold pieces. This money, it turned out, represented honorariums which Grandpa Murray had received for attending directors' meetings of various companies. After the ceremony, to be sure, the money had to be returned to the patriarch to be banked in the child's name. He continued the practice with his grandchildren, and when one grandchild said shyly to him that he had entertained forty little boys at his birthday party, Grandpa Murray said, "Any boy who has had forty little boys at his birthday party should have another twenty dollars," and handed the child another gold piece. He could also be stubborn. He never served a drink in his house until the advent of Prohibition. Then, however, he began serving cocktails every night because, as he put it, "Nobody is going to tell me what to do."

He continued to love music and singing, and each Christmas he would pay a special visit to the prisoners at Rikers Island, and sing Christmas carols for them, bringing along his children's piano teacher as his accompanist. Such deeds were, he carefully explained to his children, Corporal Works of Mercy—caring for the hungry and the needy and the orphaned and imprisoned. Whenever a board meeting at one of his companies was ended, he liked to close the proceedings with a song. In return, his board members

37

sang for him, and children at the local parochial schools always appeared on the doorstep of the Murray mansion on Christmas Eve to serenade Tom Murray.

He enjoyed taking his children for outings at the theater or to the opera in New York, and the minute the group was settled in the back seat of the big chauffeur-driven car, and it was ready to pull away from the house, Mr. Murray would remove his beads from his vest pocket and, in a solemn and stentorian voice, would begin to recite the rosary, intoning, "I believe in God, the Father Almighty, creator of heaven and earth, and of all things visible and invisible . . . and in Jesus Christ, His only son . . ." announcing all the Mysteries as he came to them, delivering a full ten Hail Marys at the appropriate intervals, pausing to cross himself whenever the car passed a church or a cemetery. The recital continued all the way into Manhattan. The children's Protestant friends were always somewhat baffled by these performances. And yet he considered this a vital ritual, and before any of the family started on a trip, or went into the water, there were prayers and blessings, and everyone was expected to cross himself. He had made, he liked to explain, only two trips to Europe in his life, and both times they had been pilgrimages to Catholic shrines. He also gave his children practical advice—particularly in the field he knew best, electricity. He lectured on how crucial electricity was to the life of New York City, how the city depended on it, and he was one of the first in the field to warn of the dangers—on city streets, where electricity controlled traffic and provided illumination, in apartment houses with electrically run elevators, in hospitals where electrical equipment kept patients alive—of massive blackouts that could occur if systems became overloaded. Long after his death, New Yorkers began to have firsthand experience of what Tom Murray had been talking about.

"Thomas Edison's invention may have been more spectacular and *showy*," one of his grandchildren says, "with the incandescent

38

bulb. But Grandpa Murray virtually invented everything *but* the light bulb—the circuits, switches, dynamos, and power systems that got the electricity to the bulb. In my opinion, it was a more important contribution. After all, if there hadn't been a way to get the power into the bulbs, how would the bulbs light up?"

Meanwhile, Mr. Murray's children were steadily making their way into New York society. Mr. Murray rather liked and encouraged this, and enjoyed clipping items from society columns about his children's appearances at this or that "swell" party in Manhattan. In this preoccupation he was, again, very Irish-American. American Jews kept to themselves, and tended to shun "society" and actively to avoid seeing their names in the papers. But America's emergent Irish families were proving themselves a socially ambitious lot, bringing with them a strong sense of pride in their Irish heritage—as, whenever an Irish or Irish-sounding name was mentioned to one Boston dowager, she would always comment, "Well, if they were one of the First Irish Families, I would certainly know them."

The Murray children were indeed attractive, and had the three prerequisites that are still needed for acceptance in society in New York: money, good looks, and good humor, which rank in importance in that order. The second-generation Murrays were all at once *very* social.

"Yes, I suppose you could say they were accepted," says one member of New York's Protestant Old Guard. "But you always knew that they were Catholics. And, socially, the Murrays always remained—well, just a little bit different, a little bit *Brooklyn*."

Chapter 4

"MURRAY BAY"

he first prominent New York Irishman to buy a summer home in Southampton, on Long Island's southeastern shore, was a New York lawyer named Morgan J. O'Brien. O'Brien—who was always called Judge O'Brien—was the first lawyer of Irish ancestry in the city to assume a place at the top of his profession comparable to the positions held by Protestants, and it is said that he paved the way for a good many other young Catholic lawyers to advance in the big "old family" firms downtown.

O'Brien bought a big Southampton place in the early 1920's, and Southampton was then, as it remains today, a resort for the second-rate rich, or at least for the *nouveau riche*. It has been said that Southampton was colonized in reaction to old-line Newport, which many younger people in society considered too restrictive and stiffly formal, but this is only partly true. The fact is that Newport's Old Guard would not accept many of the newer-rich families, who, if they wanted a strip of Atlantic seashore for themselves, simply had to look elsewhere.

Certainly, the Irish families would not have been accepted in Newport, and they knew it. A New York lady of ancient Sephardic Jewish heritage recalls visiting a gentile friend in Newport and her friend saying at one point, "I do think our two peoples are getting closer together, don't you?" The Jewish lady replied that she indeed hoped so. With that, the non-Jewish Newporter said, "Of course we'll never accept the Catholics."

Newport is, after all, in New England, and in New England—particularly in nearby Boston—the Irish experience had been quite different from what it had been in New York. The Irish immigration had disturbed big, bustling, competitive New York in only a relatively minor way, but its impact on prim old Boston had been shattering.

To begin with, Boston was a smaller city than New York, and geographically much less suited to immigrants. The suburbs could only be approached across bridges which required the payment of a twenty-cent toll in each direction, and so the hordes of arriving Irish who entered Boston Harbor during the famine years—or who struggled down from Grosse Île in Canada, both legally and illegally—were crowded into Ward Eight and the North End, districts that had formerly contained the homes of prosperous merchants. Neighborhoods were literally ruined as wealthy home-owners fled the invasion and fine old Federal houses were surrounded by jerry-built shanties and lean-tos. At one point, Paul Revere's splendid house in Ann Street was so completely encased by tenements that the house within became invisible. In the nine years prior to 1845, some 33,346 immigrants had landed in Boston, a figure which must be increased by 50 percent for those who made their way in by unrecorded or illegal means—or an average of 5,500 a year. These the city had been more or less able to absorb. In the single famine year of 1847, however, more than 37,000 immigrants arrived in Boston, "three-quarters Irish labourers," adding their poverty and weight to a city which, two years earlier, had contained a population of 114,366, and the Boston *Transcript* noted with alarm that "Groups of poor wretches were to be seen in every part of the city, resting their weary and emaciated limbs at the corners of the streets and in the doorways of both private and public houses."

The cellars of Boston, meanwhile, provided even worse housing than those of New York, and were usually windowless hollows carved out of the earth, completely without ventilation, drainage, or any form of plumbing. Families doubled and tripled up to occupy these holes, and it was not surprising to find as many as forty people living in a single tiny cavity. Drunkenness and crime and violence soared. In 1848 complaints for capital offenses increased 266 percent over the preceding five years, and assaults on police officers rose 400 percent while other forms of assault jumped 465 percent. The outraged Boston authorities declared that Massachusetts was becoming "the moral cesspool of the civilized world."

Beggars by the thousands roamed the Boston streets. The sick grew sicker and the starving died. By an ironic quirk of human logic, Boston's aristocrats had no trouble regarding the starving and dying populace in Ireland as "poor unfortunates," and the Protestant churches on Beacon Hill were filled with sermons counseling mercy and kindness for those benighted souls. And yet these same Irish, having managed to make their way across the Atlantic, were categorized as the dregs and filth of human society, a scourge and disgrace to Boston, and an intolerable burden on the taxpayer.

It is also ironic that upper-class Boston, otherwise so culturally and intellectually liberal, simply could not then—and cannot today—accept the Irish as candidates for social equality. In the pre-Civil War South, the enslaved blacks could count on the support of the Boston Brahmin abolitionists. Upper-crust Yankees throughout New England—where religion was so firmly rooted in the Old Testament (Harvard was the first college in America to offer a course in Hebrew)—could also look with kindness on the Jews (such anti-Semitism as there was always had its base in the lower classes). But there were only a very few philo-Celtic Protestants. The rest looked with utter disdain upon the Irish. As Daniel Moynihan has put it in *Beyond the Melting Pot*, "The Irish were the one oppressed people on earth the American Protestants could never quite bring themselves wholeheartedly to sympathize with. They would consider including insurgent Greece within the protection of the Monroe Doctrine, they would send a warship to bring the rebel Kossuth safe to the shores of liberty, they would fight a war and kill half a million men to free the Negro slaves. But the Irish were different." And of even such a devout supporter of minority causes as Eleanor Roosevelt, Joseph P. Lash has said that "Somewhere deep in her subconscious was an anti-Catholicism which was part of her Protestant heritage."

As the fictional George Apley in John P. Marquand's novel put it in a letter to his son in New York, "We have our Irish and you your Jews, and both of them are crosses to bear.", In Boston the luckiest Irish, perhaps, were the healthy young women who were able to find jobs as serving girls in the homes of Boston's rich. In those more spacious days, over a century ago, the top floor of every rich man's house was the servants' floor, divided into cubicles where the housemaids slept, and a strong Irish maid would work seven days a week, with time off for six o'clock Sunday Mass, for room and board and as little as four dollars a month. Household service might seem to go against the Irish grain, but it was something these girls could do with a small amount of pride. Their mothers had taught them to cook and wash and sew; they loved children, and made excellent nannies; their Church had taught them orderliness, neatness, honesty, personal cleanliness, and above all virtue. An "Irish virgin" was certain to remain that way, and it was not long before every proper Boston home had its "Bridget" in the nursery, the laundry, or the scullery.

To be sure, the servants' floor was dark, lighted only with tiny windows, and a maid's room was barely big enough to hold a single bed and perhaps a dresser, with splintery flooring and, sometimes, a single electric lamp. Plumbing and heating seldom ascended to this level of the house, and each room was provided with a chamber pot. But these girls had other advantages that they were quick to see. They were able to spend their daily lives among gentle, cultivated people, and they were able to observe at first hand the ways not only of the wealthy but of the polite and well-bred. They learned the touch of fine silver and porcelain and furniture, the feel of good linen and real lace. They also learned, from their mistresses, good manners. These were advantages that these girls would do their best to see that their children would have in the next generation.

The Irish, however, never had the security of feeling that they had a friend in court, at the top level of American society. In Boston, they felt particularly abandoned and left to their own poor resources, with only their faith and their Church for comfort. They could draw on no reservoir of automatic sympathy as, paradoxically, could blacks and Jews. This situation, once established, would continue.

Woodrow Wilson, who was President while Ireland was fighting for its independence from England, had no sympathy whatever for the Irish cause. On the contrary, Wilson was an "Orangeman," a Scotch Presbyterian, and was both anti-Irish and anti-Catholic. Wilson, on the other hand, had great admiration for the Jews, and it was he who appointed the first Jew, Louis D. Brandeis, to the Supreme Court. Some thirty years later in the mid-1940's, when Israel was in similar throes of the fight for independence, both President and Mrs. Roosevelt were hugely sympathetic to Israel's position, as was Harry Truman, who pushed the motion of independence through the United Nations. But from the beginning of their history in America, the Irish were required to make their way upward aided only by each other.

Why was this? Perhaps the answer lies somewhere in the thorny Irish "personality," the Irish orneriness and stubbornness, and unwillingness to bow, scrape, and court favor. The Irish, it might be said, were not "rewarding" victims as were, by contrast, the Negro and the Jew. The masses of Irish immigrants from the famine were clearly poor, but it was difficult to think of them as "deserving" or worthy beneficiaries of care and charity. The Irish might suffer, but they refused to show it, and even the Irish beggars begged aggressively, not obsequiously. It is difficult, perhaps, to want to rescue a porcupine from a trap, or even from an oven, nor is it easy to pity a caged rattlesnake.

All these various and subtle social forces conspired to cause new-rich Irishmen like Judge Morgan O'Brien to congregate at a summer resort in Southampton. Judge O'Brien was quickly followed by his friend Thomas E. Murray, who had been summering in various places such as Far Rockaway and Allenhurst, New Jersey, and who bought himself a large piece of property on the ocean front and started to build an appropriately large house which was to have, among other amenities, two swimming pools—a larger one for the adults and a smaller one for the children. Since the pools were to be filled with salt water from the Atlantic, it was necessary to figure out some way to keep sand from the ocean floor from flowing into the pool with the water, and so, with his stylus on a copperplate, Grandpa Murray invented a filtering system that would do just that. Grandpa Murray also installed a huge telescope on his lawn through which to survey his neighbors, and another chapel.

Not long after Grandpa Murray's Southampton place was finished, his son-in-law, James Francis McDonnell, who had begun

45

summering with his family in Westchester County, in Rye, New York, waded out into Long Island Sound for a swim and saw something floating in the water that displeased him. He returned to the Rye house and announced—in his imperious fashion—that his family would thereafter also spend their summers in Southampton. The family took over a large section of the resort's Irving Hotel while the McDonnell house was going up hard by the Murrays'. The McDonnell house had over fifty rooms, and was promptly dubbed "the hotel." Next came two more of Thomas E. Murray's children, his sons Tom, Jr. and John F. Murray, and both acquired large houses in what had become the Murray family compound. Meanwhile, another son, Joseph B. Murray, and a daughter, Julia, who had married Herbert Lester Cuddihy, acquired equally substantial places in nearby Water Mill. Eventually, there were eight houses on perhaps thirty acres of shorefront, plus garages, stables, boathouses, pools, and a polo field.

The Tom Murray, Jr.'s had eleven children, the Jack Murrays had seven, and the Joe Murrays had five. The Cuddihys had seven, and the McDonnells topped all of Grandpa Murray's offspring with fourteen. (The Pope himself, or so went a family joke, had given Anna Murray McDonnell his personal permission to have as many children as she wanted and, because it was the fashion in the 1920's and '30's for pregnant women to pass most of their time lying down, Anna McDonnell spent the better part of fifteen years in bed, while her husband had a "nervous breakdown" with the announcement of each new arrival, as though he had nothing to do with it—and with the prospect of having to make another million dollars in his brokerage business for the new child.) Thomas E. Murray's daughter, Katherine, who married J. Ennis McQuail, also came to Southampton with her more modest quota of two children, and so did another daughter, Marie, who—to confuse things somewhat—had married James Francis McDonnell's brother John, making their two McDonnell children double cousins of all the other McDonnell children. When President Theodore Roosevelt publicly decried the increasing number of small families among the "best" American family stocks, warning of the dangers of "race suicide," Grandpa Murray sent Roosevelt a photograph of his own huge clan, to approve of and to autograph. The President returned the picture with his signature.

It was no wonder, however, with this onslaught of Murrays, that Southampton was soon—perhaps spitefully—being referred to as "Murray Bay." In fact, the only one of Grandpa Murray's eight children who did not join the patriarch in Southampton was brother Daniel Murray, who, after a brief but brilliant career at Georgetown,.had fallen from a polo pony, sustained a head injury, and become an incompetent. Whenever Uncle Daniel's face showed up in an old family photograph, and the children asked who he was, they were told, "He died." He had, in fact, not died, but had been placed at McLean Institute outside Boston, where Grandpa Murray had provided him with a house of his own on the hospital grounds, servants, and a nurse-companion. His brothers and sisters paid him regular visits, but the children were never told of these.

It would be pleasant to suppose that all these relations gathered together along these balmy summer miles of beach would have composed One Big Happy Family, but of course this was not the case. There was constant squabbling within and without this vast—and, by now, quite wealthy—family group. Most of the fights were about money, now that there was so much of it, and these usually centered on the fact that Grandpa Murray's sons, who worked for his companies and other scattered interests, always seemed to have more money than his daughters, who didn't. Thomas E. Murray, Jr. was the martinet of the next generation, and the strictest Catholic, and he was forever lecturing his brothers, sisters, and their respective wives, husbands, and children on what he considered their religious laxity. The children, who resented this, often gath-

47

ered on the Southampton streets at night and conducted parodies of the Mass.

The Thomas E., Jr.'s took themselves very seriously and seemed to consider themselves the grandest of the clan. And so the other Murrays enjoyed circulating the frivolous rumor that Uncle Tom had met his wife, who had been a Miss Brady, while she had been doing his laundry. Uncle Jack and Uncle Joe Murray were more outgoing and fun-loving than their more strait-laced brother Tom. Uncle Joe had a particularly jolly nature, and Uncle Jack liked to slip out of church on Sunday morning before the sermon started and head for the golf course. At the same time, some Murrays looked down their noses at Uncle Jack's wife, who had been a model, and who had also been an orphan, and of unknown parentage.

Certain Murrays, in the meantime, tended to look down on the McDonnells as parvenus and upstarts, and it was assumed in the family that the two McDonnell brothers who had married the two Murray sisters had done so only for the Murray money. And once a young Murray child watched, in tears, while two of his older McDonnell cousins entered the house and proceeded to beat up his mother. Comforting the child afterward, his mother said, "Those McDonnells are nothing but stupid Micks—don't worry about it."

In fact, life was far from harmonious at Southampton. Each of the families had many automobiles, and letting the air out of the tires of cars belonging to their relatives was a popular sport among the children. The McDonnells alone had three sport coupés, five station wagons, three limousines, plus numerous Fords and Chevrolets for the children. One of the McDonnell cars was an exotic Lancia, which, to the nephews' and nieces' great delight, would never work properly, and the children enjoyed chanting over and over "Sell the Lancia" to the tune of "Valencia," whenever a McDonnell appeared within earshot. Once, for amusement, the

Thomas E. Murray children vandalized the John F. Murrays' boathouse, and Mrs. Murray, who had witnessed the act, complained about it to her brother-in-law. "Nonsense," said Uncle Tom, "they couldn't have done that. They both received Communion this morning."

The Cuddihys—Mr. Cuddihy was in publishing—were considered "snooty" and "intellectual," and were accused of putting on airs about it. A narrow strip of grass separated Uncle Joe's driveway from the Cuddihys' garage in Water Mill, and the Cuddihy children, in their various cars, took to driving casually back and forth over the grass between two trees. One day they discovered that Uncle Joe had placed a length of sturdy wire between the trees, and so they merely detoured between the next two. Presently, Uncle Joe's wire was extended, and then extended again, until the entire strip of grass was barricaded to traffic. Looking at the wire, Mr. Cuddihy said, "I'll tell you what let's do. Let's get all the oldest rags and underwear we can find and hang it up on Joe's clothesline." This was done, and the garments remained there— with no comment from next door—for several weeks. Finally, when the Joe Murrays were expecting some important guests for dinner, Mrs. Murray called her sister-in-law and said, "Please take your laundry down."

Uncle Tom Murray, meanwhile, had taken to raising chickens on his place; there were tax advantages to be had if his house could be considered a working farm. The other Murrays took an exceedingly dim view of this, and one morning Uncle Tom was surprised to discover that his laying hens had laid no eggs at all. The culprit was eventually found—a young nephew—leading someone to compose the mocking family rhyme:

> Tommy-Tommy Tittlemouse
> Stole the eggs from Murray's house,
> Hid them in McDonnell's cellar.
> Now wasn't he the naughty feller?

The fact that Auntie Katherine McQuail seemed to play a great deal of golf with Monsignor George H. Killeen, the ruddy-faced, heavily jowled pastor of a Southampton Catholic church, was the cause for frequent comment among others in the family. "I'm absolutely sure that golf is *all* that's going on between them," her relatives said, "even though Father Killeen *does* look a bit like Spencer Tracy."

In the McDonnell household, Tom, the family chauffeur, was a troublemaker. Once he reported to his mistress that he had seen Mrs. Edward T. Stotesbury drive by, and said, "Mrs. Stotesbury has a chauffeur in maroon livery, and a second man 'on the box' " —i.e., seated beside the driver. Thereafter Tom, too, was accompanied by a footman riding "on the box." But Tom clearly disliked chauffeuring and, at his urging, little Jim McDonnell one day chased his nurse around the house with an air rifle. The nurse, understandably, gave prompt notice following this episode, and Tom took over her job. The children adored him. The senior McDonnells liked to retire early, but the children would sit up until the wee hours with Tom, in the maids' dining room, reading tea leaves and going over the racing form, picking out winners on the next day's races—for which Tom placed their bets. There was a huge uproar, and a general revamping of the McDonnell household, when it was discovered that the servants, who had gone out weekly with huge shopping lists, had been receiving kickbacks from various Southampton stores.

Still, every effort was made to keep up dignity and decorum, and to maintain a standard of what had come to be known as gracious living. "Always go First Class," James McDonnell used to counsel his children. "Always be the best at everything you do, and never accept anything that's second-rate." Everybody dressed for dinner, and little boys were never permitted at the dinner table without a clean shirt, jacket, and tie. Self-improvement was stressed, and a map of the world always hung on the McDonnell dining room wall, to help the children learn geography. When it was time to move back into the city, and go back to school— the girls to the Sacred Heart, the boys to Georgetown prep— Anna Murray McDonnell, in her continuous state of *accouchement*, always required her children to line up at her bedside each morning for clothing inspection. The little girls always carried rosary beads in their purses, and the boys carried them in their jacket pockets. They were fitted for coats by a man who came to the house from Rowe of London, and the little girls' dresses were hand-made creations by an outfit called Fairyland in Paris, or from a fashionable New York dressmaker named Marcelle Julienne. De Pinna, then a stylish New York clothing store, also received a great deal of Murray-McDonnell-Cuddihy custom for ready-to-wear.

"There was something almost mesmerizing about Southampton in those early days," recalls one woman who married into the Murray clan. "I had never seen anything like it—the clothes, and the jewels the women wore. I'd feel naked if I went out without dozens of bracelets, and they wore diamond earrings to play golf. Of course it was all very *nouveau riche*, nothing at all like the way the older money lived on the North Shore, or at the Piping Rock Club." There was also something "almost feudal" about Southampton on a Sunday, when the fleet of Murray and McDonnell cars lined up to transport the families to morning Mass. The front pews on the left-hand side of the Sacred Hearts of Jesus and Mary Church were always reserved for the Murrays, McDonnells, and Cuddihys, who assembled solemnly to listen to one of Father Killeen's two favorite sermons—the one on the evil of birth control or the other on the importance of sending children to Catholic schools.

Socially, there were a few snubs from the Protestant summer residents of Southampton, and there was talk of "this Irish invasion." "Oh, so you're a Catholic," said a Southampton lady to Mrs. Murray. "That's what my cook does on Sundays. She's taught me quite a lot about the Catholics." "I suppose you'd also ask your cook," said Mrs. Murray crisply, "which corner of a visiting card to turn down." From a dressing room at Foulke & Foulke's dress shop in Southampton, one of the McDonnells overheard a customer saying to Mrs. Foulke, "Isn't it dreadful—all these Irish we're getting here?" "At least they pay their bills," replied Mrs. Foulke. This was true. Anna Murray McDonnell, who never liked to be remiss about anything, would never leave her desk in the morning until every single bill was paid. And there was a certain amount of commotion within the membership of the Southampton Beach Club when Grandpa Murray and his voluminous offspring wanted to join. A sign, borrowing the phrasing of the famous Boston snub, "No Irish Need Apply," was briefly hung on the club's front door. But the Beach Club also wanted to build a salt-water pool, and faced the same sand-filtering problem that Grandpa Murray had. At last the club agreed to let the family join, provided Grandpa Murray would share the secret of his invention with them. In Southampton it was soon being said, "If you're an Irish Catholic here, you've *got* to be rich."

"We overcame by sheer numbers," recalls Mary Jane Cuddihy MacGuire. "After all, we were about sixty strong. We were our own defense, and nobody could touch us. If someone wanted a partner for tennis or golf, they practically had to ask one of us. And those were wonderful, glorious days. We literally didn't have a care in the world. We danced, we swam, we went to parties. Meyer Davis always played. There was very little drinking. Maybe we had some innate fear of inheriting the 'Irish curse,' I don't know, but we always frowned on anyone who drank, and anybody who got drunk was ostracized. There were always friends dropping in, and house guests, and if we ran out of beds people slept on the piano or on the billiard table. It was marvelous fun. We cared nothing at all about money. We were never *taught* anything about money. We just spent it. When I was sixteen, I was given an allowance of three hundred dollars a month. I promptly went out and ran up fifteen hundred dollars' worth of bills on clothes. Daddy took my allowance away for a while, but then he gave it back. I can't tell you how many five-hundred-dollar chiffon dresses I've ruined jumping into pools at parties. I remember when my husband asked me to marry him, he told me he was making only twenty-five dollars a week. I said to him, 'But that's *plenty* of money to live on—isn't it?' " And so, in this gay and carefree manner, the new-rich American Irish families made their way into what passed for New York society or, more properly, Café Society. When Mary Jane Cuddihy, in the late 1930's, danced without her shoes at the old El Morocco, her picture was published around the world, even in Nazi Germany, where the photograph was offered as testimony of "the extreme state of poverty in the U.S."

Grandpa Murray did not have long to live in his great Southampton house. He had developed a fondness for yellow taffy almost to the point of addiction. A box of yellow taffy was almost always within his reach, and he passed out taffy to his children and grandchildren. At Southampton, he became ill with diabetes, and he died in his house there on July 21, 1929. He was not quite sixty-nine. At the time of his death, reports of the size of his fortune varied wildly. Some placed it at over $50 million, while others said it was only $5 million. The figure of $10,044,070 was later published. He died, of course, just a few months before the great stock market crash, and so that event diminished the value of his holdings sharply. The estate entered a lengthy period of litigation, during which the family lawyers argued with the state and federal tax authorities over the amount of taxes to be paid. The *New York Times* commented that "The appraisal shows a wide gap in the valuation set by the family, and those of the State." The Revenue people wanted, naturally, to tax the estate on its size at the time of Thomas E. Murray's death. The family, naturally, wanted it taxed on the lower figure of what the estate would be worth at the time of its distribution to his heirs, after the Crash. The trouble was that nothing of the sort had ever happened before in the taxation of large fortunes, and so there was no precedent to go by.

A few things were certain, however. The former lamplighter from Albany who had gone to Brooklyn, and then had gone from Brooklyn to the ample splendors of Southampton, had died a very rich man. At the time of his death it was noted that Grandpa Murray held some eleven hundred separate patents, a record in the world that was second only to his friend and former associate, Thomas Edison. He also left eight children and thirty-seven grandchildren.

"Money can divide a family," Grandpa Murray used to warn. He was right, of course, and scrambling for a rightful share of his money would cause even more family squabbling and dissension. But he had died wealthy at a time when the rest of the country was plunging into a long period of economic disaster. As one of his grandsons puts it, "When everybody else got poor, we got rich."

Chapter 5

MR. McDONNELL'S GIMMICK

cDonnells today—perhaps some ten thousand strong—are scattered across Ireland, with the name variously spelled McDonnell and MacDonnell. The most numerous Mc-Donnells are those descended from a Scottish clan in Argyle, whose chief was known as Lord of the Isles, and these McDonnells came to Ireland in the thirteenth century as a military body and, having established themselves as galloglasses—or mercenary foot soldiers—for the most powerful chiefs in the North of Ireland, they were presently acquiring territory of their own, both by grants for military service and through marriage. An ability to marry well has been a McDonnell family trait for five centuries. By the middle of the fifteenth century the McDonnells had become one of the leading families in County Antrim, in Ireland's northeast corner, and, in 1620, the head of the family, Randal McDonnell, was created Earl of Antrim. There have been a number of distinguished McDonnells. In the sixteenth century,

Sorley Boy McDonnell was famous as a life-long foe of the British, and, in the seventeenth century, Francis McDonnell became a well-known politician. Sir Anthony McDonnell, in the nineteenth century, was a noted revolutionist, fighting to give the Irish a say in their own affairs, and, in literature, Sean Clarach McDonnell (1691–1754) was considered the leading poet of Munster. There has even been a McDonnell world chess champion—Alexander McDonnell, who achieved his title in 1833. All the Irish like fondly—and often vaguely—to suppose that they descend from lofty or even noble lineage. But the McDonnells of Drumlish who arrived in New York in the mid-nineteenth century have some reason to make this claim.

The Wall Street firm of McDonnell & Company became, in 1917, the successor to Byrne & McDonnell, which James Francis McDonnell had helped form twelve years earlier. By no small coincidence, Mr. McDonnell was able to buy out Mr. Byrne within a year after his marriage to the wealthy daughter of Thomas E. Murray, though exactly how much of his wife's money may have gone into the creation of the new company is unknown; it eventually became several million dollars.

In the early days there were, just as there are today, specialists in certain stocks. One brokerage firm might specialize in U.S. Steel, another in General Motors, and another in the stocks of banks or insurance companies. But James Francis McDonnell had come up with a somewhat special gimmick. The idea of a *right* had just been initiated (in those days), and stock rights work this way: When a company sells securities by privileged subscription, each stockholder is mailed one right for each share of stock he owns. With a common-stock offering, these rights give the stockholder the option to purchase additional shares according to the terms of the offering. The terms specify the number of rights required to subscribe for an additional share of stock, the subscription price per share, and the expiration date of the offering. The holder of rights has three choices: he can exercise them and subscribe for additional shares; he can let them expire; or he can sell them, since they are transferable. When a right is sold, it sells at only a fraction of the price of the stock itself. Rights have a limited life, and expire after a specified period of time.

Suppose, for example, that a person owned eighty shares of stock in a company, and that ten rights were required to purchase an additional share. With his eighty rights, this person could purchase eight full shares of stock, or he could sell them. People who want to play the stock market can, of course, buy stock directly. Let us suppose, if they do so, that the price of the stock is $40 a share. If the stock goes up to $60, the purchaser can make 50 percent on his original investment. If he buys 1,000 shares at $40, he puts up $40,000. If he sells them at $60, he has made $20,000 on a $40,000 investment—again 50 percent.

But rights can offer additional leverage to the speculator. If you can purchase for $2, say, a right to buy one share of the same stock within a one-year period, and you buy 1,000 rights, at the end of the year—or at any time during that year—you can buy 1,000 shares of stock at $40 a share. Effectively, then, the cost of the stock to you is $42 a share. Suppose, again, that during the year the stock has increased from $40 to $60. There has been a 50 percent increase in the price, but since the rights only cost you $2,000, you have made a profit of $18,000 on a $2,000 investment. That is, you have made 900 percent rather than just 50 percent.

James Francis McDonnell had a dour and somewhat unaccommodating nature—they called him "Little Caesar" in the family behind his back. He was not a financial genius, or even a brilliant trader. But he was one of the first men on Wall Street to recognize the value of rights, and to see the extra leverage inherent in these rights offerings. He was also among the first to see that lots of speculators would be interested in buying rights to any common stock. And so he became a specialist in rights trading. It was a simple system, perfectly legal, and not at all a laborious way to make money. With his particular gimmick, and with relatively

57

little else, James Francis McDonnell was able to make the promised million dollars for each new child as it arrived, and to keep his family in the large houses in New York and in Southampton, their cars and parties and polo ponies. As they watched their brother-in-law's climb to success, other Murrays, Cuddihys, McDonnells, and McQuails gradually began letting James Francis McDonnell's brokerage house handle their money. Seemingly without effort, he made money for them. His business prospered throughout World War I, continued to prosper throughout the twenties, and, with the lucky windfall of Grandpa Murray's inheritance in 1929—the Murray heirs eventually won their case, and were allowed to compute their taxes on a lower base—the 1930's continued serenely. There was no reason to suppose that McDonnells and Murrays would ever stop making money, and prospects throughout the thirties seemed eternally rosy. No one stopped to consider the fact that McDonnell & Company, trading rights for clients, and handling family accounts, was really not doing anything more than prospering. It was developing no particular talent or expertise in business management. It didn't need to. "Just let Jim handle it" became the casual family-business watchword. "He has a gimmick."

The combined families continued, meanwhile, their steady climb into society. Joseph B. Murray's marriage to Theresa Farrell was easily the most socially auspicious in the second Murray generation. Joe Murray was a suave and handsome young man who had graduated from Stevens Institute and the Yale Scientific School, where his charm and good nature had won him the nickname "Jo-Bo Murray-O," and where, one Saint Patrick's Day, he was presented with a bottle of rye and a bit of doggerel that went:

> To Joseph Murray of Irish descent
> This little token we present.
> If perchance you are troubled with snakes,
> Run like hell for heaven's sakes!

Both Joe Murray and his brother Jack showed clear promise of inheriting their father's talents as an inventor, and after Yale Joe Murray had been placed with Grandpa Murray's Brooklyn Edison Company, where he quickly rose to the position of general manager. Theresa Farrell, meanwhile, was a dark-haired beauty, whose father, James A. Farrell, was also a self-made man. Farrell had started as a mechanic in a Pennsylvania steel mill, and had been spotted by the steel king, Charles M. Schwab. Both the Farrells and the Murrays loved publicity, particularly social publicity, a trait that was becoming quite distinctive among the American Irish rich (in contrast, again, to such emerging Jewish families as the Schiffs, Loebs, Lehmans, and Warburgs, who considered publicity anathema and actively worked to keep their pictures off the society pages, even of the Jewish-owned *New York Times*).

For weeks beforehand, the newspapers were filled with details of the upcoming Farrell-Murray nuptials. The wedding was to take place at St. Joseph's Church in South Norwalk, Connecticut, with a huge breakfast reception following at the Farrells' nearby estate, "Rock Ledge." There were to be sixty people in the bridal party alone, plus hundreds of guests including all the "top" New York Irish Catholic names—Nicholas Brady, Judge Morgan O'Brien, and assorted Gormans. A special train would depart from Grand Central Station for South Norwalk on the morning of the wedding, just to transport the guests. The wedding pages would wear white knee-stockings and patent-leather pumps with colonial cut-steel buckles. Meanwhile, three large rooms of the Farrell mansion were filling up with wedding presents—"The silverware especially was remarkable!" the press gushed—and James Francis McDonnell's gift to his future sister-in-law was a rope of pearls reported, with some degree of exaggeration, to be "the size of hens' eggs." The honeymoon couple would take a six weeks' automobile trip around the United States, and would then make their home, of course, on Park Avenue.

But on the day of the wedding, June 19, 1916, the deluge of publicity took a decidedly unpleasant turn. After the throng of guests had left the church, and had gathered in the garden of "Rock Ledge" and the festivities had begun, a sudden puff of smoke burst from the roof of the big house, followed by a column of flame. Almost before the guests' eyes, the entire Farrell house seemed to explode into fire. "Save the wedding presents!" was suddenly the cry, as the men tried vainly to push their way into the burning house and attempted to douse the flames with bottles of champagne, and the women clutched at their rosary beads. But it was no use. The combined fire departments of South Norwalk and Rowayton could not extinguish the blaze, and the great house burned to the ground, taking with it $100,000 worth of furnishings and all the wedding gifts, valued at $30,000, the remarkable silver pieces melted into lumps. Repeated attempts were made to save the presents, but when the walls of the house began to crumble the bride's father refused to let either firemen or guests go inside, crying gallantly, "Don't worry! It's all insured!"

Later, it was concluded that the fire was the result of "the extraordinary amount of cooking being done" in the Farrell kitchens. But there were some who wondered worriedly: Was the fire the doing of a stern Deity who was punishing the Farrells and the Murrays for the sin of pride? In any case, the press commented that the fire left the couple's honeymoon plans "somewhat up in the air."

But two more rich Irish-American families were now joined in marriage, in what would become an increasingly complicated interfamily linkage. Mr. Farrell later commemorated this union by adding "Braised Breast of Lamb à la Murray" to his Farrell Line menus, which already offered such quaintly designated dishes as "Farrell's Dublin City Prime Ribs of Beef" and something called "O'Camembert." And Farrell-Murray family accounts were gradually added to the list of those handled by McDonnell & Company.

The firm's business continued to burgeon. Soon there would be McDonnell & Company offices in twenty-six different American cities, in every major money capital in the United States, with three separate offices in New York alone, and another in Paris. Throughout all this, no one seemed to worry about the fact that this was a business founded on a single gimmick that happened to work well. No one seemed to think it surprising, either, that what might have seemed an excessive amount of money was being spent on decorating McDonnell & Company's offices, which were lavishly furnished with imported chandeliers, thick carpets, and French and English antiques. Along with this went an increasing sense of the family's social importance. In the early 1930's, one of the Murray children heard one of his parents remark that Mrs. So-and-so was "from the wrong side of the tracks." What, the child wanted to know, did this expression mean? "New Jersey" was the reply.

Chapter 6

THE GREATEST
NOSE COUNT OF THEM ALL

 singular fact about the Irish in America has been that they have been able to succeed in a wide variety of fields. There is a "difference," again, between the Irish and the Jews—the latter having tended to distinguish themselves in retailing, investment banking, and, later on, in dress manufacturing and show business. The Irish, on the other hand, have managed to be successful not only in politics (with a concentration on elective offices, while the Jews have seemed to prefer appointive ones) but also in banking, insurance, engineering, industry, and show business, as doctors and lawyers and stockbrokers and advertising men—a whole spectrum of endeavor. Proud and scrappy and ambitious, the Irish quickly got into everything. Joseph P. Kennedy, for example, made money not only in finance but in whiskey and the motion picture industry. In the case of New York's Cuddihy family—which would soon ally itself, through marriage, to the ubiquitous Murrays—the money was made in publishing.

Isaac Kauffman Funk, the founder of the *Literary Digest*, was a Lutheran clergyman who had retired from the ministry in 1872 to become a publisher of religious tracts and sermons, and a magazine called *Metropolitan Pulpit*. In 1877, Funk was joined by a former schoolmate named Adam Willis Wagnalls, who had been a lawyer in Atchison, Kansas, and in 1884 Funk & Wagnalls began publishing a Prohibition journal called *Voice*. In 1888 the firm took over another religious periodical called *Missionary Review of the World*.

From the beginning, a kind of missionary zeal marked all the new publishers' ventures, even though neither Mr. Funk nor Mr. Wagnalls had any qualms about lifting and republishing previously published matter—material that had been printed in England, for example, or that had gone into public domain. Since this was before the advent of an international copyright law, this sort of thing was, though perhaps deceptive to readers, more or less legal, and when Funk & Wagnalls was attacked by a reporter from the New York *Evening Post* for highhandedly reprinting the entire *Encyclopaedia Britannica* in a cheap edition, Funk sued the reporter for his story and won his case. In 1890 Funk & Wagnalls brought out a new magazine called the *Literary Digest*, but only the title of the publication was really new. In line with Mr. Funk's policy of borrowing freely from the work of others, the *Literary Digest*, in the beginning, was nothing more than a compilation of stories and articles that had been published before by others. Even the format of the magazine was stolen from the then popular Washington magazine *Current Opinion*. At the outset, the magazine was only a moderate success and sold only a few thousand copies at ten cents each, or three dollars a year, and consisted of unstimulating columns of gray type, no illustrations, and three or four pages of advertising per issue.

Robert Joseph Cuddihy had gone to work for Funk & Wagnalls as an office boy at age sixteen, several years before the *Literary*

Digest came into existence. Cuddihy was poor and an Irish Catholic, and both Mr. Funk and Mr. Wagnalls were wealthy Protestants. At the same time, Cuddihy's devoutness and sense of moral rectitude were very much in line with Isaac Funk's ethical Lutheranism, and the older man took the younger one under his wing. Cuddihy was also tough, aggressive, and fiercely ambitious, and his rise in the firm was rapid. Wagnalls, meanwhile, was showing only a dilatory interest in the company, and Funk was spending more and more time investigating psychic phenomena and spiritualism. In 1905, Robert Cuddihy was named publisher of the *Literary Digest* and, though Funk made occasional appearances in the office, Cuddihy was in charge of things.

Robert Cuddihy's two main drives for the fledgling magazine were to maintain a high moral tone and to build circulation through advertising promotion. To establish the former, Mr. Cuddihy dictated that male and female personnel could not occupy the same offices, nor were men and women editors permitted to lunch out with one another or be seen together after hours. Both smoking and drinking were rigidly banned, and divorce was punished with quick dismissal. To achieve his second goal, Cuddihy believed in spending money, and in 1906 he bought the magazine *Public Opinion*, merged it with the *Digest*, and embarked upon an advertising campaign so expensive that it is said to have "terrified" his partners—but it boosted the *Digest*'s circulation to 200,000 by 1909, and to double that figure seven years later.

The *Digest*'s coverage of the events of World War I perhaps did more than anything else to establish it among the front-runners of American magazines. Its maps, prepared by professional cartographers and printed in two or three colors, were marvels of clarity and precision, and brought the details of overseas battles stunningly home to American readers. With this grew the *Digest*'s reputation for absolute and strict impartiality; if it quoted a Republican newspaper editorial on any issue, it was always careful to give an equal and balancing amount of space to a Democratic source, and the same to an Independent voice. At Robert Cuddihy's—or "R.J." as they called him in the office—insistence, no trace of bias or prejudice was ever to be discernible in the *Digest*'s pages, whether the subject at hand was politics, religion, economics, history, or literature, and by the 1920's hundreds of thousands of Americans had learned to believe that if you saw it in the *Digest* it was not only so, but fair.

By the end of the war the *Literary Digest*'s circulation had climbed to 900,000, and, under the Cuddihy aegis, it continued to climb until, by 1927, it had reached 1,500,000, when it was topped only by the mighty *Saturday Evening Post*. Its success at garnering advertising pages was one of the wonders of the era, and in a single issue in 1920 it contained 174 pages, with many issues of 150 or more pages following, while the weekly price for the magazine— out of Mr. Cuddihy's staunch respect for his readers' pocketbooks —remained at ten cents. By the late 1920's the *Literary Digest* had become a publishing phenomenon, and its boss a legend and a rich man. At one point during this great success Robert Cuddihy offered Mr. Funk $5 million to buy out Funk's 40 percent interest in the publication. Funk turned the offer down. He would live to regret his cavalier decision. But then, at the time, the *Digest* was making a profit of $2 million a year.

One reason for the *Digest*'s enormous popularity was Robert Cuddihy's innovative idea, in 1916, of conducting "straw votes." Voters in key areas were polled by mail as to their stands on various political issues; their individual responses to the questionnaires were then tallied, analyzed, and a "prediction" of the political outcome was reached. The first poll was of members of state legislatures on their choices of party nominees for President. Charles Evans Hughes and Woodrow Wilson would be the two candidates, the *Digest* announced—and they were. Next, in the autumn of that year, the *Digest* polled labor-union officials as to the outcome of the impending election, and followed this with a pole of fifty thousand *Digest* readers in Illinois, Indiana, Ohio, New Jersey, and New York—on the basis of which the *Digest* was able to announce that Wilson would be the winner. When the election results were in, the figures were astonishingly close to the *Digest*'s projection, with Wilson, of course, the winner. It began to seem that the *Digest* was an infallible barometer of public opinion.

Nothing at all like the *Literary Digest* polls had ever been done before in publishing, and from the outset the polls were hugely successful for at least three different reasons. They were, to begin with, highly interesting to *Digest* readers, who enjoyed looking into the magazine's crystal ball, and they increased circulation. Also, the results of each *Digest* poll were published in newspapers across the country, and thus provided a vast amount of free publicity for the magazine. Furthermore, every ballot that went out was accompanied by a *Digest* subscription blank, making the polls a gimmick through which to gain subscribers.

In 1920 the *Digest* predicted Harding over James M. Cox—again correctly—and in 1924 picked Coolidge over Davis. The *Digest* continued to be right in 1928 with Hoover over Alfred E. Smith (interestingly enough, R. J. Cuddihy himself, though normally nonpartisan, went to the Republican convention in Kansas City that summer to help nominate Hoover, instead of supporting Smith, the first Catholic candidate for President in American history). And in 1932 the *Digest* correctly stated that Hoover would be defeated by Franklin D. Roosevelt. The *Digest*'s winning streak at picking winners and losers was extended into other areas besides Presidential elections. In 1922, 1930, and 1932, from eight to twenty million ballots went out to car owners and telephone subscribers on the issue of Prohibition. The results showed an eventual victory for the "wets"—again an ironic contrast to the magazine's Prohibitionist management, but it underscored Robert Cuddihy's policy of editorial impartiality.

R. J. Cuddihy himself was a small-boned, fine-looking man who dressed conservatively and shunned publicity. He hated to be photographed, and only four pictures are known to have been taken of him in his lifetime. In 1886, still a rising young man at Funk & Wagnalls, he had married a Miss Emma Frances Bennett. When their son, Herbert Lester Cuddihy, was born, Mr. Cuddihy again showed the independent and impartial side of his nature by deciding that, when the time came, his son would not be sent to a Catholic school or college. His son Lester was sent to Lawrenceville and Princeton. When the boy left college, he went to work for an advertising tycoon, Baron Collier. Anxious to have his son join him at the *Digest*, R. J. Cuddihy told the young man that he would double his Collier salary if he would come over. Explaining this situation to Mr. Collier, Herbert Lester Cuddihy suggested that Collier double his salary. Collier did, and then, to lure his son away, R. J. had to double the double. But it hardly mattered. The Cuddihys were by now quite rich. R. J. Cuddihy had acquired a yacht, and Lester soon owned a town house in East Seventy-third Street that had its own elevator—very much a novelty in private houses in those days.

One of his son's first notions for the *Literary Digest* was to reduce the size of its pages by one-eighth of an inch. Even such a tiny reduction would, the younger Cuddihy pointed out, lower the *Digest*'s bulk weight in the mails and would result in a substantial saving in postage. The senior Cuddihy was reluctant to tamper, even in so slight a way, with a successful product, and was certain that the move would bring a storm of protest from readers. But he let his son have his way and the reduction was made—and no one noticed it. Only one reader, in fact, wrote in to complain. Another hugely successful Funk & Wagnalls venture was the publication, in 1922, of a volume titled *Etiquette* by a socially prominent New York divorcee named Emily Price Post. Mrs. Post's book went into hundreds of printings and new editions, and made Emily Post a rich woman and Funk & Wagnalls an even richer company. The

Cuddihys found Mrs. Post a somewhat prickly author to deal with. She was intensely jealous of her name and her product, and when she spotted an advertisement for a deodorant cream called Etiquet, she clipped the ad and wrote indignantly across the face of it, "Dear Mr. Cuddihy—is there no way to check this association with 'Etiquette'? Few things could be more revolting! At least could the illustration—" it showed a young woman stroking her underarm—"be forbidden? Certainly it is a *revolting* offense against 'Etiquette.' As a matter of fact, I was asked to go on a radio program by these manufacturers . . ." (The rest of her angry scribble is indecipherable.)

R. J. Cuddihy's favorite philanthropy was a center for cancer patients run by a Catholic order which had been started by Rose Hawthorne, daughter of Nathaniel, herself a convert and thus "more Catholic than the Catholics." Mr. Cuddihy approved of Miss Hawthorne's zeal, and to aid her cause he regularly carried about on his person a hefty wad of large bills. Whenever he encountered a rich Catholic friend, Mr. Cuddihy would produce the wad, tap it significantly with his finger, and suggest that the friend fatten the pile with a few big bills of his own. Among Mr. Cuddihy's well-heeled friends were members of Chicago's Cudahy family, including Michael Cudahy himself, who had gone to work as a butcher at the age of fourteen, and later revolutionized the meatpacking industry by developing the process for summer curing of meat under refrigeration; the result was the Cudahy Packing Company. Cudahy once dropped in on Cuddihy in New York just to ask him for a semantic explanation of the different spellings of their name—clearly the field of Mr. Cuddihy, the publisher, and not Mr. Cudahy, the butcher. R. J. Cuddihy told his Chicago kin Cudahy, "Both our families came over in the forties from the same county, Kilkenny, and the same town. Only there was this difference between our two sets of forebears: *ours* knew how to spell. The officials at Ellis Island thus recorded your name phonetically

—that is, incorrectly—as *Cudahy*. Our name we ourselves wrote—
to wit, *Cuddihy*." After imparting this information, Mr. Cuddihy
took Mr. Cudahy to lunch. Meanwhile, back in Kilkenny, the
name turns up in various guises, from Cuddy to McGillicuddy.

Mr. Cuddihy was equally precise in other matters. His grandson
Jack recalls bringing a schoolmate home one weekend from Portsmouth Priory. At lunch, Grandpa Cuddihy asked the friend,
"Where are you from, George?" The young man replied, "Man-
chester, New Hampshire, sir." "Ah," said Mr. Cuddihy, "Man-
chester, New Hampshire—population 233,563," or whatever it
was at the time. The young man was dumfounded that Mr. Cuddihy had the figure right to the last digit.

At the same time, Mr. Cuddihy was consistently reserved in respect to his religion, and was careful never to discuss his faith with
his non-Catholic friends and business acquaintants, nor to prose-
lytize in any way, nor to get into religious arguments. This was not
so much a matter of conscience as it was in line with the *Digest*'s
editorial policy of strict neutrality in all matters. Few non-Catholics who knew him suspected Mr. Cuddihy's affiliation with the
Church, and, in fact, one of his best friends was a Baptist minister
named Justin D. Fulton, D.D. Obviously, Dr. Fulton did not realize that his friend was a devout Catholic because, on one occasion,
Dr. Fulton presented Mr. Cuddihy with a little book he had written, and which had been published in 1893 by something called
the Pauline Propaganda Company. The book, warmly inscribed to
Cuddihy by Fulton, was called *How to Win Romanists*, and was
dedicated:

To
The Youth of America
confronted by
Lost and undone Romanists journeying
To an endless death, to whom
few speak and for whom

few pray . . .
in the hope and with the prayer
that it may show them
how to win Romanists to Christ

Fulton's little book, a polemic of anti-Catholic bigotry, was filled with lurid tales of human sacrifice, of nuns being violated by priests in convents, of onanism among monks in monasteries, of the fallibility of the Pope, and blamed the Catholic Church for everything from slavery to the labor movement. Quite typically, R. J. Cuddihy accepted the gift and thanked his friend, and never let Fulton know the considerable gaffe he had committed.

Under Mr. Cuddihy's stern and proper exterior he, too, was a sentimental Irishman. Like his partner, Mr. Funk, Cuddihy was quick to instigate lawsuits against any detractors of either Funk & Wagnalls or its precious *Literary Digest*. But when he won his cases, he inevitably paid the damages for which his opponents were assessed. In his strictly run offices, he would call errant employees into his chamber, dress them down thoroughly for their misdeeds, and then follow the scolding with an apology and an invitation to lunch. There is a persistent Funk & Wagnalls tale that one afternoon Mr. Cuddihy happened upon two of his *Digest* editors merrily fornicating among the *Digest* files or, as he discreetly put it later, "going at it." Mr. Cuddihy muttered a confused apology, retreated from the scene, and then, after a decent interval had elapsed, summoned the fellow whom he had caught *in flagrante* to his office. "Young man," he announced sternly, "you are going to have to accept a reduction in salary!" And it was done.

A Father Wynne, a Jesuit priest, once said of him, "Catholics in New York as elsewhere are crushed under the burden of their churches and schools, but there is in this town one Catholic who has never said 'No' to anybody. . . . I mean Mr. Robert Cuddihy. His *Literary Digest* has an extraordinary influence in the United States."

And so indeed it did. After the *Digest*'s correct forecast of the outcome of the 1932 Presidential election, the editors of the Kansas City *Journal-Post* trumpeted, "Not even Franklin D. Roosevelt can feel more triumphant than the editors of the *Literary Digest*." And the *Digest* editors themselves, in a rare moment of pride and self-congratulation, added a paean of their own to their magazine, saying, "When better polls are built, the *Digest* will build them!"

In the early spring of 1936, the Robert J. Cuddihys celebrated their fiftieth wedding anniversary with a special Nuptial Mass in the Lady Chapel of St. Patrick's Cathedral, which was then at 460 Madison Avenue. There was a big family party afterward, with relatives gathered from all corners of America. R. J. Cuddihy was seventy-three years old, and the Great Depression had affected his great fortune, and his great magazine, very little. The three Cuddihy sons, Paul, Lester, and Arthur, were now all connected with the *Digest*, and had made brilliant marriages to prominent (and rich) Irish Catholic women—Lester Cuddihy to Grandpa Thomas Murray's daughter Julia. (At the time of the courtship, when Grandpa Murray was told that the Cuddihys were big in publishing, the great inventor said, puzzled, "Publishing? What is publishing exactly?") The Cuddihys' four daughters had also made good Catholic marriages—Mabel to T. Burt McGuire, Helen to William J. Ryan, Alice to Thomas Guerin, and Emma to Kenrick Gillespie. Grandpa Cuddihy's money had built the elegant apartment house at 1088 Park Avenue, and his son Lester had had the idea of adding the large and fountain-filled central garden-courtyard, which makes 1088 Park one of the singularly pleasant addresses in New York today. (At first, it looked as though the building would be a financial failure, and so it became inhabited largely by other Cuddihys, McGuires, and Gillespies.) There were summers in Water Mill and cruises on Grandpa Cuddihy's yacht, the *Polly*, and trips back to boarding school on the boat for the grandsons, when Father Diman himself, head of Portsmouth Priory, would come out and stand on the bluff to greet and bless the boys as the Cuddihy yacht sailed into Portsmouth Harbor. Meanwhile, the *Literary Digest*'s pollsters were busily at work on the upcoming November election, a contest between Alfred Landon and Roosevelt for a second term. And presently the results of the poll were out: It would be a landslide victory for Landon, with Landon carrying all the big states—New York, California, Ohio, Illinois, New Jersey, and so on. The result of twenty million *Digest* ballots showed that Landon would win four votes out of every seven.

What went wrong? Was it the sin of pride again? Because when the results were in, Landon had carried exactly two states, Maine and Vermont. It was an overwhelming victory for Roosevelt. *Time* magazine printed a picture of Grandpa Cuddihy with the caption, "Is Our Face Red!" And in its wisecracking style, *Time* noted that "The *Digest* mispredicted a Landonslide." A solemn American political maxim used to be "As Maine goes, so goes the nation." The joke became "As Maine goes, so goes Vermont."

Prior to 1936 the *Digest* had sent out the ballots for its polls to telephone subscribers, automobile registration owners, and to its own subscription list. In the 1936 poll, however, the telephone lists were largely abandoned, since it was felt that telephone books went quickly out of date. Perhaps that was the reason for the gigantic error. But some *Digest* people felt that there were other, more subtle, reasons. One editor commented that he felt that the *Digest* had become "punch-drunk," and had begun to believe too completely in the myth of *Digest* infallibility which it had sponsored. ("When better polls are built . . .") Others said that the *Digest* had gone wrong by failing to reach "the lower economic brackets" of the voting population. There had been other ominous notes. During the early Depression years, *Digest* circulation had dropped more than the *Digest* cared to admit, and profits were down accordingly. The *Digest* had also begun to feel the competition of newer, sprightlier weeklies such as *Time, Newsweek,* and

The New Yorker. The *Digest*'s own explanation was a somewhat mysterious one: Republicans, it said, answered questionnaires more readily than Democrats. This left the reason in the realm of the occult. But one thing was absolutely certain: The *Literary Digest*, which had a few days earlier been a great and trusted American institution, was suddenly a national laughingstock, and all over the world *"Literary Digest* jokes" proliferated, rather the way Polish jokes spread in the early 1970's. On the day of the debacle, Mr. Funk and the three Cuddihy sons either avoided the office altogether or else put in only momentary appearances. Mr. Robert J. Cuddihy, however, came into the office at the usual hour and went about his business as though nothing had happened.

H. Lester Cuddihy, who had been for Landon, wired his young son Jack at Portsmouth Priory, saying simply, "Ha ha." But Lester Cuddihy's wife, Julia, sent another telegram to Jack, saying, "Don't write anything fresh to Grandpa. He feels very badly. Mom."

By the issue of July 17, 1937, things at the *Digest* were in such dire shape that Funk & Wagnalls actually gave the *Digest* away— to the publisher of *Review of Reviews*, and the combined result was called by the unwieldy title of *The Digest: Review of Reviews Incorporating the Literary Digest*. It did not do well. By October of the same year, this amalgam was sold, and the name *Literary Digest* was reapplied to the new result. This attempt at a resuscitation was also a failure, and with the issue of February 19, 1938, publication was suspended—temporarily, it was hoped—and a pathetic letter was sent out to ten thousand subscribers which begged:

Literary Digest is not just another magazine; it is an American Institution of major importance. *It cannot be allowed to die.* . . . We ask you to put a dollar in the enclosed return envelope. . . . Your dollar will be credited to your subscription as an increase in rate.

Quite a number of dollars floated in, along with several outright gifts. But for soliciting and accepting this sort of charity, and tampering in an irregular way with rates and circulation methods, the

Digest attracted the attention of the newly created Audit Bureau of Circulations. Funk and Cuddihy had fought against the creation of the Bureau, and its goal to create a standard and uniform method of tabulating magazine circulations, throughout their entire professional lives. Now it was the ABC that would administer the *coup de grâce* to the *Digest*. The ABC demanded that the cash gifts be returned, and petitioned the court to reorganize the magazine under the Bankruptcy Act. *Time* gleefully reported the death statistics:

Against liabilities of $1,492,056 (including a $60,000 demand note to Funk & Wagnalls—original *Literary Digest* publishers—$63,000 for paper, $30,000 for printing, $612,000 to readers for paid up subscriptions), the *Digest* listed assets of $850,923: cash on hand, $222,293; mailing lists, furniture, machinery, $377,794; deferred charges, $160,821; goodwill, $90,015.

This last figure sounds the saddest of all. After three months' suspension, *Time* took over the *Digest*'s 250,000 unexpired subscriptions.

Funk & Wagnalls—and the Cuddihys—at least still had Emily Post and *Etiquette*. And, as someone had commented at The Players Club on the day the news was released of the *Digest*'s sale to the *Review of Reviews*, "All I know is that when R. J. Cuddihy lets go, you know that the cow has been milked dry."

Chapter 7

THE ORIGINAL BUTTER-AND-EGG MAN

he Cuddihy family tree becomes a rather confusing one to contemplate, not only because of the profusion of children and grandchildren, but also because one is required to remember that Mr. R. J. Cuddihy's daughter, Mabel, married T. Burt McGuire, and one of his granddaughters, Mary Jane (Lester Cuddihy's daughter), married James Butler MacGuire— no kin, different spelling—which makes the tree sprout with a collection of both McGuires and MacGuires, and which union (the Cuddihy-MacGuire union, that is) brought the Butler family fortune into the wealthy Murray-McDonnell-Cuddihy family complex. One way to sort out the McGuires from the MacGuires is to remember that the MacGuires today are all descendants of both Grandpa Murray and Grandpa Cuddihy, while the McGuires are descendants of Grandpa Cuddihy only.

The MacGuires, meanwhile, would be nobodies if it had not been for Grandpa Butler. James Butler was born in County Kilkenny in 1855, where the Butlers had been farmers for fifteen generations. The original Butler, it is said, was a Norman officer who came across with William the Conqueror. He was William the Conqueror's butler, and the French branch of the family is called Le Boutillier. In 1328 a Butler was created Duke of Ormond, and lived in Kilkenny Castle, and the American Butlers today use (for this somewhat tenuous reason) the royal Ormond family crest. James Butler's antecedents, however, were not royal, but the family must have had some small amount of property, and were not impoverished tenant farmers, because when James Butler emigrated to the United States in 1875 at the age of twenty he had inherited a hundred pounds (then about five hundred dollars) from an uncle, and had received some education at the parish schools near his family's farm outside the village of Russelltown. This small nest egg was sufficient, when he came ashore in Boston, to keep him in an inexpensive rooming house—and not force him into one of Boston's notorious cellars—while he looked for a job.

Because young James Butler had been a farm boy, he first went to work for a farmer named Dresser near Goshen Mountain, Massachusetts, where he started out tilling land with a hoe. One of his brothers, meanwhile, had also come out of Ireland and had gone to Urbana, Illinois, to work in a railroad hotel. After a year or so behind the plow, James Butler followed his brother there and got a job in the same hotel as a steward. From there he went to Chicago, where he joined the staff of the Sherman Hotel, working in the kitchen and learning a bit about the purchasing, preparation, and storage of food. Gaining confidence as a hotel man, he next went to New York, to work for the old Windsor Hotel, where he was given the job of preparing President Grover Cleveland's first inaugural banquet. "I was the busiest man in the United States that night," he used to say of the experience. (Twenty-four years later, he would decline an engraved invitation to President Taft's inaugural, saying, "I don't even like to think about inaugurations!")

From the Windsor, he moved on to the old Murray Hill Hotel, and he might well have remained a hotel man for the rest of his life had he not moved into a rooming house operated by the mother of a young ex-reporter named Patrick J. O'Connor. Patrick O'Connor was a melancholy fellow who had been told by his doctor that he must get into some business that was less "nerve-racking" than newspaper work. O'Connor had opened a small grocery store, but in the evenings, around the boarding-house dinner table, he moaned and complained about how poor business was. "It's in a bad part of town," he would say sadly, "and I can't afford to move to a good one." Finally, James Butler had had enough of this, and said, "O'Connor, stop complaining. How much do you need to move to a good part of town?" O'Connor replied that he would need at least two thousand dollars. James Butler, who, even then, was exercising a trait for which he would become famous—a dislike of spending money, and a habit of squirreling away every penny he could in savings banks and mattresses—said, "All right, I'll stake you."

Together, the two new partners scouted for a new location, and found one at 857 Second Avenue. Since both partners were Irish, Butler suggested that they paint the storefront green, and the little green-fronted grocery store called P. J. O'Connor & Company opened for business on September 2, 1882. For a while, James Butler wore two hats, buying food for the Murray Hill Hotel and groceries for the store, but as the store with the eye-catching front began to prosper and to consume more and more of his time, he quit the hotel business and gave his full energy to groceries. In 1883 the partners bought a second store and painted it green at Tenth Avenue and Forty-fourth Street, and a year later James Butler bought his partner out. He was twenty-nine years old, and his own man.

At the outset, his stores—now called James Butler, Inc.—were designed to offer quality merchandise at more or less carriage-trade prices. Butler stores offered generous credit, and made deliveries.

But as he expanded—with a third green-fronted store, and then a fourth—he decided that credit and deliveries were "a lot of damned nonsense." He cut out the nonsense, slashed prices, cut out deliveries except to a few housebound old ladies, and concentrated on quantity sales at a small margin of profit. To keep his overhead low, he staffed his stores with just two, or at the very most three, young clerks, and to keep his overhead even lower, he hired only young Irishmen—many of whom he would buttonhole as they came down the gangplank—who were eager and hungry and would work hard for small wages. As his profits increased, he bought more stores. By 1909 he owned or controlled two hundred stores, all painted green, doing $15 million worth of business a year. He had become not only the first, but the largest, grocery-chain-store operator in the United States and had acquired, in the process, a considerable amount of New York real estate. By 1929 James Butler was personally worth more than $30 million, an impressive gain on his original investment, and in the summer of that year he outwitted the stock market by selling $1 million of property at peak, pre-Crash prices. Before he was through, there would be eleven hundred stores.

In 1883, James Butler had married a sweet-faced Irish girl named Mary Rorke, who bore him, all told, eleven children, only four of whom survived birth or childhood diseases. All that child-bearing must have taken its toll, because Mary Butler died in her early forties. But the loss of his wife was the only thing that occurred to mar his dream, which, he often said, had from the outset been a fourfold affair: "To become rich, to raise a family, to own a stable of thoroughbreds, and to add to the glory of the Catholic Church—with a good room in Heaven waiting for me at the end." James Butler's first horse had been a mare that he had ridden on the farm back home in Ireland, and it is said that a love of horses is in every Kilkenny man's blood. In 1894 he bought his first trotter, which he named Russell T. (after Russelltown), and he began driving in amateur races. When, in the early 1900's, he bought 350 acres of rolling Westchester farmland, and built himself a huge Victorian country house, surrounded by porches, on the property which he christened "East View Farm," he bought more trotting horses and began shipping them off to races at Belmont Park, on Long Island. Mr. Butler—who, now that he owned a big estate in Westchester, liked to be called "Squire Butler"—was not overly generous with his wife in terms of money, nor did he believe in betting on his own horses. But whenever his wife wanted money to buy something for the house, or for herself, or for the children, he would give her a tip on the horse likeliest to win, and see that her bets were placed properly. She usually won. In those days there was no parimutuel system, and bets were placed with bookmakers who skulked around and about the racetrack. At the family breakfast table, Mrs. Butler would inevitably ask, "Well, what shall we pray for today, dear?" "Pray for good weather and a fast track" was his usual reply.

Shipping horses all the way from Westchester to Long Island was, the Squire soon realized, a costly business. There must be a cheaper way. The cheaper way led him to acquire, in 1902, the land on which to build what he named the Empire City Racetrack, in nearby Yonkers. At first, Empire City offered only harness races, but Squire Butler decided that there was more money to be made in racing thoroughbreds, and so he switched to that. This immediately put Squire Butler at loggerheads with the New York Jockey Club, which, having supreme control over New York racing, refused to give him a license. The Jockey Club was also one of the strongholds of New York's Protestant Establishment, and James Butler was an Irishman, a Catholic, and an outsider to the little circle. Led by such New York bluebloods as John Sanford (of the Bigelow-Sanford carpet fortune) and Harry K. Knapp, the club went out to do battle with the doughty Squire, never suspecting that they might have met their match. Butler

complied with every legal requirement for operating a thoroughbred racetrack and, after a court battle that lasted from 1904 to
1907, he won. Needless to say, James Butler became the first figure in thoroughbred racing who was never asked to join the club.
"To hell with them," he used to say.

Empire City soon became known as a "homey" track, plain and
comfortable as an old shoe, quite the opposite of the fancier and
more social Belmont. It offered thoroughbred racing for the common folk, but it quickly became one of the most profitable tracks
in the East. Some of its profitableness was directly due to its owner's now-famous economies. It became known as "The little track
beside the water tower," and it faced Yonkers's Central Avenue.
When the buildings and the fence around the track needed painting, Mr. Butler directed that only the side that was visible from
the avenue be painted; the sides that could not be seen received no
paint. On dry days, the crowds from Empire City would emerge at
the end of an afternoon of racing covered with dust, because
Squire Butler would not buy a watering rig. When, at last, he
decided that he would have to buy a rig or lose attendance, he
bought one, but he personally supervised every watering operation, periodically shouting to the man in charge, "Don't waste my
water! Don't waste my water!" In the early days of Empire City, a
band would appear to play "The Wearing of the Green" whenever a Butler horse won. But when the band became too expensive, Squire Butler fired them all. When someone asked him,
"Who'll play 'The Wearing of the Green' now, Jim?" he replied,
"The crowd can whistle it." Though he was a millionaire, he
always drove to the track in an ancient and dilapidated Ford car
that terrified his passengers and that he refused to turn in for a
new one.

With his Empire City Racetrack, the Squire began buying race
horses in quantity, the way he bought groceries for his stores. He
was out to prove, he said, that fine horses could be bred and raised

in the Northeast as successfully as they could in the traditional "bluegrass country" of Kentucky and Virginia, and he proved it. Among his more successful horses were Direct and Directum Kelly. Directum I, a pacer, and son of Directum Kelly, sold for $40,000 in 1915. The Squire had paid $8,250 for Direct, who went on to become the unbeaten champion of old-style sulky racing. Driving King Direct, one of Direct's descendants, Mr. Butler himself broke the world's amateur sulky racing mark by doing a mile in 2.0475 minutes. Other noted thoroughbreds were Pebbles, Spur, Sting, and Questionnaire, the last of which won both the Empire City and Brooklyn Handicaps, plus the Metropolitan in 1931, and the Paumonok at the opening of the 1932 racing season at Jamaica. Between the years 1914 and 1933, Butler horses won a total of $649,573. Squire Butler's favorite horse was Sting, and in 1925, after Sting had won a number of important races, Mr. A. C. Bostwick, through an intermediary, offered Mr. Butler $125,000 for him. Butler replied, "That's a nice offer, but you tell Mr. Bostwick that there are a lot of men in the world who have that much money but there is only one man who has Sting. I wouldn't take a million for him. I'm a sentimental Irishman, and Sting will stay here until his dying day." Stay Sting did, and after his dying day a bronze statue of him was erected on the lawn at East View Farm.

Other horse breeders, jealous of the parvenu Mr. Butler's great success and noting his pronounced penuriousness, liked to circulate stories that he fed his horses short rations, and that he would rather see a crate of Butler eggs spilled on the sidewalk than see a race horse pampered or overfed. But no one who really knew him could say that his love of horses was not genuine, even though he was well aware of the value of each of them, and watched the performance of each with a hard eye on the ledger sheet. He once turned "white as a ghost" when handed the news that three of his prize horses had been killed simultaneously by a bolt of lightning. "All men are equal, on the turf or under it" was one of his favorite sayings. No one could deny, either, that the Squire was tightfisted. One of his business tactics was to have periodic picnics for his grocery clerks at Empire City. After the picnic, the "boys" were instructed to "clean up the place," which they did, enabling Mr. Butler to charge the cost of the outing as a business expense for "rubbish removal."

At one point a rumor got around—circulated, no doubt by jealous rivals in the grocery business—that Mr. Butler was in the habit of "levying" a dollar a day on each one of his stores (the implication was that there was something evil and un-American in the practice). "Ridiculous!" said Mr. Butler indignantly. "If I had a store that didn't pay me more than a dollar a day, I'd close it." He was, on the other hand, lavish in his spending when it came to horseflesh and racetracks, and he eventually acquired a large share of Laurel Park, in Maryland, and helped put up the track at Juarez, Mexico, where he once spent a pleasant afternoon chatting with Pancho Villa.

There were, meanwhile, repeated confrontations between the Squire and members of the Old Guard racing world, and Old Guard society. Once Mr. J. E. Widener (whose father had got his start as a butcher in Philadelphia) met the Squire and said, somewhat loftily, "Ah, Mr. Butler—how are your groceries?" The Squire, who always spoke with a bit of a brogue, answered, "Sure an' they're fine. How's yer meats?" He refused to join clubs—calling them more "nonsense"—and refused "to have truck with" either society or politics. Once both Tammany and anti-Tammany groups wanted to put up James Butler's name for Mayor of New York, and William L. Ward, the Republican boss of Westchester, asked him to run for Congress. The Squire would have no truck with either offer. "I'm a butter-and-egg man" was his reply to that. He refused to be listed in *Who's Who in America*, and would not let his name be used as a dummy on any board of directors. The only club he joined was the Andiron Club on Seventy-second

Street, where he liked to play poker and lift a glass or two of Irish whiskey. He did, however, become a good friend of his Westchester neighbor, John D. Rockefeller, whose estate adjoined East View Farm. Mr. Rockefeller enjoyed listening to Mr. Butler's salty and vociferous opinions on "high finance," for which the Squire had very little use. He had little use, either, for tennis or golf, and once when Mr. Rockefeller invited him over for a round on his private course, the Squire snorted, "Golf! That's a rich man's game."

His interest in horseflesh in no way diminished his interest in groceries and, as his business continued to flourish and expand, he worked at it at a whirlwind pace. He built a two-million-dollar warehouse in Long Island City which contained 500,000 feet of floor space, and included a bakery, a coffee-roasting and a canning department, a printing plant for labels—including his East View Farm—brand egg and dairy products—and numerous other divisions. Big as his operation had become, the Squire's hand was in every phase of it. He made periodic visits—always unannounced, of course—to each of his stores, checking on things, and on anniversary-sale days he often showed up on the loading platform of the Long Island City plant as early as six in the morning, when the early shipping crew was going to work. An admiring friend, commenting on the Squire's almost magical ability to juggle dozens of different projects at once, told of how he would simultaneously "bargain for one hundred thousand eggs, buy the output of a vineyard in France, order the entire product of a canning factory, keep four or five lawyers busy with the technical details of a vast amount of litigation, discuss the best points of trotting horses, buy a farm, receive a delegation seeking help in some municipal undertaking (which usually meant money), and give ready and sympathetic response to appeals from churchmen to aid worthy cases of distress." The Squire once boasted that he had not taken a day's vacation for seventeen years.

The Squire's philanthropic activities were almost exclusively confined to the Catholic Church, and when he entertained at East View Farm, or at his big town house in the city, it was usually for Cardinals, Bishops, or other Catholic dignitaries, and he often opened the place for Fresh Air Fund picnics and parties for Catholic orphans. He founded Marymount School and College in Tarrytown, New York, which was headed for years by James Butler's first cousin, Mother Marie Joseph Butler, who became known as "Mother Butler of Marymount." Although the "Mary" in the school's name refers to the Virgin, Mr. Butler liked to think of the institution as a memorial to his wife. In 1926, James Butler purchased the old Florence Vanderbilt Burden house at Fifth Avenue and Eighty-fourth Street, and presented it to Marymount so that the school could have a city unit. Once, at Christmastime, after he had presented his cousin with a million-dollar piece of property in addition to the Burden house, Mother Butler murmured to her staff, "Santa Claus has been very good to us this year." He was equally generous with his gifts to New York's St. Patrick's Cathedral, and today the Butler family pew—Number 11—is the only one still in private family ownership. The walls of Squire Butler's bedroom at East View Farm were covered with photographs of Church figures, family, race horses, as well as with pictures of saints, the Blessed Virgin, Christ, and religious relics and crucifixes. For his contributions and devotion to the Church the Pope made James Butler a Knight Commander of the Order of Saint Gregory in 1912, an honor he was to take with great seriousness all his life.

Raising his motherless children, he was a strict and sometimes stern parent, and his offspring regarded the patriarch with awe and not a small amount of dread. As he had done with their mother, he insisted that the only spending money that the children could have was what they could win by placing two-dollar bets on Butler horses. He left a stern—some of his heirs thought too stern—and tough-minded will which, after a bequest of $100,-000 to the Sacred Heart Convent in Tarrytown, gave each child $100,000 at age twenty-five, an additional $125,000 at age thirty, and the balance of the inheritance at age thirty-five, minus $250,-000 that was to be set aside in an unshatterable trust. "None of my children will be spendthrifts," he used to say. When the Squire died in 1934, and was gathered to his "room in heaven" and his mortal remains were placed in the Butler crypt at Marymount, beside his wife's, over three thousand people turned out for his funeral at St. Patrick's.

There was "some question" as to whether his oldest son, James Butler, Jr., who shared his father's interest in horses, would be taken into the exclusive Jockey Club. But, after a certain amount of grumbling from some of the Old Guard, the younger Butler was accepted for membership. By the third generation, all the old feuds were forgotten and James Butler III went sailing into the club with no difficulty whatever. Squire Butler's oldest daughter, Beatrice, had meanwhile married a prominent New York physician, D. Philip MacGuire, and it was their son, James Butler MacGuire, who married Mary Jane Cuddihy, tying up the Butler connection with the Murrays and McDonnells and the Funk & Wagnalls fortune. The first brush of scandal ever to touch any of the interconnected families occurred in 1947 when one of R. J. Cuddihy's grandsons, T. Burt McGuire, Jr. (the other McGuires), married actress-singer Lillian Roth, the author of a confessional book called *I'll Cry Tomorrow* which dealt candidly with her bouts with alcoholism. Not only had Miss Roth been a vaudeville performer, but she was Jewish, and had had four previous husbands and divorces. At the time of the McGuire-Roth nuptials, it was announced in the newspapers that the pair had met at a meeting of Alcoholics Anonymous. Miss Roth told reporters, "He has given me a love beyond my worth," and Mr. McGuire revealed that when his wife struggled with insomnia he lulled her to sleep by sitting at her bedside and repeating "The Good Lord wants you to sleep" over and over again until she slept.

As if all this weren't bad enough, several years later the Mc-Guires were all over the newspapers again, this time battling for a divorce. Mr. McGuire accused his wife of "mental cruelty, physical violence, and habitual intemperance." He claimed that Miss Roth had once attacked him with a knife at their Palm Springs, California, house, and that he had had to escape from her fury by locking himself in a bedroom and leaving the house through a window. "I'm afraid of this woman," he declared. "When she drinks, she becomes violent, and I'm afraid of her." In her countersuit, Miss Roth charged Mr. McGuire with adultery. To the chagrin of the Cuddihys, it was all very messy. What would Grandpa Cuddihy, such a stickler for moral rectitude within and without the *Literary Digest*, have thought of such proceedings? Heaven alone knew.

Through it all, Mr. McGuire repeatedly denied that family pressure had anything to do with his wish to divorce Miss Roth, or that he was trying, through the divorce, to obtain more funds from his family. There was no Cuddihy trust, he insisted, that was in any way contingent upon the marriage. But the fact was that when T. Burt McGuire, Jr. married Lillian Roth, his Cuddihy relatives ostracized him thoroughly from their midst. After the divorce, albeit reluctantly, the clan readmitted him.

Out in Hollywood, meanwhile, one of the Chicago meat-packing Cudahys, young Michael, was creating headlines with his well-publicized romance with Joan Crawford. When Michael, an enthusiastic playboy, suddenly died, Miss Crawford stole the show at the funeral by arriving in not one but two huge limousines. The second was filled with nothing but flowers. The first contained Miss Crawford, in full mourning, draped in black veils from head to toe and clutching a silver cross.

Chapter 8

THE WEDDING OF THE CENTURY

When Grandpa Thomas E. Murray warned his children that "money can divide a family," he might have added that another divisive influence among the F.I.F.'s would certainly be the contentiousness and scrappiness of the Irish nature. Squabbles between the various members of Grandpa Murray's family had become, by the early 1930's, a consistent fact of family life both in Southampton and in New York. Each of his children had his or her own distinct personality, and that, of course, did not help.

Uncle Joe Murray was a shy Murray, the quietest and most retiring of Thomas E. Murray's sons, devoted to his garden and his boxwood hedges, and the author, in his spare time—while not conscientiously toiling for his father's companies—of a number of scholarly articles on the cross-pollination of different varieties of ilex, and the quiet resister, with lengths of wire, of his nieces' and nephews' motorized excursions across his precious lawn at Water

Mill. His wife, the former Theresa Farrell, was also a shy and somewhat nervous person, a meticulous housekeeper—not in the *Craig's Wife* sense, but rather out of her innate fear of offending or upsetting the "help," which she had a great deal of trouble managing. Her five daughters, for example, were never permitted to have any breakfast if they appeared at the table later than 9 A.M., lest the servants object or a "fuss" be created in the kitchen. As a result, "the Joe Murray girls," as they were called, were always trooping across the drive on summer mornings to Aunt Julia's house, where they were cheerfully fed. (Though not without some grumbling from Nat, Aunt Julia's butler, who was often heard to say, "Some household they've got here—breakfast at one end of the table, lunch at the other.")

Aunt Julia, Uncle Joe's sister (Mrs. H. Lester Cuddihy), ran a much more relaxed establishment in her big house, and Mrs. Joe Murray used to say that she "could never see how Julia did it." Julia Cuddihy's servants seemed to adore her, there were never any below-stairs fusses, and the help would change their plans at the wave of their mistress's hand. Aunt Julia had (and was able to keep) an excellent cook, and the Cuddihys were famous for the food they served. If friends dropped by for cocktails, they were almost automatically expected to stay on for dinner, and even when as many as a dozen extra places had been set at table at the last minute, the meal was always faultless and faultlessly served. Once—it was a Friday night—on his way into the dining room, Mr. Cuddihy asked his wife, "What's for dinner?" She replied, "Lester, you asked for broiled lobster." "But what I really feel like," he said "is a Spanish omelet." Without a word, Mrs. Cuddihy stepped into the kitchen with her husband's request. The others at the table were served their lobsters, and Mr. Cuddihy got his Spanish omelet.

Uncle Jack Murray, meanwhile, Thomas E. Murray, Sr.'s youngest son, was an altogether different sort. Jack was known as a "wild" Murray—handsome, definitely a blade, and a bit of a hell-raiser, who was often criticized by the other Murrays for "living high off the hog." This may have been because he was clearly his father's favorite. Jack was not without talent as an inventor and, in 1915, when he was only sixteen, received Patent Number 951,486 for a baseball game-playing apparatus based on the gravity principle, invented when he was eleven, which had prompted Thomas A. Edison to write him a handwritten note that said:

> This is pretty good for a boy of
> only 11 years to have invented. It's
> "going some."
>
> EDISON

Jack Murray loved sports, and had been a star lacrosse player at Stevens Institute. But he had bowed to his father's wishes after college, and had gone to work for the Murray enterprises. Though neither of his brothers—Tom and Joe—ever took so much as a glass of Dubonnet until very late in life when they were ordered to by their respective doctors, Jack Murray enjoyed strong whiskey, parties, and pretty women, all of which preferences caused raised eyebrows among others of his conservative family. And when, in the spring of 1918, he eloped with and married a beautiful girl named Jeanne Durand—who was an orphan and therefore of "questionable" heritage—there was criticism from the other Murrays, particularly his older brother Tom. The wedding took place in, of all places, Hoboken, where the bride was described as "popular in 'frat' parties," and announcement of the union was withheld until almost three months later.

It would not be fair to call Jack Murray the black sheep of the Murray family, because, while he worked for his father's various companies, he personally succeeded in securing some two hundred patents for his own inventions. But, after his father's death in 1929, there was a bitter quarrel between Jack and his older brother Tom as to which man would control the family interests.

The feud became so bitter that the two brothers barely spoke, and in 1930 Jack Murray left the company to go into politics. He was named Commissioner of the Port of New York Authority twice— once under Governor Franklin D. Roosevelt and again under Herbert H. Lehman. And, in 1934, he managed Lehman's campaign as incumbent Governor, Lehman's theory being that a good Irish name was needed in the fight to offset his own Jewishness. He was, of course, successful. Following this, Jack Murray bought himself a seat on the New York Stock Exchange. He had a brokerage office at 11 Broadway, but stockbrokerage did not suit his restless, active mind. He died in 1937 at his Brooklyn home the day before his thirty-eighth birthday, leaving his wife and seven young children.

With his death, the rift between the Jack Murrays and the other Murrays did not heal. Perhaps if Jack Murray's widow had been willing to accept the family leadership that had been somewhat autocratically assumed by Tom, it would have been different, but the snubs which Jeanne Durand Murray had suffered from the family in the past still rankled, and she refused to turn to her brother-in-law for help or advice, as he clearly expected. Tom Murray, Jr. was the most like his father of all the Murray sons, and, as self-appointed head of the clan, he expected to be deferred to and to be consulted in all matters. Needless to say, the others in the family resented this and begrudged him his role as paterfamilias. At the time of Jack Murray's death, it was discovered that Jack had been dipping heavily into capital. In his will, Grandpa Murray had given each of his three sons (excluding Daniel, who was by then institutionalized at McLean and "dead" to the family) a sizable sum "off the top" before the balance of the estate was divided. This in itself was bad enough—dividing the Murray sons and the Murray daughters over the matter of money—but when it appeared that brother Jack had spent his share, matters were only made worse. Tom Murray took the stand that his brother had "squandered" his inheritance, and that therefore Jack Murray's widow and her children were not entitled to any further financial aid from the family. The Jack Murrays, understandably, did not enjoy being relegated to the role of poor relations. Whenever they encountered the Toms or the Joes—which was often in the family compound on Long Island—there was an undercurrent of hard, heavy feeling, all based on the disparity in their financial status.

As family head, Tom Murray, Jr. also considered himself the "conscience" of the combined Murray-McDonnell-Cuddihy families, and he was always offering counsel and advice—some thought pompously and condescendingly—on money. He also counseled them on religious matters and was, if anything, more pious than his father. Tom Murray maintained not one but two private chapels—one at New York and another at Southampton. But, whereas his father had received two Papal decorations, Tom Murray, Jr. had received *three*—which is the most that a single individual can ever receive. Once, when Tom Murray went to Rome for an audience with Pope Pius XII, and posed for a photograph with the Pontiff, one of his nephews commented slyly, "I see the Pope is posing for a picture with God."

Tom Murray often lectured his relatives on the importance of sending their children to Catholic schools, and in this regard he was often at loggerheads with his brother-in-law, Lester Cuddihy, whose feelings toward the Church were somewhat ambivalent. Whenever Lester Cuddihy encountered a Jesuit, for example, he would inevitably say, "Why don't you have *one* college that doesn't have to bow its head to the names of Yale and Harvard and Princeton?"—always maintaining that the secular universities were scholastically better than the Catholic ones. Lester Cuddihy had also somewhat startled the family when he had bitten a Cardinal. It was none other than Francis Cardinal Spellman, and the occasion was a reception at the home of Mrs. Robert L. Hoguet.

Mr. Cuddihy was about to kiss the Cardinal's ring, and the Cardinal said, "Ah, Lester, I see you have some new teeth." Mr. Cuddihy hissed, "I'll teach you to call attention to my new teeth!" and bit the Cardinal on the finger. During Mass at Southampton, Lester Cuddihy and Joe Murray both regularly stood at the back of the church, and always walked out when it came time for Father Killeen's sermon, Cuddihy explaining that, "Technically, the sermon is not a part of the liturgy," whereas actually both men wanted a cigarette.

Tom Murray disapproved of all this, and would not even send his sons to Portsmouth Priory because it was considered "the most Protestant" of the Catholic boys' schools. He did want them to attend Georgetown University. (From Portsmouth, boys often went on to sinful—and secular—Harvard.) Both Tom Murray and his brother Joe had gone to Yale Engineering School, and once when their sister Julia had been asked for a date by one of their Protestant classmates, she had asked her father for permission. Grandpa Murray's reply had been "No." She had said, "Just because I go out with him doesn't mean that I'm going to marry him." He had said, "I'm not going to give you the chance." Tom Murray, Jr. adopted the same firm line with his own four daughters. It was not, perhaps, pure religious fanaticism. It was that, to Tom Murray, the Faith was a precious and inheritable treasure—as money and social position might be for others—something to be passed on from one generation to the next, pure and undiluted, as his father had passed it on to him. Out of devotion to the memory of his father, whose namesake he was, Tom continued to use the designation "Jr." Even after his father's death in 1929, and finally consented to abandon it only in the late 1940's.

Though he reprimanded others of his family for what he considered excessive spending, Tom Murray, Jr. was not himself above spending money on costly trifles that amused him. In 1941, for example, he bought the entire ice-skating rink from the New

York World's Fair, and had it shipped to his Southampton place—freezing plant and all—so that his children could enjoy summer skating. Lester Cuddihy, meanwhile, was a friend of Mr. Robert Moses, and Moses presented the Cuddihys with illegal slot machines that had been confiscated by his Commissioner's office. One was set up in the entrance hall of the Cuddihys' Water Mill house. It was a constant problem to keep the Cuddihy servants from depositing their life's savings in the device, but Father James Keller, visiting from Maryknoll, once won the entire jackpot from a twenty-five-cent investment, proving that the Lord watches over those who pray. Uncle Tom, on the other hand, had in 1932 been named receiver of the Interborough Rapid Transit Company, and remained in that capacity until the city took over the subway lines in 1940. *He* brought home all the nickel slugs that were extracted from the subway coin boxes, but these, he told his children, were for use only in the Cuddihy slot machines.

While all this bickering was going on among the Murrays, the McDonnell cousins seemed to be doing nothing but becoming richer, led by their doughty family patriarch, "Little Caesar" James Francis McDonnell and his McDonnell & Company. The obvious prosperity of the McDonnells was the cause of still more jealousy among the various Murrays, who, though they might consider themselves the "grander" family in terms of background and lineage, could not seem to hold a candle to the McDonnells when it came to wealth. Nor were feelings between the Cuddihys and McDonnells eased when the Lester Cuddihys had a weekend guest from Smith & Watson, the antiques firm, who, after visiting both the Tom Murrays' and the James Francis McDonnells' houses, and inspecting both with his expert's eye for "wood," declared that while Uncle Tom Murray's furniture was terribly good, Aunt Anna McDonnell's was truly of museum quality. The Murray and Cuddihy houses had all been elaborately decorated by McMillen, but, declared the Smith & Watson man, Mrs. McDonnell's furniture was so magnificent that no decorating was really necessary.

If there was one thing that could bring the disparate and feuding members of the large and interrelated families together, even briefly, it was the prospect of a family gathering, or wedding. And, early in 1940, such a prospect was at hand with the announcement of the engagement of blonde and beautiful Anne McDonnell to the young and handsome Henry Ford II. At first, Uncle Tom Murray was highly displeased with this news—Ford had been raised an Episcopalian—but he was quickly mollified when it was explained to him that Ford had agreed to accept religious instruction, and to convert to Roman Catholicism. To an America grown weary of dispiriting war news from Europe, and tense with apprehension over entering another war, the impending union of two attractive young people from two of the country's richest families came as a kind of intoxicating relief, and no sooner had the engagement been announced than newspapers across the land began extolling the approaching marriage as "The Wedding of the Century." Perhaps, indeed, it was, and only the romance, a few years earlier, between Mrs. Wallis Warfield Simpson and King Edward VIII of England received wider national and international coverage.

For months before the July 13 wedding date, the newspapers were filled with news of Fords and McDonnells, along with peripheral social doings of McDonnell relatives—Mary Jane Cuddihy being squired at the Stork Club by Harry K. Smith and Claudine Goodwin; Patricia and Jeanne Murray at this or that fashionable party; a note that Mrs. H. Lester Cuddihy and Mrs. Joseph P. Kennedy, a relatively recent arrival on the New York scene, would be copatronesses of the Barat Settlement House dinner—and so on. Elaborate attempts were made in the press to sort out, for readers, who was who in the McDonnell-Murray clan—that the bride-to-be had sixty-two first cousins, six aunts, and six uncles on her mother's side alone. On her father's side, she had twenty-one more first cousins, three aunts, and three uncles. She also had thirteen brothers and sisters, or a grand total of 116 new in-laws for young Henry Ford. Ford, meanwhile, had only two brothers, a sister, and one aunt. Henry's parents, it was pointed out, were Episcopalians, and his father, Edsel Ford, was a Mason. "But the Fords like Anne," the *Daily News* reminded its readers.

Social credentials were also trotted out—that Anne McDonnell was a graduate of the Convent of the Sacred Heart, and had studied at the Grotanelli School in Siena, Italy. Henry Ford, a graduate of the Hotchkiss School, was Yale '40, where he had managed the crew and been a member of Book and Snake and Zeta Psi. The papers omitted the fact that Henry Ford II had not quite made it through Yale, but had been asked to withdraw after submitting a paper that had been prepared for him by "Rosie," the well-known ghost writer for Yale undergraduates.

Much was made, needless to say, of the Ford family fortune, and of the story that Henry Ford had once sat for four hours in a New York night club because he was afraid to offer his personal check for three dollars for two beers. (He finally did, and it was accepted.) The McDonnell money was not overlooked either, and the newspapers wrote enthusiastically of the fifty-room McDonnell house at Southampton, with its pool, tennis court, and polo field, and of the twenty-nine-room New York apartment which had a separate kitchen just for the children. The McDonnell automobiles were listed—three sport coupés, five station wagons, three limousines, uncounted Fords and Chevrolets for the children, and a custom-built Chrysler with a special body and red-leather upholstery. It was noted that the Joseph B. Murrays, the future bride's aunt and uncle, had been threatened by kidnapers in 1938, and that their chauffeur carried a gun.

Next came the public announcement that Henry Ford would indeed become a Catholic, over only minor objections from his father, that the wedding would be in St. Patrick's Cathedral, and that none other than Monsignor Fulton J. Sheen would handle Ford's conversion—a process that would involve anywhere from forty to a hundred hours of religious instruction. Immediately a quarrel broke out between two newspapers, the New York *Mirror* and the *Journal*, over which publication had carried the conversion story first. The *Journal*'s Cholly Knickerbocker claimed that he had published the story first, on March 16, 1940. Not so, replied the *Mirror*'s Walter Winchell, insisting that he had reported the news more than a month before, on February 15.

Next came the news of Henry Ford, Sr.'s gift to the wedding pair—not surprisingly, it was to be a superspecial custom-built Ford car, complete with its own chauffeur. Then the list of bridal attendants: Catherine McDonnell, the bride's sister, maid of honor; Charlotte McDonnell, another sister; Marie and Rosamund Murray, both cousins (Uncle Tom's and Uncle Joe's daughters); Jeanne Murray (Uncle Jack's daughter); Cousin Mary Jane Cuddihy; Josephine "Dodie" Ford, the groom's sister; and Dorothy Morgan, Helen Macdonald, Mavis Coakley, and Kathleen Kennedy, daughter of the Joseph P. Kennedys, all bridesmaids. Benson Ford would be his brother's best man, and the twelve ushers would be brother William Ford; the bride's brothers James F. McDonnell, Jr., and T. Murray McDonnell; Raymond Peter Sullivan (fiancé of Catherine McDonnell); Buckley Byers of Sewickley; Jesse Davis, Jr. of Baltimore; Harry Quinn of Lebanon, Pennsylvania; Hood Bassett of Palm Beach; Ralph Browning of New Rochelle; Jerome DuCharme and George R. Fink, both of Detroit; and John MacSpovran of Orange, New Jersey. It was also rumored that usher Buckley Byers would soon announce his engagement to cousin Rosamund Murray (it was true, and they would marry a few months later), and it was noted that "Bucky" Byers's father, J. Frederic Byers, the Pittsburgh steel magnate, had once been sued by an ex-show girl named Kitty Ranelett who claimed that the senior Byers had promised her $31,000 for medical care for her dead daughter—but that the case had been tossed out of court. Of the Murrays and McDonnells, the newspapers commented, "None has been sued. None has been divorced. None has been the object of a whispered scandal."

Still another rumor was of the engagement of Anne McDonnell's sister Charlotte to young John Fitzgerald Kennedy. This engagement, which lasted only briefly, was thoroughly disapproved of by the Murrays and the McDonnells, particularly Uncle Tom Murray, who considered the Kennedys upstarts. They regarded Jack Kennedy as a "moral roustabout," and his father as a "crook and thorough bounder." Needless to say, that marriage did not take place. "If he had married me," Charlotte McDonnell says today, "I'm sure he would never have become President," meaning that her own freewheeling and party-loving style of life would have perhaps not been an asset to the White House. Several years later, the then Senator Kennedy was riding up in an elevator in New York with Mrs. James Francis McDonnell to attend some Catholic function. "Did you know I almost married your daughter?" he asked pleasantly. "I did," said Mrs. McDonnell, "and I'm happy you didn't."

As the date of the wedding approached, there was breathless news that the church had been changed from St. Patrick's to the Church of the Sacred Hearts of Jesus and Mary in Southampton, but Monsignor Sheen would still say the Mass. A wedding trip to Honolulu was planned. Three days before the ceremony, the Edsel Fords arrived in Southampton in their yacht, the *Onika*, and anchored in Peconic Bay. There was a hectic gaggle of prewedding parties, and a terrible crisis when it was discovered that the church would seat only five hundred people, although already there had been over eleven hundred acceptances. Sixteen armed guards were required to protect the two roomfuls of wedding gifts. The night before the ceremony, Henry Ford II took his first Holy Communion.

Among the hundreds of wedding guests were John F. Kennedy,

97

the Alfred E. Smiths, three Bishops, and dozens of priests. Speaking the words, Monsignor Sheen said, "Your marriage bond is *unbreakable* . . . because it is modeled upon the union of the divine and human natures in the unity of Our Lord . . . for all eternity . . . that timelessness which only death can dissolve into the eternal rebirth of the love of God." Afterward, while little Barbara and Sean McDonnell gathered up the rose petals that had been scattered after the bridal pair, crowds of the curious uninvited thronged onto the McDonnell lawn, trying to peer under the canopy of the huge reception tent for a glimpse of the young Henry Fords. In the press of onlookers, one woman narrowly escaped suffocation. Inside the tent, where the bride was arrayed in flowing white tulle showered with orange blossoms, a morning-coated Henry Ford, Sr., then seventy-seven, danced with his new granddaughter-in-law to the strains of Strauss's "Tales of the Vienna Woods." Photographs of the dancers went around the world, and newspapers praised "a Catholic wedding of people with their feet on the ground." Mary Jane Cuddihy caught the bridal bouquet. If it was not the wedding of the century, it was certainly the last of the great weddings in America before World War II.

Only one slightly adverse public comment was made. It came from the Old Guard's Mr. Barclay Beekman, who said, a bit loftily, "The Murrays and McDonnells hadn't made the grade fifteen years ago. Their social aspirations were resented by the snooty. But they're kindly people who don't snub climbers."

Uncle Tom Murray was at the Ford wedding, of course. But it was a different story, later that year, when his niece, Rosamund, was married to Mr. Byers, also a Yale man and a member of the crew. This was a mixed marriage, without a conversion on Mr. Byers's part, and Uncle Tom rather pointedly stayed away, even though every effort had been made to make the ceremony appear as Catholic as possible. It was held in the Murrays' East Side town house, one room of which had been converted into an improvised chapel, complete with stained-glass windows and other ecclesiastical trappings imported from the bride's maternal grandfather's house—"Steel King" James Farrell. For similar reasons, Uncle Tom had removed himself from the marriage ceremony of his own sister, Marie, when she married Mr. Elgood M. Lufkin after her first husband, John Vincent McDonnell—a brother of James Francis—had died. Uncle Tom announced that he considered the Lufkins "mysterious"—as well as Protestant. The Church might condone mixed marriages, but he did not. Nineteen-forty was to be a big year for family weddings. In November, Catherine McDonnell married Peter Sullivan, and in December her cousin Mary Jane Cuddihy married James Butler MacGuire—both girls to proper Catholics, and both in fashionable New York churches, the first at St. Ignatius Loyola and the second at St. Vincent Ferrer. But after the Ford wedding, everything seemed an anticlimax, and these weddings received only routine society-page coverage.

"Scandal" might never have touched the Murray or McDonnell families at the time of the Ford wedding, but it was certainly to come, and it involved, of all people, Uncle Tom's son Frank. Young Frank Murray had been dispatched, by his father, to Los Angeles to "get something started" on the West Coast for Murray Manufacturing. Frank was a handsome lad and, in Hollywood, he became involved with a motion picture actress named Eva Bartok. What happened next provided the press with a spicy, if somewhat confused, account. At 11 P.M. one April night, according to young Frank Murray, Eva Bartok and her ex-husband, a movie producer named Alexander Paal, barged into Murray's Hollywood apartment and tried to bully Frank Murray into marrying Eva, a Hungarian national, so that she could remain in the United States. The immigration authorities agreed that Miss Bartok was having certain "problems," which marriage to an American might solve, and that her visa needed extending. Frank Murray claimed that in order to force him to the altar Paal knocked him down three or

99

four times and chased him around the house with a poker. The police were called when Frank Murray ran to a neighbor's house crying, "There's a crazy Hungarian who's trying to kill me!" Murray charged Paal and Miss Bartok with extortion. In her counter-charge, Eva Bartok claimed that Murray was trying to "ruin my career"—she had made one film, called *Ten Thousand Bedrooms*—and that she had gone to Frank Murray's house to tell him that she was through with him, and that he had invited her in. As for extortion, Miss Bartok said, "Ha! I make five million dollars for a picture and he makes a hundred and fifty a week!" Mr. Paal claimed that he had seen Frank Murray knock Miss Bartok down and that, in her defense, he knocked Murray down. "He went right down—he's such a baby," said Paal. Two days later, charges were dropped, but at the time of the publicity Uncle Tom could only shake his head in bewilderment and say, again and again, "Not our Frank . . . not our Frank!"

And it was not long after the Ford wedding that the Jack Murrays' daughter Constance announced her decision to become a Holy Child nun. In Catholic society, there are generally two reasons given for a girl's decision to enter a convent. Either a girl has very few young men friends or she has so many beaux that she cannot decide among them. In Connie Murray's case, her mother announced to the press that "She has a true vocation." At the time, the *Daily News* noted that she "graciously gave in to her family" and made her debut before taking the veil. Whatever the true reasons for her decision may have been, there were those who suggested that she wished to become a nun "to atone for the sins of her relatives."

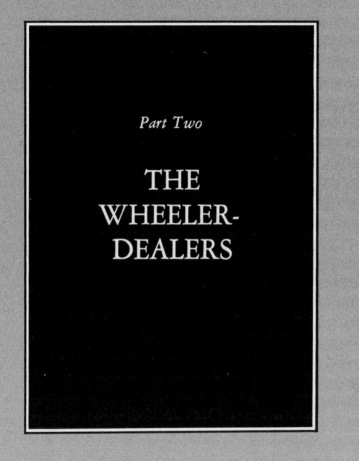

Part Two

THE WHEELER-DEALERS

Chapter 9

"MA AND PA D."

or all their feuds and fallings-out—and the occasional
eruptions of bad press—families like the Murrays and
McDonnells and Cuddihys strove earnestly to achieve
an aura of respectability to accompany their wealth. They wanted
to be regarded as "kindly people." They also wanted to be honest
and churchgoing and devout, daily communicants. Because they
were aware of the Irishman's reputation for drunkenness, they
were teetotalers or, at the most, cautious drinkers. They conducted
themselves in much the same way as the "Uptown" German Jews
—Schiffs, Loebs, Lehmans, and Warburgs—anxious to develop
a proper self-image and to define themselves as against the Lower
East Side "newcomers" from the *shtetl* of Eastern Europe. Even
such families as the Joseph P. Kennedys cared enough about
being accepted socially to move out of Boston, where they knew
they could never make the grade, and follow the example of the
Murrays and McDonnells and come to New York, where they

settled in Bronxville and where the Kennedy daughters made society debuts, and the Kennedy sons were invited to all the best parties. But, at the same time, there were other Irish-Americans who cared less about probity and the impact they made on society, and who concentrated almost single-mindedly on amassing huge fortunes. One of the most successful of these entrepreneurs was Mr. Edward L. Doheny.

Born in 1856 in Fond du Lac, Wisconsin, the son of a poor Irish immigrant who had headed westward in a vain search for success, Ed Doheny ran away from home at the age of sixteen and worked, variously, as a booking agent, a fruit packer, a mule driver, and a waiter in the Occidental Hotel in Wichita, Kansas. At the age of eighteen he began what was to be his life-long occupation—searching for wealth underground—and became a gold prospector. He wandered about Texas, Arizona, New Mexico, and Mexico, sometimes striking it rich, sometimes going broke. It was a rough-and-tumble existence in the one-street towns of the Southwest, and Doheny developed a reputation as a rough-and-tumble character. He had learned early how to use a gun, and was quick to reach for his holster in tough situations, and it was rumored that he had once killed a man—or possibly several. In New Mexico, Doheny was known as the man who had cleaned up the little town of Kingston of local cattle thieves and bad men, one of whom was said to have fired sixteen bullets at him before Doheny was able to disarm and overpower him. As a prospector, however, he employed more mystical methods and, for a while, his principal mining tool was a divining rod. When the rod quivered and dipped in his hand, Doheny stopped on the spot and began digging for gold, sometimes finding it and sometimes not.

In 1892, when he was thirty-six years old and when prospects for discovering a real bonanza had begun to look exceptionally dim, Ed Doheny turned up in the still-raw city of Los Angeles. His mining adventures in Arizona and New Mexico had all lost money, and he was virtually penniless. But then one of those strokes of incredible luck that have marked the beginnings of so many American fortunes occurred to Ed Doheny. Passing in the street one day, he noticed a black man driving a horse and wagonload of black, tarry stuff. Doheny asked the man what the substance was, and was told that it was *"brea"*—Spanish for pitch— and that it bubbled from a pit on the edge of town, and that the poorer families of the city collected it and used it for fuel. From his diggings around the West, Doheny knew enough to recognize the *brea* as crude oil, and set off to investigate the bubbling pit. He located it in Hancock Park, decided it looked promising, and, with a small amount of hastily borrowed cash, leased the land. Within a few months he had brought in one of the first gushers ever to flow in the city of Los Angeles. Armed with this success, he went on to drill other wells in other parts of California and, within five years' time, practically controlled the entire oil production in the state.

He next turned to Mexico, where he had prospected as a young man, this time in search of oil, not gold. He found profitable lands in the jungles beyond Tampico and leased over a million acres there. His Mexican Petroleum Company cleared the jungle, built roads and railroads, docks, pipelines, shops and houses for laborers and, from lavish bribes to Mexican officials, earned the intense good favor of the Mexican Government. By 1922 Doheny's income from his Mexican company alone netted him $31,575,937, and his total worth was reported to be more than a hundred million dollars. By 1925 he was reliably reported to be even richer than "the richest man in America," John D. Rockefeller.

As a rich man, Edward L. Doheny, former Southwestern gunman, affected a monocle, a walrus mustache, British tailoring, and an autocratic manner. He also became devoted to prodigious spending, and bought a large portion of what is now downtown Los Angeles which he converted into a vast park and estate called

"Chester Place." His yacht, the *Casiana*, was one of the most luxurious in the country. He surrounded himself with an entourage of servants and bodyguards, and "Chester Place" was so heavily protected that once, when a fire broke out in one of the many buildings on the estate, the Los Angeles Fire Department had difficulty getting through the security at the main gate. His second wife, who had been his secretary, was decked out in ropes of sapphires, emeralds, diamonds, and rubies. Mr. Doheny was not particularly philanthropic, but he did contribute heavily to the Irish Freedom Movement and to the Democratic Party. In fact, it was probably his wife, who was shrewder about the handling of money than her husband, who was responsible for conserving Ed Doheny's fortune, and for seeing to it that it was not all spent as rapidly as it was made. Once, surveying a gathering of her children and stepchildren, "Ma D.," as she was called, commented, "None of them would have anything if it weren't for me. I'm responsible for every penny they have, right down to that big diamond ring on Lucy's finger."

Ma D. was the undisputed empress of "Chester Place." She had been made a Papal Countess and enjoyed using the formal title, "Countess Estelle Doheny." Physically, she resembled Queen Victoria—small, ugly, and imperious, with a decidedly Victorian manner. At "Chester Place," one descended a long, wide marble staircase lined with footmen and maids to be ushered into the presence, or Presence, of Ma D. Though she became almost totally blind, one was never permitted to comment on, or to remind her of, her infirmity, and small, carpeted ramps were built across the thresholds of doorways and up steps so that Ma D. could move through the rooms of her house unaided. For all her grand ways, Ma D. had a middle-class American's love of showing off her home to visitors, leading her guests along the vast marble corridors, into the Pompeian Room where she pointed out the vaulted ceiling covered with gold leaf and her priceless collection of antique watches, into the conservatory which was big enough to contain tall trees as well as her prize-winning collection of orchids. For her dining table, a long silver centerpiece was created just to contain the specimen orchids, which were changed daily. Before each meal, Ma D. memorized the name of each variety of orchid up and down the centerpiece so that she could recite to her guests the names of the blooms which she could not see. Inevitably, each tour of the house ended with an elevator ride up two stories to Ma D.'s private chapel with its magnificent reliquary and where the Eucharist was reserved. Outside the chapel entrance stood two tall Spanish armoires filled with hats and scarves in a variety of styles and colors from which ladies could choose in order to cover their heads before going inside.

Like royalty—or like the parish priest—Ma D. believed, when paying calls on her friends, that it was unnecessary to announce her visits ahead of time. Once, when actress Loretta Young and her husband, Tom Lewis, were living in a house hard by "Chester Place," Miss Young's upstairs maid nervously announced that Mrs. Doheny had just appeared downstairs, and was waiting in the drawing room to be received. As rapidly as she could, Miss Young attended to her hair and make-up, but, for a reigning movie star, this took a bit of time. By the time she got downstairs, Mrs. Doheny had departed.

On the other hand, whatever philanthropies are associated with the Doheny name in California are largely attributable to Ma D. These include an eye hospital named after her, a Catholic church which she built in Adams Street, Los Angeles, and the Doheny Library at the University of Southern California.

One of Pa D.'s cronies from his prospecting days was a young fellow from Kentucky named Albert Bacon Fall. Like Doheny, Fall had had little formal education and a checkered career after heading west as a youth. Fall had worked as a cowboy, a farmhand, a prospector, and a miner, and had wound up in New Mexico when it was still a territory and where, after studying law in his spare time, he had settled, been admitted to the bar, and gone into politics. He had been an early supporter of President Grover Cleveland, and the latter had rewarded him by appointing him to be a judge of the Supreme Court of the Territory of New Mexico. It was here that Fall and Doheny first met, and became card-playing friends and drinking companions. But, as a judge, Fall had a tendency to take the law into his own hands, as happened one day when he leaped down from the bench to lead a posse that was out to lynch a bandit. When word of this escapade reached President Cleveland's ears, Fall was summarily removed from his judicial post.

Unlike his friend Doheny, Albert Fall never had the luck to strike it rich. With the outbreak of the Spanish-American War, Fall joined the infantry, rose to the not particularly exalted rank of captain and, at the war's end, came home to New Mexico and announced that he had switched his allegiance from the Democratic to the Republican Party. When New Mexico was admitted to the Union in 1912, Albert Fall ran for and was elected New Mexico's first United States Senator.

As a Senator, Albert Fall provided Washington with almost a caricature of the Western hombre. He had cold blue eyes and thin lips from which a large cigar usually drooped. He spoke with a drawl and wore wide-brimmed hats and shoestring neckties. A Washington newspaperman wrote of him, "With a long drooping moustache, he looks like a stage sheriff of the Far West in the movies. His voice is always loud and angry. He has the frontiersman's impatience. From his kind lynch law springs." Though Fall represented the opposite side of the political fence from his friend Doheny, the two men had a number of beliefs in common. Both were strong advocates—Doheny with particularly good reasons—of armed intervention in Mexico to protect American investments there. Both were also ardently in favor of the immediate and complete exploitation by private interests, such as Doheny's, of the nation's natural resources, such as oil. In the Senate, because he spoke a little Spanish, Albert Fall presented himself as an expert on Mexican affairs. Also in the Senate, Fall became a card-playing chum of the easygoing Republican Senator from Ohio, Warren Gamaliel Harding. When, in 1920, Harding became one of the unlikeliest Presidential candidates in American history, Albert Fall was one of his staunchest supporters. So, at Fall's urging, was Ed Doheny, who contributed $25,000 to the Harding campaign, and paid for national newspaper advertising which featured full-page photographs of Harding's mother and father—designed to counteract rumors to the effect that Harding had "Negro blood," in addition to his more obvious shortcomings.

When Harding was elected to office by an overwhelming majority—carrying thirty-seven of the forty-eight states—Harding asked Fall if he would like to be his Secretary of the Interior. Harding had originally considered Fall for Secretary of State, but had been persuaded by his advisers that the Senate would not approve a Southwesterner for the top Cabinet post. In offering Interior to Fall, Harding apologized for not giving him the bigger job. Fall, on the other hand, was not at all disappointed. Interior was known as one of the Cabinet positions most susceptible to graft, and where important money could be made on the side. It was also rumored at the time that Interior was "owned" by the nation's big oil interests. Fall's appointment was greeted with cheers and applause on both sides of the Senate floor, and Fall went sweeping into the job without the usual formality of having the appointment sent to committee. Of his Cabinet appointments Harding had announced that he was picking "the best man" for each job, and the *New York Times* replied editorially that the new President was obviously appointing not the best men but his best friends.

About three years before Harding's election, Ed Doheny had had another meeting that was to prove fateful. His son, Edward L. Doheny, Jr., was a young lieutenant in the Navy assigned to the U.S.S. *Huntington*, and while the *Huntington* was in Pensacola Harbor, the vacationing Mr. Doheny came aboard to visit him. While on board, the oil millionaire was invited to the quarters of the ship's commanding officer, one Captain John Keeler Robison. The visit lasted for about two hours, and the main topic of conversation was, naturally, oil. Oil was of vital importance to the Navy. Nearly all its vessels had been converted from coal- to oil-burning, and to ensure that the fleet would have a ready supply of fuel in cases of emergency—and fuel that could be obtained at much lower cost than if it were bought on the open market—the Navy Department, under President Taft, had been given some 78,791 acres of oil lands situated in three principal locations: at Elk Hills and Buena Vista Hills, both in Kern County, California, and at Teapot Dome in Natrona County, Wyoming. Ever since the Taft order, private oil interests, including Doheny's, had been trying to obtain leases to drill and exploit this highly valuable acreage, but had thus far been successfully resisted by the Naval Fuel Oil Board, which had maintained that the land should be kept strictly by the Navy and strictly for Navy use. Captain Robison, an Annapolis man and a career naval officer, may not have known much about oil wells, but he was proud of his Navy, and he commented to Mr. Doheny that he thought the Navy was doing a pretty good job in keeping and maintaining its precious oil reserves. Doheny gave the Captain a little smile and said, "Well, it is being handled very well for the people you have for neighbors. But you are not going to have any property there in a very few years." Captain Robison asked him what he meant by that, and Doheny explained that neighboring oil companies, operating on the periphery of the Navy lands, were rapidly pumping out oil that was "leaking" from the Navy oil fields into other fields nearby.

Doheny depicted the invisible situation underground as one of a series of huge bathtubs with interconnecting drains. When oil ran out of one tub, it simply drained in from the next.

Captain Robison was aghast at this news. It opened his eyes, he said later, to a problem that he had never dreamed existed. Testifying before a Senate investigating committee, Robison said that Mr. Doheny's words carried particular weight because they did not come "from some $2,500 clerk," but from a man "who had made millions knowing how." He assured the Senators, "That is the kind of information I believe."

The meeting aboard the *Huntington* had been an exceptionally fruitful one. When Harding became President, he appointed Edwin Denby as his Secretary of the Navy, replacing Josephus Daniels, who had served under Wilson. Denby's chief qualification for the Cabinet post seemed to be that he had served as a Marine in the First World War. Denby then placed none other than Captain John Keeler Robison in the post of Chief of the Navy's Bureau of Engineering, and put him in complete charge of the naval petroleum reserves, with the temporary rank of rear admiral.

The problem of "drainage," meanwhile, was not at all a new one to Navy petroleum engineers. It had been studied under Secretary Daniels, and it had been concluded that while a certain amount of drainage might occur in certain areas of certain fields, the situation was nowhere near as dire as Doheny had painted it to Captain Robison. There was no danger of the Navy's oil simply leaking away. The pressure from private oil interests to obtain leases on Navy land had also been applied upon Secretary Daniels, and, in June, 1920, Daniels had been persuaded to ask Congress for authority to lease to private operators certain Navy lands where "important" drainage might be apt to occur. Congress passed the act, but the small amount of the appropriation—$500,000—was an indication that Congress had not intended to open up the Navy lands to complete exploitation. Under Daniels, only a very few leases were granted to private companies. Still, under the Wilson administration the door to exploitation had been opened a crack. Under Harding, with Edwin Denby as Secretary of the Navy and Albert Fall as Secretary of the Interior, oil men like Doheny saw a chance to push it fully open. But, Fall explained to his friend Doheny, it was a question of first things first. If Fall was going to do his best job for his friends in the petroleum industry, it was important that he, Fall, first get control of the naval oil reserves into the hands of his own department, which he intended to run as a one-man operation. To do this, he would have to go to work on Denby. Even more important, he would have to go to work on his friend the President. With neither man did Fall foresee any real difficulty.

As a President, Warren G. Harding was a man who, at his best, was never exactly certain what the office entailed. Once, when a problem involving taxation had come to his desk, Harding complained to an aide, "John, I can't make a damn thing out of this tax problem. I listen to one side and they seem right, and then— God!—I talk to the other side and they seem just as right, and here I am where I started. I know somewhere there is a book that will give me the truth, but, hell, I couldn't read the book. I know somewhere there is an economist who knows the truth, but I don't know where to find him, and haven't the sense to know and trust him when I find him. God, what a job!" Most administrative decisions, he admitted, gave him a headache, and he eagerly delegated as much authority as he could to the members of his Cabinet, most of whom were his card-playing cronies. In the White House poker games, on the other hand, Harding was exceptionally lucky— which was perhaps not too surprising; it may have been to the advantage of men like Fall and Denby to let their boss be a frequent winner. As a Secretary of the Navy, Edwin Denby was a man who preferred to have as little to do as possible, and was always pleased when a problem could be shuttled from his desk to someone else's. When Fall approached Denby about transferring the naval oil reserves from the Department of the Navy to the Department of the Interior, Denby was delighted. It was one less chore for him.

Others in the Navy Department were less sanguine about Fall's notion. Admiral R. S. Griffin, who was then Chief of the Bureau of Engineering, which administered the reserves, reminded Denby that the Navy had been struggling for over a decade to keep its oil, and said "if he turned the administration over to the Interior Department we might just as well say good-by to our oil." But Secretary Denby told the Admiral that the President was in favor of the scheme, and within a few days Fall was able to write to his friend Doheny in California:

There will be no possibility of any further conflict with Navy officials and this Department, as I have notified Secretary Denby that I should conduct the matters of naval leases under direction of the President without calling any of his force in consultation unless I conferred with himself personally upon a matter of policy. He understands the situation and that I shall handle matters exactly as I think best and will not consult with any officials of any bureau of his department but only with himself and such consultation will be confined strictly and entirely to matters of general policy.

Originally, Doheny had wanted the entire naval oil reserves for his own company, but Fall decided that it was more to his advantage if at least one other company was involved and, after all, Doheny wasn't Fall's only friend. Another was the Eastern oil magnate, Harry F. Sinclair, head of the Mammoth Oil Company. Doheny eventually agreed to split the pie with Sinclair, and Sinclair received leases on the entire Wyoming acreage at Teapot Dome, with Doheny getting the two vast tracts in Kern County. As if by sleight of hand, all the Navy's emergency oil supply thus went into private hands.

Sinclair was obviously not as good a friend of Fall's as Doheny was, and so, for a smaller number of acres, Sinclair had to pay Fall a considerably higher price. Altogether, Sinclair paid the Secretary close to $400,000 in cash and bonds for his good deed, and also presented him with six prize Holstein heifers, a yearling bull, two six-month-old boars, four sows, and an English thoroughbred horse for the Secretary's New Mexico ranch. Doheny, meanwhile, managed somewhat to mollify Navy officials who were horrified over the transfer by agreeing to build the Navy some oil-storage tanks in Pearl Harbor, Hawaii, that the Navy had long wanted but had been unable to get from Congress. Now it was time for Doheny to pay Fall or, as Fall put it in a telephone call to Doheny, "I am now prepared to receive that loan."

Doheny sent for his only son, Edward L. Doheny, Jr., and instructed him to go to the brokerage firm of Blair & Company, where both father and son had accounts and in which the former owned a considerable interest, and to withdraw from the younger Doheny's account $100,000 in cash, giving two checks for the money. Doheny told his son to take the bills, wrap them in paper, put them in a small black valise, and carry them personally to Secretary Fall in Washington. In November, 1921, young Doheny carried out this mission and arrived, with his little black bag full of banknotes, at Secretary Fall's apartment in the Wardman Park Hotel. Doheny, with his secretary, watched as Fall counted out the money and then—or so he claimed later—received Fall's note for the amount. At the time, Doheny said, he remarked to Fall that no interest rate had been placed on the note, and Fall had loftily replied that his old friend Ed Doheny could insert any rate he wished to.

Within days, Secretary Fall was back home in New Mexico, where he paid cash for a large piece of property adjoining his Three Rivers Ranch. During this visit, his daughter testified later, she walked into her father's room and saw large piles of money lying on his desk. She snatched one of the piles and cried, "Here's my trip to Mexico!" and started out of the room with it. But her father ordered her back, and to return the money, saying that it was to pay off the mortgage on their house. Secretary Fall's New Mexico neighbors were somewhat surprised at the Fall family's sudden affluence—a relatively hardscrabble ranch being expanded into something of a showplace, with prize cattle and thoroughbred horses. But then it was known that Albert Fall had many rich friends and occupied a high position in the government.

On January 9, 1923, Fall had completed all his various deals and announced his intention to retire from public life. To the press, President Harding expressed profound sorrow at Fall's decision and said that, to keep him in Washington, he had offered Fall a judgeship on the United States Supreme Court. But Fall had turned the offer down, saying that he wished to return to the land and the humble chores of tending his little Southwestern ranch. And well he might have wished to get out of Washington. He had collected some half a million dollars in bribes and payoffs, and his only regret may have been that he sold himself too cheaply. At the time, when for a mere $100,000 Doheny had acquired roughly 30,000 acres of proven oil lands whose contents were estimated to be between 75 and 250 million barrels of oil, Doheny had commented, "We will be in bad luck if we do not get $100 million in profit. But that will depend on the price of gasoline."

At the time also, though he did not show it, Albert Fall may have been one of the most frightened men in the United States. There had already been rumblings of dissatisfaction in Washington about the turnover of oil leases to Doheny and Sinclair, and dark mutterings about corruption. There had also been a curious meeting between Mrs. Fall and the President, when Harding was passing through Kansas City and Mrs. Fall appeared and asked to see him. She arrived at the President's hotel suite looking nervous and agitated, and, after a private conversation behind locked doors that lasted for a full hour, the President emerged looking haggard and shaken. What the two talked about has never been revealed, but it cannot have been a pleasant topic, and the next day, speaking with William Allen White, editor of the Emporia, Kansas, *Gazette*, Harding said to White, "In this job, I am not worried about my enemies. I can take care of them. It's my friends who are giving me trouble."

President Harding accepted Fall's resignation "with deep and sincere regret," and Fall departed—but not without first ordering that the elegant Jacobean antique furniture, with which his Washington office had been supplied from taxpayers' money, be shipped to his home in New Mexico. The transfer of the furniture was all perfectly legal. Fall wrote out his check to the government for $231.25 to pay for it. It was worth about $3,000.

Chapter 10

THE BUBBLE BREAKS

The Doheny family of Los Angeles has never, for all its wealth, been a particularly "social" family—in the American sense in which society survives almost entirely on publicity. Even before the scandal which became known as Teapot Dome (after the quaintly named Wyoming town where a dome-shaped rock looked, to the pioneer settlers, a little like a teapot) and their involvement in it, the Dohenys disliked seeing their names or pictures in the paper, and tried to conduct their lives and businesses as discreetly and quietly as possible in the secluded and policed vastness of "Chester Place." With Teapot Dome, however, all attempts at family privacy came abruptly to a halt.

The mounting corruption of the Harding administration was dramatically punctuated by the President's sudden death on August 2, 1923, while his wife was reading him a *Saturday Evening Post* article praising him. The cause of his death was said to have been some bad crab meat he had eaten on a trip to Alaska (though there was grisly speculation that he had been poisoned by a "friend"), and all the problems of his administration—of which Albert Fall's activities were only a part—descended upon the shoulders of his taciturn successor in the White House, Calvin Coolidge. And, slowly and laboriously, under President Coolidge, the legislators in Washington began to investigate some of the things that had gone on during the Harding regime. The Senate Committee on Public Lands and Surveys—organized to look into what had become of the naval oil reserves—held its first hearing on October 23, 1923. The chief examiner was Senator Thomas J. Walsh, a Democrat from Montana, and the first witness called was Albert Fall.

As a witness, Fall was arrogant, contemptuous, and evasive, taking the position that everything he had done had been for the good of the government and the glory of America and had, furthermore, been done on instructions from his President. He suggested that Walsh "look at the records"—which, of course, was difficult to do because the records of the Harding office had been so sloppily kept that it was almost impossible to tell what the President had ordered and what he had not. Walsh pressed Fall to admit that in such matters as the Navy's oil lands, and national security, it was proper to consult the Congress and not highhandedly take matters into his own hands, and did succeed in getting Fall to admit that he had not sought any legal opinions in connection with his maneuvers. "But I'm a lawyer myself," Fall added, and then said that, "law or no law," he would have done anything in his power to prevent the Navy's oil from draining away into neighboring fields. Asked why he had turned over Teapot Dome to Sinclair without any competitive bidding, Fall's haughty reply was "Well, I did it."

He told the first of many lies. "Did you get any compensation at all?" Senator Walsh asked him. "I have never suggested any compensation at all and have received none," Fall answered. Not a penny from Sinclair. Not a penny from Doheny. "So long as I was in an official position," he said, "I did not feel I could accept any gift of any kind." No horses, no cattle, boars, or sows. "I shall go into no further detail in discussing this matter," he added. "The entire subject, of course, is more or less humiliating even to refer to." When asked about his obviously improved life style, Fall admitted that he had received a $100,000 "loan" from a friend, but lied again when he said that the loan had not come from Doheny, or from anyone connected with the oil industry, but had come from another friend, the Washington publisher Edward B. McLean, husband of Evalyn Walsh McLean of Hope Diamond celebrity. Hastily, Fall got in touch with McLean and got him to promise to "back me up in this."

Ed Doheny made his first appearance before the Walsh committee on December 3. He was then sixty-seven years old, but still full of restless, bristling energy. After a brief lecture to the assembled Senators on the dangers of oil leakages, he stated that he "knew" that the Navy had lost at least one hundred million barrels of oil from its California reserves prior to the Doheny takeover. He, he said, had stepped in out of sheerest patriotism to save America's oil. When Senator Walsh asked him why the Bureau of Mines had not been aware of this grievous loss, Doheny said flatly, "No man on earth has access to the same information I have, because my information comes from twenty-nine years of close study of the proposition, such as no other living man has given to the business. That sounds egotistical, I grant you, but that is absolutely the truth, since you have asked me the question." Doheny admitted that, though a Democrat, he was "sometimes a Republican," and had contributed $25,000 to the Harding campaign and paid for the advertisement portraying Harding's parents. But there was nothing wrong with that. Asked whether he had ever given Fall any money, Doheny replied, "Not yet. I want to say right here, though, that I would be very glad to take Mr. Fall in my employ if he ever wanted to come to us." Technically, of course, he was telling the truth since it had been his son, not he, who had presented Fall with the $100,000.

The hearings wore on, with other witnesses called—they would continue, all told, for the better part of four years—and Doheny's next appearance was in January, 1924. He appeared voluntarily, and, because it was rumored that he was now about to "tell all," the Senate Caucus Room was packed to capacity. He did not tell all, exactly, but he told a bit more than he had told before. Yes, he admitted, he had loaned Fall $100,000 because Fall was an old friend and needed money to improve his ranch. He told about the cash and the little black bag. Wasn't that, Walsh wanted to know, an unusual way for a businessman to carry out a financial transaction? Not at all, said Doheny. In the last five years alone he had carried out at least one million dollars' worth of cash transactions in Mexico because it was difficult to deal with banks from one country to another. But, Senator Walsh reminded him, they were talking now of a transaction between Washington and New York, where there was no international banking problem to deal with. Doheny countered by saying that, after all, $100,000 to him was the equivalent of pocket change, and amounted to "no more than $25 or $50 to the ordinary individual." Walsh replied dryly that he could see Doheny's point but that $100,000 was still a lot of money to a man in Fall's position. "It was indeed," Doheny admitted, "there is no question about that." He then added, "And I am perfectly willing to admit that it probably caused him to favor me," in terms of granting the oil leases. Was the loan directly responsible? the committee wanted to know. Doheny replied that he didn't think Fall was "more than human," a remark that drew laughter from the spectators. Pressing on for more details about the loan, Walsh wanted to know whether Fall had paid Doheny any interest on it. No, Doheny said, he had not, but Doheny was perfectly willing to hire Fall for his company and let him work off the indebtedness. Yes, Doheny said, Fall had given him a note for the loan, but Doheny had misplaced it somewhere and couldn't find it.

Doheny's appearance concluded with an odd scene. Walsh asked him if he had communicated with any member of the Senate committee prior to the hearing, and Doheny replied that he had not. "I was told that Senator Smoot handed you a note as you were coming in the room," Walsh said. Doheny hesitated, and then admitted that this was true. "Let us see the note," Walsh demanded. Certainly, said Doheny, smiling broadly, and reached into his jacket pocket and withdrew a clenched fist. With a dramatic gesture, he opened the fist and scattered a small snowstorm of shredded paper onto the green baize table. The contents of the note, he said haughtily, would make "very painstaking" reading. "Can you *tell* us what was on it?" the Senator asked him. "Yes," said Doheny. "After we finish, I would like to see you in my room." In disgust, Senator Walsh dismissed the witness.

Pieces of paper had a curious habit of getting torn when in Ed Doheny's possession. When he made his second appearance before the committee in January, 1924, he had found Fall's note for $100,000. It had, it seemed, been in his wallet all along. But, for some reason, the lower half of the document, which had contained Fall's signature, had been torn off and was missing. Why was this? the Senators wanted to know. Doheny offered a strange and rambling explanation. Before leaving New York for California after receiving the note, he said, he and Mrs. Doheny had been afraid that their train might have an accident. If that should happen, and he and his wife were killed, it had occurred to Doheny that the executors of his estate might find the note and demand immediate payment on it from his old friend Fall. This, of course, would be a dreadful state of affairs—disaster piled upon disaster—and so he had torn the note in half, given the lower portion to his wife to carry, and she had unfortunately lost it. As evidence, Fall's note—if

121

it indeed was Fall's note—was meaningless. The Senators remarked that they had been "very greatly misled" by Doheny, who shrugged and said he was sorry they felt that way.

On June 30, 1924, a Washington grand jury handed down four indictments against Fall, Sinclair, Doheny, and Doheny's son. Fall and the two Dohenys were charged with felony in entering into a conspiracy to defraud the Government of the United States in an effort to control the Elk Hills oil reserves in California. Fall and Sinclair were charged with similar conspiracy in connection with Teapot Dome. The third indictment charged Fall with accepting a $100,000 bribe from Doheny, and the fourth charged Doheny with giving the bribe to Fall. The first civil case involving the oil scandals came to trial in Los Angeles on October 21, 1924.

At the time, it was noted that the local press was showing a certain amount of favoritism to the Dohenys. Partly, it was because Mr. Doheny, as one of the town's richest citizens, had become something of a local favorite son. (A Los Angeles street, cutting across Beverly Hills, would be named Doheny Drive.) But one reporter openly admitted that he had been instructed by his editor to write only nice things about the Doheny family because, the editor pointed out, the newspaper would not want Doheny's oil companies to cancel any advertising. The press was further aided by Doheny's chief lawyer, a shrewd little fellow Irishman named Frank J. Hogan, who saw to it that all pieces of evidence favorable to the Doheny side made their way promptly to the press table as soon as they were offered in court. Doheny's appearance at his trial was also in his favor—that of a jovial, white-haired, bright-eyed, and distinguished-looking gentleman, the picture of merry innocence. Hogan's large staff of lawyers was housed in suites of rooms at "Chester Place," where they led an active after-hours social life and enjoyed such facilities as the Dohenys' private gymnasium, bowling alley, and swimming pool, and where the members of the press were frequently asked to parties.

After nine days of testimony, the government rested its case, and the Dohenys' lawyers embarked on their defense, relying heavily upon pathos, patriotism, and even bringing in the Yellow Peril. Of Doheny's oil tanks in Pearl Harbor, which had been built for the Navy as part of his deal with Fall, the defense made much of the fact that these provided a vital national force to protect the Pacific—including the California coastline—from America's "enemies" in Asia (enemies who did not materialize until nearly twenty years later). In a ringing voice, one of the Doheny lawyers told the court, "America can sleep tonight secure from danger of being overrun by a Mongol country because of the patriotism of such men as E. L. Doheny, Edwin Denby, and Admiral John K. Robison and their work in establishing a great naval oil base in Hawaii. These men have been humiliated and vilified because they endeavored to save you and me and our country." The trial lasted about two weeks and ended on November 12, 1924, after a five-day summation. Judge Paul J. McCormick retired to deliberate the case.

The judge's deliberations took him until the following May. In his 105-page decision, he decided that the leases to the Elk Hills land were null and void, and that the contract for the Hawaiian storage tanks was equally illegal, having been obtained through fraud. He also held that President Harding had exceeded his authority in turning over the Navy's lands to Fall's Department of the Interior. He held further that Doheny's payment of $100,000 to Fall was "against good morals and public policy, and tainted with fraud." He ordered Doheny's company to pay the government for all the oil it had taken out of Elk Hills. It was a clear and unexpected setback for Ed Doheny, but there was some comfort in it. Judge McCormick ordered that the government had to repay Doheny for the storage tanks. The Doheny lawyers immediately appealed Judge McCormick's decision, and this may have been a mistake. The Court of Appeals, in October, not only upheld Mc-

123

Cormick but took away Doheny's reimbursement for the tanks. Once more the lawyers appealed—this time to the United States Supreme Court.

Doheny and Fall, meanwhile, would have to stand trial again, in Washington, on the bribery charge, which, since it was a criminal case, might end up not only costing them money but also sending them to jail. For his Washington trial, which opened in November, 1926, Mr. Doheny was even better prepared than he had been in Los Angeles. His lawyer, Mr. Hogan, marshaled an even larger staff of lawyers. A huge suite of rooms was leased on the third floor of the Columbia Building, opposite Judiciary Square, and this was fitted out as a private club for the Doheny legal aides as well as the press. A staff of waiters was hired and a chef, and the press were fed with a steady stream of releases—all taking, naturally, the Doheny side. A personal press agent accompanied Ed Doheny into the courtroom to facilitate this flow of laudatory news. A few days before the trial was to begin, several jurors complained of threatening and otherwise disturbing telephone calls from strangers. One juror, who was told that his caller was "the court," was asked questions about his bank account, his real estate, his family, his social and religious affiliations, and his relations with women other than his wife. Because of this, the presiding justice, Adolph A. Hoehling, ordered that the jury be locked up during the entire lengthy proceedings. While Doheny and his lawyers partied in the Columbia Building, the jurors languished in locked hotel rooms, guarded by marshals. The jurors were not even permitted to join their families for Thanksgiving dinner, nor could they go to church on Sundays. Instead, they were given Bibles to read. At the time, someone in the press slyly remarked that the jurors were the only ones involved in the entire Teapot Dome mess who had thus far been placed behind bars.

Ed Doheny was now seventy years old and, when he took the stand on December 9, it was for the first time noted that he looked shaken, exhausted, and ill. He had been suffering from an infection in his arm, was wearing a sling, and rested his arm on a cushion. Before her husband testified, Mrs. Doheny was called and repeated the story of the torn note with the missing signature. Edward Doheny, Jr. also went over the tale of the trip to Washington with the cash in the little black bag. Neither Mrs. Doheny nor her son was asked any questions by the prosecution.

Once again, Doheny's testimony, when he reached the stand, stressed his patriotic intentions. He was merely trying to "save" the Navy's oil to keep America safe and strong. He insisted that he expected no profit whatever from his machinations with Fall, despite the fact that he had once announced that he assumed his profits would exceed $100 million. He explained that he had selected his son as the courier to deliver the cash to Fall because "I was endeavoring at that time to work him into every phase of the business of handling the fortune that I expected sometime or other he would handle all of." Doheny was asked whether he considered his son's rather simple mission to Washington an important part of the young man's financial education. "Yes, sir," Doheny replied. "Even if he had been held up on the way he would have learned something. He would have had something in experience." Doheny's was a mind that seemed frequently to contemplate disaster.

After some three weeks of testimony, Frank J. Hogan was ready to sum up for his client and to demonstrate his particular mastery of the Irish gift for oratory. With flashing eyes and a voice that filled the courtroom, Hogan told the jury that what it had heard against Doheny amounted to "as wholesale and as vicious a vilification as ever polluted the atmosphere of a court of justice." He asked the jury, "Do you think that a man who has left his home at the age of sixteen and followed the trails of the pioneer West, who dug in mother earth for the minerals hidden therein, who with pick and shovel sunk wells that he might bring out the gold and liquid that today mean safety for worlds, would, even if he himself could, stoop so low as to bribe an official of his government, the friend of his youth and his former days, would, if he could, stoop so low as to bribe a Cabinet officer of the United States of America in order that he might swindle and cheat the land that had given him plenty?"

For more than five hours Hogan besieged the jury with his rhetoric, once becoming so overwrought with emotion that he had to pause and dry his eyes. He brought in the horrors of World War I and young Ned Doheny's valiant service in it. Doheny, Sr. had not only given America its riches from underground but had also "offered that young man's life upon the altar of patriotism. He went on the turbulent and submarine-infested oceans in his country's service—the only son, the only child. And you are asked to believe that when Edward L. Doheny, near the end of his life, corruptly intended to bribe Albert B. Fall, a Secretary in the Cabinet of Warren G. Harding, he deliberately used as an instrument therefor his son, the pride of his youth, the hope of his maturity, the solace of his old age!" He invoked the memory of the dead President, calling Harding "as able and loving and as fine-hearted a President as we have ever had, or will have," and saying that "From his sacred tomb in Marion, Ohio, I stand his splendid figure before twelve of his fellow men. . . . He stands here today as the best silent witness in this case." Before he was finished, Hogan had compared his client's situation to the Crucifixion in Jerusalem, and Edward Doheny to Jesus Christ himself.

After seven hours of deliberation, the jury had not reached an agreement and the jurors were locked up for the night. At ten-fifteen the following morning, they came in with their verdict: not guilty. Immediately, a wild demonstration broke out in the courtroom and chairs, tables, and desks were overturned. Lawyers, friends, and well-wishers rushed up to shake the defendants' hands. Old man Doheny wept with joy. His daughter-in-law also wept, as did Fall, Mrs. Fall, and the Falls' daughter, who had not yet got her trip to Mexico. In her hotel room, where she received the news, Ma D. burst into tears as well, and cried out, "My prayers have been answered!" The Doheny family returned in triumph to Los Angeles, where a welcoming throng of some four hundred people had gathered on the station platform to meet their train. Doheny was given a huge testimonial dinner by the city to celebrate his acquittal, and the principal speakers at the gala were the mayors of both Los Angeles and San Francisco, and Doheny's victorious lawyer.

Of course there were some observers who saw through the smoke screen of celebration and congratulation. Rollin Kirby, the topical cartoonist for the New York *World*, produced a cartoon which depicted a row of four prison cells, variously labeled "Rich Man," "Poor Man," "Beggarman," and "Thief." Three of the cells overflowed with prisoners. A fourth cell stood conspicuously empty.

Chapter 11

THE DECLINE OF MR. FALL

In the long legal struggle to untangle the knotted web of Teapot Dome, and to get back the United States Government's property, there would be more trials, more hearings, more testimony, more decisions. On February 8, 1927, the United States Supreme Court upheld the Los Angeles court's decision against Doheny, ordering him to pay for all the oil he had extracted from Elk Hills and further declaring that he had no right to the $11 million which Doheny claimed the government owed him for the storage tanks his company had built at Pearl Harbor. The entire proceedings, the Court declared, had from the beginning been thoroughly stained with "fraud and corruption." It was a scathing and unanimous opinion.

Now it was Albert Fall's turn to stand trial for accepting the bribe. He had taken the precaution of hiring Doheny's lawyer, Mr. Hogan (Doheny had made Fall a gift of $5,000 to help him pay for his defense, and Doheny had also purchased Fall's ranch from him for $168,250). Fall arrived at the District of Columbia Supreme Court building looking terrible. He still wore his wide-brimmed Western hat, but underneath it his face was gaunt and haggard. His color was bad, and he looked much older than his sixty-seven years. A heavy overcoat and baggy trousers hung on his emaciated frame, and he was in a wheelchair. A nurse and doctor were required to lift him, clutching a cane, from the wheelchair to a special leather easy chair that his doctor had ordered placed in the courtroom. The court proceedings had barely started when Fall slid from the leather chair and collapsed on the floor. He was helped out of the courtroom by the nurse, the doctor, his wife and daughter, and the senior Dohenys. It was discovered that he had suffered an internal hemorrhage.

The next day, while his lawyers were in the process of obtaining a postponement of the trial due to Mr. Fall's ill health, the doors to the courtroom suddenly opened and in wheeled Fall, looking even worse. With help, he staggered to the leather chair, where a nurse covered him with a blue lap robe. He insisted on going through with the trial because, as Hogan explained to the court, Fall wanted "vindication before he passes into the Great Beyond." Implicit in the scene was the possibility that Hogan had staged the whole thing in order to obtain the jury's sympathy for his sick and aging client.

One of the many lurid details surrounding the whole Fall-Doheny oil scandal had been the murder, just a few months before Fall's trial, of young Ned Doheny by his male secretary, Robert Plunkett. In the days that followed, it was whispered that it had been because Doheny had resisted a homosexual overture of Plunkett's, but such rumors can never be corroborated because Plunkett, immediately after killing Doheny, shot and killed himself. In Fall's trial, Hogan attempted to make emotional capital out of this tragedy when, in questioning the elder Doheny, he mentioned his dead son's name. The old man broke down and wept on the stand,

and the court had to be recessed until Mr. Doheny had sufficiently gathered himself together to go on. Hogan also, it seemed to many observers, made excessive use of Mr. Fall's failing health in his remarks to the jury, and other theatrical elements were supplied by the fact that throughout his testimony Fall was solicitously hovered over by his wife, his daughter, both Mr. and Mrs. Doheny, his doctor, and his nurse. Hogan also brought up a number of Fall's friends and neighbors from New Mexico to be character witnesses (significantly, no one in Washington could be persuaded to come forward and speak for Fall). On the day of Hogan's summation, Mrs. Fall even brought Fall's tiny granddaughter to the courtroom. The little girl seemed also to be able to cry on cue.

In his summation to the jury, the prosecuting attorney reminded the panel that the state of Mr. Fall's health was immaterial to the question at hand. "It is all simple," he said. "There are four things of a controlling nature for you to remember. One is that Doheny wanted the lease of the Elk Hills. The second is, Fall wanted money. The third is, Doheny got the lease, and the fourth is, Fall got the money." As for drainage of the oil lands, he said, "The only drainage in this case was from Doheny's to Fall's pocket."

In *his* summation for the defense, Mr. Hogan seemed not quite able to repeat his past performance for Doheny. Although he relied again on the twin themes of pathos and patriotism ("Patriotism," the prosecution had told the jury, "is the last refuge of the scoundrel"), and talked emotionally of Doheny and Fall as two old pioneering and prospecting pals, he chose one unfortunate simile when he said, "National security runs like a thread of gold" through the Elk Hills and Pearl Harbor deals. In his charge to the jury, the judge said, "Counsel has urged you to send this man back to the sunshine of New Mexico. Neither you nor I have anything to do with sunshine. You are here to decide this case on the evidence and nothing else."

Refugees fleeing from the Great Famine. (New York Public Library Picture Collection)

Worshipers at a *scalán,* or a clandestine Mass station. Under British rule, Irish Catholics were forbidden to build churches. (John Murray Cuddihy)

"Honest Dan" Bradley.
(John Murray Cuddihy)

His wife, Julia.
(John Murray Cuddihy)

Grandpa and Grandma Thomas E. Murray and their children. Boys *(from left)*: Tom, Joe, Dan, Jack. Girls *(from left)*: Julia, Marie, Katherine, Anna. (Mrs. James Butler MacGuire)

Thomas A. Edison *(center)*, with Grandpa Murray *(to his right)*, Walter P. Chrysler *(to his left)*, and friends and relations. (John Murray Cuddihy)

Grandpa James Butler and his grandson, James Butler MacGuire.
(Mrs. James Butler MacGuire)

Thomas Fortune Ryan.　　(New York Public Library Picture Collection)

Mrs. H. Lester Cuddihy, Sr. as
a bride in Brooklyn.
(Mrs. H. Lester Cuddihy)

Mr and Mrs George Bryden
request the pleasure of the company of
Mr and Mrs Ted Coley and Family
at the marriage of their daughter
Elizabeth Jane
to Robert A Cuddihy
at Trinity Church Lockerbie
on Friday 31st July 1970 at 3 o'clock
and afterwards at Lockerbie House Hotel
R S V P
38 Victoria Park
Lockerbie
Dumfriesshire

The uncommon invitation to
Robbie Cuddihy's wedding
(Protestant) in 1970.
(John Murray Cuddihy)

Edward L. Doheny, *(right)* and Albert B. Fall outside the courthouse where the Teapot Dome hearings were conducted, 1926. (Culver)

The James C. Flood mansion in Menlo Park, California. (Culver)

James G. Fair's house in San Francisco, and his two daughters,
Mrs. W. K. Vanderbilt, Jr. and Mrs. Hermann Oelrichs. (Culver)

San Francisco's "Irish Big Four": *(top, from left)* William S. O'Brien, James G. Fair; *(bottom)* John W. Mackay, James C. Flood.   (Culver)

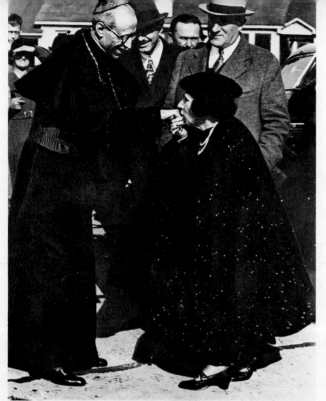

The Duchess Brady with Eugenio, Cardinal Pacelli, future Pontiff. (Wide World)

Evalyn Walsh McLean's Hope Diamond.
(New York Public Library Picture Collection)

John Murray Cuddihy, outfitted by Rowe of London, as painted by Robert
Henri, circa 1928.
                                                                    (Mr. Cuddihy)

"Wedding of the Century," Anne McDonnell to Henry Ford II.
(John Murray Cuddihy)

The picture that went around the world: Mary Jane Cuddihy dancing barefoot at the old El Morocco.   (Jerome Zerbe)

Wedding breakfast for the girl who caught the Ford bouquet, Mary Jane Cuddihy MacGuire. *(From left)* Al Smith, Grandma R. J. Cuddihy, Grandpa Cuddihy, Mrs. Smith.   (Mrs. James Butler MacGuire)

The boys at the wedding. *(From left)* Bob Cuddihy "The Roué," John M. Cuddihy, Thomas E. Murray II, Tom Cuddihy. (Mrs. James Butler MacGuire)

Mrs. William F. Buckley, Sr., her children, and a few of her grandchildren at "Great Elm."

(Black Star—Dan McCoy)

The children in Southampton, circa 1929—thirty-five of an eventual forty-nine. *(From left)* the Elgood Lufkins' Tom and John; the Joe Murrays' Marcia, Theresa, Joan, Rosamund; the John F. Murrays' Catherine, Jake, Pat, Tom II, Jeanne; Auntie Katherine Murray McQuail with Ennis; the H. L. Cuddihys' Mary Jane, Tom, Bob (always in motion), John, H. Lester Jr.; the Thomas E. Murrays' Tommy Jr., Anne, Marie, Bradley, Paul, Jane, James, Baby Frank; the James Francis McDonnells' Gerry, Murray, Charles, Genevieve, Charlotte, Anne, James and Morgan, Catherine and Sheila.

(John Murray Cuddihy)

The jury was out for eleven hours without a verdict, before retiring for the night. This length of time was regarded as a heartening sign by the Falls and Dohenys and their lawyers. (Doheny had an important stake in this case: if Fall was found guilty of accepting the bribe, he would have to stand trial again for giving it, and might yet be sent to jail.) But when the jury came out at eleven the next morning, its verdict was: guilty. There was widespread weeping and sobbing. The Falls wept, and Doheny wept and then swore at the judge, saying something about "this damned court." One of Fall's many lawyers immediately fell to the floor unconscious, and was given a heart stimulant by Fall's doctor. Frank Hogan lost his composure as completely as he had lost his first criminal case. He banged his fists on the table and shouted incoherencies at the judge. The judge sentenced Fall to a year in prison and a fine of $100,000. On July 18, 1931, after more than a year of unsuccessful legal maneuvers to keep him out, Fall was driven by police ambulance to the penitentiary at Santa Fe, where he became convict Number 6991 as well as the first Cabinet member in American history to be convicted of a felony, and to serve a prison sentence. In November of that year, he became eligible for parole. This was denied on the grounds that parole did not apply to a man who had committed "so grave an offense against the government and civilization."

Now, of course, it was necessary for Ed Doheny to stand trial again, again for bribery, his fourth and final court battle. Once again, Hogan was defending him, and was back in his old tearjerking form. Reading from previous testimony of Doheny's dead son ("a voice from the tomb"), he managed to imitate the young man's speech. Hearing him, Mrs. Doheny collapsed in tears, sobbing, "It's Ned . . . it's Ned!" Mr. Doheny wept along with her. The testimony contained almost nothing that was new, and reiterated everything that had been said before, but Doheny did add one new touch to his explanation of the $100,000 loan to Fall. Once, Doheny said, in the year 1886, he had fallen down a mine shaft and broken both legs. His old friend Fall had loaned him some lawbooks so that he could study law while he was recuperating. That was one reason why, thirty-five years later, he had helped Fall out with $100,000.

The trial lasted barely ten days, and Frank Hogan once more drew widespread weeping with his summation ("Ned Doheny says from the grave," etc.). The jury was out for barely an hour before returning with its verdict: not guilty.

The very same court, in the very same building, presided over by the very same justice, Mr. William Hitz, had declared Edward Doheny innocent of giving the very same bribe that Albert Fall had been found guilty of taking. It seemed, to some, all very queer —but not to those who had long regarded the ways of American jurisprudence with a cynical and jaundiced eye.

Ill health or no, Albert Fall survived for twelve more years after his release from prison, and died in March, 1943, at the ripe old age of eighty-three. Edward L. Doheny had died nine years earlier, on September 8, 1935, at the age of seventy-nine, having been almost completely bedridden at "Chester Place" for three years. The last years of his life had involved a welter of stockholders' suits as a result of his Elk Hills and Pearl Harbor activities and, in all, he had been required to pay back the United States Government $47,137,696.28 for oil he had taken out of Elk Hills, and more millions had to be paid in income taxes, interest, and penalties on the money had had made from Elk Hills. But he was still a very rich man. At Ma D.'s suggestion, he had divided up his fortune among his wife and relatives, giving his family $75 million in trusts and keeping $10 million for himself.

And he was to have two more gala receptions to his credit. On his return from Washington to Los Angeles after his second acquittal, over five hundred people were at the platform to meet him—naval officers, clergymen, dignitaries, and motion picture stars. And his funeral, at St. Vincent's Cathedral, which Doheny money had built, drew a capacity crowd of twelve hundred friends and admirers, while another two thousand stood outside the doors of the church, paying tribute.

After Ed Doheny's death, the Doheny companies which owned Fall's ranch served Fall with an eviction notice, an ungrateful gesture. Surely the two who had been such pals in life cannot any longer be pals in heaven, or wherever they are.

Today the United States Navy has its oil lands back. They are regularly checked for drainage. It has been minimal.

Ma D. survived her husband for a number of years, living quietly and avoiding publicity in the vast reaches of her estate, surrounded by guards and watchdogs. Finally, she was taken ill and brought to a hospital, where doctors advised that she had only a short time to live. A priest was summoned to administer Last Rites, and was told to make all possible haste. When he arrived at the hospital, he was told that death was perhaps only moments away. He ran down the corridor, struggled with the heavy, handleless hospital door, managed to push it open, and then skidded across the highly polished floor of the room and fell forward, elbows first, across the patient's bed, landing on her stomach. With that, Mrs. Doheny expired.

It is quite easy to see what kind of a man Albert Fall was, but what kind of a man was Ed Doheny? Was he a fool or a knave? Was he a hard-nosed hypocrite or merely naïve? Had he become so used to bribing and paying off governments—as he had done with such success in Mexico—that he simply believed that this was one of the more practical ways of doing business? Or did he envision all governments as basically corrupt, and therefore corruptible? Or was it simple self-faith? Had he become so rich, and so accustomed to the lavish use of money, that he had begun to believe his own myth and that he could do no wrong, no matter what he did or how he did it? Had he developed the same blind and implicit trust in his own mystic or psychic powers that he had once placed in his prospector's willow wand? Or was he at heart an honest man, who honestly believed that what was good for Doheny today was good for the country tomorrow, and the next day the world?

One man, long associated with the Doheny family, was asked once what he thought was the secret of Ed Doheny's character and his success. "The ability to smell a dollar bill a mile away" was the answer. "He was not a nice man."

Chapter 12

THE SILVER KINGS

an Francisco has always taken both a dim and a lofty view of Los Angeles, and San Francisco money is considered to have acquired more "refinement" than that of the larger city to the south. The famous Big Four—Charles Crocker, Mark Hopkins, Collis P. Huntington, and Leland Stanford—who founded considerable San Francisco fortunes were, however, of origins no more genteel than Edward Doheny's. Nor were San Francisco's *second* Big Four, or Irish Big Four—James C. Flood, William S. O'Brien, James Gordon Fair, and John William Mackay—the "Silver Kings" of the Comstock Lode in Virginia City, Nevada. From its discovery in 1859 to its final depletion twenty years later, the Comstock was the largest and most valuable single pocket of silver ever discovered in the world, and from its mines poured, all told, more than $500 million worth of shiny metal, which made multimillionaires not only of the four Irishmen themselves but also of several others, including Adolph Sutro, William Sharon, and William Ralston.

Jim Flood, described by Dixon Wecter as a "poor gamin of the New York streets," had gone west with the Gold Rush and settled in what was then a rough-and-tumble frontier town with rutted streets and ramshackle houses, and set about to make his fortune. In San Francisco, Flood met another young fortune-seeker named Will O'Brien, and the two went into partnership with a local bar and grill called the Auction Lunch Rooms. Flood's job was to mix the drinks, which he did in generous proportions, and O'Brien worked behind the stove, where he soon achieved a certain neighborhood celebrity for his Irish fish chowder, thick with potatoes. Presently the Auction Lunch Rooms was a popular gathering spot for miners who periodically came down from the hills to disport themselves at the city's lively fancy houses, and to partake of hearty food and drink. In addition to their cooking and bartending skills, the two men had sharp ears, and they listened to miners' stories and, in return for a drink or a cup of broth, took a mining tip or two. The Comstock sounded like a particularly good one, and, taking John Mackay and Jim Fair in with them as investing partners, they set off for Virginia City to stake a claim. When the Comstock came in, bartending and chowder-making days were gone forever.

Will O'Brien dropped out of the quartet early, but the others stayed in, and perhaps no other American catapulted himself from squalor to glittering splendor in so short a time as Jim Flood. Instant riches, to Flood, demanded instant luxury, and one of his first orders was the construction of a massive brownstone mansion on the very top of Nob Hill. Flood's house was so sturdily built that it was one of the few buildings in the city to survive the Great Earthquake, and it stands today exactly as it was, as the prestigious home of San Francisco's Pacific Union Club. Flood also built another palatial house in suburban Menlo Park, which became known locally as "Flood's Wedding Cake," and was described by the late Lucius Beebe as "a miracle of turrets, gables, and gingerbread." So much carpeting was required to cover the floors of these two houses that John Sloane, the carpet manufacturer from New York, found it necessary to send special representatives to California to handle the order, and soon it seemed simpler just to open up a branch store on the West Coast. Sloane's today is where much of San Francisco buys its rugs and furniture.

Jim Flood's daughter, Jennie, became the instant belle of San Francisco, a dark-haired beauty famous for her wit, charm, and devastatingly large and flashing eyes. In 1879, Jennie Flood was courted by no less than a United States President's son, Ulysses S. Grant, Jr., and the prospect of a match so pleased her father that he promised to build the pair a huge château in Newport as a wedding present. But young Grant, it seemed, had an eye for other ladies and, returning from a trip east, he delayed so long before reaching Jennie's house—"dallying along the way with Dora Miller and other adorables"—that Jennie angrily broke the engagement. Later she was admired and squired about by the British Lord Beaumont, but this, too, came to nothing and, in the end, Jennie Flood never married at all, though she remained a colorful and popular figure in San Francisco.

A later James Flood also cut a wide social swathe in the Western city, and his own big house—later to be given to the Order of the Sacred Heart—was the scene of some of the town's most lavish parties. The most famous of these was called "The Original Costume Ball," and was tossed, with no expense spared, in the Depression year of 1938. As described by a contemporary reporter, Julia Altrocchi:

The great pillared entrance hall had been transformed into a garden of azaleas and blossoming fruit trees. The costumes represented both old and current "characters." Mrs. Flood wore an old-fashioned crinoline of magenta silk. Her son, Jimmie, acted the part of Pop-Eye the Sailor Man. Mrs. Harold McKinnon was "charming in the wedding gown of her grandmother." . . . "One of the loveliest costumes

137

of the evening was that of Mrs. Willard Somers who went as the ark. Her pale blue gown was painted with animals two by two and her ark hat had a dove of peace in front and Noah's three brothers in the back." Charles Theriot [who had married one of the daughters of newspaper publisher Meichel H. de Young], as a newsboy, "distributed a one-page edition of the *Chronicle*" describing "floods" in the city, and specifically Jimmie Flood and his yacht, *Dorade*, which had just won the San Pedro to Honolulu race in 1936. The prize for the most amusing couple was awarded to Mrs. George A. Pope, Jr., as "a Floradora girl in pale pink over a chemise and over that an old-fashioned black satin laced corset," and to her partner Tallant Tubbs, as "a second baseman of the Seals." First prize for women went to Mrs. Sheldon Cooper, who arduously represented the framed picture of the Dauphin, and first men's prize to Dick Magee who "entered the ballroom as a muleteer—with a live mule."

The most popular of the Comstock's Big Four, however, was John William Mackay, a tall, slender, handsome man with a gentle nature and a generous heart. After his first big strike in the Mother Lode, in which he made $200,000, he announced that this was enough money for any man, and that "the man who wanted more than that was a fool." Later, of course, finding himself a two-fifths owner of the giant Comstock, he managed to change his mind. He had been born virtually penniless in Dublin in 1831, and emigrated to America at the onset of the famine at the age of nine. He first worked in New York as an apprentice shipbuilder, but when tales of Western gold began to circulate, he headed for California. There he worked as a pick-and-shovel man for four dollars a day, but he shrewdly insisted on receiving only part of his pay in cash, and the rest in stock of the mining company. Thus, when the Mother Lode came in, he found himself all at once a moderately rich man. In 1867, after the Comstock had made him a hugely rich man, he heard a sad tale of a poor widow in Virginia City named Louise Hungerford Bryant, the daughter of a New York barber, who had married, gone west with her husband, and been left with a small daughter and a younger sister and virtually without resources. Mackay organized a collection for her, and, going to her house to present the money to her, he promptly fell in love with her. When he asked her to marry him, he warned her to judge him for his qualities as a man, not on the basis of his money, because, as he reminded her, "Circumstances in the mining business change quickly." But even if he lost everything he had, he promised, "I can always dig a living with my bare hands," and he swore to protect her—"with my fists, if need be."

Mackay not only did not lose all his money but went on to make a great deal more. In 1874 he and his wife moved to San Francisco and, two years later, came east to New York. Though neither Mackay had any formal education to speak of, nor any "breeding" in the social sense, they were both endowed with gentle and soft-spoken Irish attractiveness. Being rich didn't hurt them either, and they made friends easily. Nevertheless, they were snubbed by New York society, but, when they moved on to Europe, they were welcomed. With their good looks and manners, they charmed everyone, including the Prince of Wales, who called John Mackay "the most unassuming American I have ever met." Through all of what Mackay called their "top-of-the-heap living," he and his wife remained steadfastly in love. In 1883 he formed the Commercial Cable Company, and went to battle against Wall Street titan Jay Gould's Western Union telegraph monopoly. The financial community was certain that Gould, known as an unscrupulous and dirty fighter, would destroy "the Irish upstart," and was filled with awe for Mackay when Mackay won. He was twice nominated to the United States Senate and, both times, modestly refused. But he was still a fighter, and, in 1891, when he was sixty years old, he had a chance to make good his early promise to his wife. A series of articles about her had been appearing in newspapers in both the United States and England stating that she had been, at first, a washerwoman and, later, had sunk "even lower than that," and that she had sent her tiny daughters into the streets of Virginia City begging with tin cups. Mackay set out to find the instigator of the stories, a man named Bonynge, and, one day, spotted him through a window of the Bank of Nevada, chatting with the bank's president. Mackay let himself into the bank through the back door and headed straight for Mr. Bonynge, who was taken completely by surprise. "I struck out with my right," Mackay reported later, "and hit him in the left eye. Then I hit him again. . . . I'm not so handy with my fists as I used to be twenty-five years ago on the Comstock, but I have a little fight in me yet, and will allow no man to malign me or mine."

Of the Irish Big Four, Mackay was also by far the most philanthropic, and the complete tally of his giving will probably never be known because, when he gave to a charity that interested him, he nearly always insisted on absolute anonymity. He gave and loaned millions of dollars to friends and business associates, and these were also unrecorded. Two of his biggest gifts, however, could not be hidden—the Mackay School of Mines in Reno and the building of the Church of St. Mary's in the Mountains in Virginia City. Throughout his life, he refused to discuss his money, and, when he died in 1902, his business manager told reporters, "I don't suppose he knew within twenty millions what he was worth."

One of John Mackay's stepdaughters and a sister-in-law married titled Europeans, which displeased him. But real tragedy was to strike John and Louise Mackay with the death of their son, Willie, at the age of twenty-five. Willie, an accomplished horseman, was riding a race horse at his private track in France, and the horse, startled by a shot, shied at a turn and Willie was hurled headfirst over the fence and into a tree, shattering his skull. A second son, Clarence Mackay, made a brilliant society marriage to the elegant Katherine Alexander Duer and settled down on a huge Long Island estate called "Harbor Hill." "Harbor Hill" in the 1920's was the scene of one of the most publicized balls of the decade, which the Mackays gave for the visiting Prince of Wales. Despite the sumptuousness of the house, its decor, food, furnishings, and art collection, the only object in which the Prince—who would later become the Duke of Windsor—expressed interest was a small statue by Gutzon Borglum of John Mackay, whom an earlier Prince of Wales had found so "unassuming."

Clarence and Katherine Mackay had three children—John William, Katherine, and Ellin. Ellin Mackay began publishing articles and short stories in *The New Yorker* in 1925 and, in one of them, wrote, "Modern girls are conscious of their own identity, and they marry whom they choose, satisfied to satisfy themselves. They are not so keenly aware, as were their parents, of the vast difference between a brilliant match and a mésalliance." Shortly after these words appeared in print, and to the consternation of her family, Ellin Mackay proved that she meant what she said when she married a young Russian-Jewish composer from the Lower East Side named Irving Berlin (born Israel Baline). Though this union horrified her father, Clarence Mackay, long since divorced, later took his daughter's advice, and married a singer named Anna Case.

The story of San Francisco's Fair family is considerably less glamorous. If John Mackay was the most likable of the Irish Big Four, James Gordon Fair was easily the least, and Fair managed to win the nickname of "Slippery Jim" very early in his career. Born in Belfast in 1831, the same year as Mackay, Fair came first to Chicago at the age of twelve, and then moved westward at the age of eighteen. By the age of thirty he had a mill on the Washoe River in Nevada, where he became chiefly responsible—making many enemies in the process—for driving San Franciscans out of Nevada development, which he then managed to take over himself. With his Comstock millions, he got the Nevada State Legislature (which in those days elected U.S. Senators) to appoint him to the Senate, where his career was undistinguished. "He made no impression on the Senate," Frederick Logan Paxton has said, "save to advertise it as a haunt of millionaires, and he rarely took part in its debates. . . . But the gaudiness and irregularity of his life and the social ambitions of his family, to which his wealth allowed full gratification, attracted much attention for two decades."

In 1861 Jim Fair had married an Irish girl named Theresa Rooney, by whom he had four children—Theresa ("Tessie"), Virginia ("Birdie"), Charles, and James. After an acrimonious divorce, Mrs. Fair retained custody of Tessie, Birdie, and Charles, and Mr. Fair got James. His young namesake hated and dreaded his father and, soon after the divorce, committed suicide. Charles Fair made a youthful marriage which so angered his father that he disinherited him, and shortly after, Charles and his young wife were killed in an automobile accident. Birdie Fair married William K. Vanderbilt, but this, too, was disastrous and ended in divorce. ("Vanderbilts often marry Catholics," says one of the Vanderbilts, "and always divorce them.") Tessie Fair married Hermann Oelrichs in a huge San Francisco society wedding—to which her father was scrupulously not invited—and went on to become a reigning dowager of Newport for many years until she underwent a mental breakdown. In his own last years Slippery Jim Fair lived alone in a San Francisco hotel, solitary, bitter, and completely without friends, estranged from his entire family. When he died in 1894, his personal and financial affairs were in such a hopeless tangle that his will offered fifty dollars apiece "to any widows or children" of his who might be able to prove themselves such.

Though the Fairs are no longer prominent in San Francisco, the Floods and Mackays currently decorate the pages of the *Social Register*. Of the third-generation James Floods who live in the horsy suburb of Woodside, a friend says, "The Floods today are all ladies and gentlemen. Nobody cares at all that his grandfather was a bartender and his grandmother was a chambermaid." Nobody cares, perhaps, but everybody in San Francisco remembers.

Unlike his contemporaries in Nevada and California, Tom Walsh was not so quickly lucky as he poked about with his pick and hammer in search of gold in the hills of Colorado. Born in Clonmel, County Tipperary, in 1850, Tom Walsh came to America in 1869 and, for a while, worked as a carpenter in Worcester, Massachusetts. At the age of twenty, however, he, too, was struck with what he called "the mining fever," and headed west, where one of his first mistakes was to turn down a half-interest in a mining venture called the Homestake. The Homestake turned out to be one of the world's largest gold mines, yielding all told nearly $300 million worth of ore, and became the foundation of the fortune of George Hearst, the father of William Randolph Hearst. Still, young Walsh was persistent, moving about from town to town—towns with such unprepossessing names as Leadville and Deadwood. In Leadville, he met a girl named Carrie Bell Reed, and married her in 1879, and this couple went to live in Sowbelly Gulch, where their first home was an abandoned boxcar which had been lifted from its tracks and placed on a foundation of logs with an earthen ramp leading up to the front door. Tom Walsh cut holes in the boxcar for windows, for which his wife made curtains of checked gingham, and planted windowboxes. Even then Mrs. Walsh must have had visions of grandeur. She found the name of Sowbelly Gulch "eructative," and for a while tried to get the town to change its name to "St. Keven's."

In 1880, off on a prospecting trip in the Frying Pan district west of Leadville, Tom Walsh came upon an abandoned cabin and mine shaft. The roof of the cabin had been covered with the dirt that had been hollowed out to make the cabin floor, and, picking about in this, he noticed promising flashes of quartz, indicating the presence of silver. He took a sample of the cabin roof, had it as-

143

sayed, and found that the roof contained hundreds of ounces of silver to the ton. What had happened, it seemed, was that the earlier prospectors had built their cabin squarely on top of a promising silver vein, and then had proceeded to sink their shaft fifty feet away, into barren rock. Walsh bought the cabin site for next to nothing and within two months had mined silver worth $75,000.

From Sowbelly Gulch, the family—which now included two small children, Evalyn and Vinson—moved on to Ouray, Colorado, where they settled in a small frame house. It was there, barely nine miles from home, in his Camp Bird Mine, that Tom Walsh chipped into a rocky hillside and found gold. He was forty-six years old, and had been searching for more than a quarter of a century. His wife, by then, had begun to suffer from headaches and melancholia—a condition defined as "neuralgia"—and spent much of her time in a darkened room. His son Vinson was too young to understand. And so it was to his ten-year-old daughter, Evalyn, that Tom Walsh first confided his "secret," tiptoeing into her bedroom and whispering, "Daughter, I've struck it rich!"

Of course, Tom Walsh's secret did not remain a secret long, as the Camp Bird Mine promptly made him a multimillionaire and he moved his family back east, to Washington, D.C., where the Walshes installed themselves in a huge fortress at 2020 Massachusetts Avenue, which Walsh built for one million dollars. Nor could the news of riches have fallen on more receptive ears than those of little Evalyn. From that moment, Evalyn Walsh embarked upon a life-long love affair with money, and all that money could buy. And it would, she discovered, buy a great deal. Tom Walsh was an indulgent husband and gave his wife everything she asked for—furs from Gunther, jewels from Cartier, gowns from Worth in Paris—which did much to assuage the lady's melancholia. He was equally indulgent with his daughter. When little Evalyn found that walking to school in Washington was "trying for my dignity," she asked her father if he could "afford to hire a horse and carriage." A day or so later, she was presented with a blue victoria and a pair of matched sorrels with silver bits, along with a coachman in a silk hat and gloves. "For a moment I was speechless," she wrote later, "then jumped into Father's arms and hugged him."

At the age of twelve, at a dancing class, Evalyn met Edward Beale McLean, the son of the wealthy Washington *Post* publisher. For "Ned" McLean, it was love at first sight, according to Evalyn, but she kept putting him off until, after being engaged "dozens of times," she suddenly married him in Denver. There followed one of the most incredible honeymoons in marital history. The two fathers—Tom Walsh and John McLean—vied with each other as to how much money each should put up for the wedding trip, finally agreeing to giving them $100,000 apiece for "the young people to enjoy themselves." It was a prewar sum that most Americans would have found difficult to spend, but not the newlyweds. For example, "One day in Leipzig," Evalyn Walsh McLean recalled in her memoir, *Father Struck It Rich*, "we lost patience with the fact that we had only one Mercedes and went overnight to Paris and bought an extra one." Earlier, Evalyn had met Chicago's Mrs. Potter Palmer, who had let her play with her jewelry— "She let me finger to my heart's content her necklace of emeralds and diamonds, and seemed to understand the passion in my eyes as I looked at them." On their honeymoon, to gratify this passion, Ned McLean bought Evalyn the first of her famous diamonds—the fabled Star of the East. That pretty much took care of the $200,-000, and the couple had to cable home for money to pay their hotel bill. They left Europe with hundreds of unpaid bills in their wake, and successfully smuggled the Star of the East past customs into the United States.

It was not long before Evalyn Walsh McLean, through the good offices of Pierre Cartier, and for $154,000, became the owner of the most famous diamond in the world, the blue 44½-carat Hope, set

145

in the center of sixteen other large stones. The purchase alarmed her mother because of the Hope Diamond's reputation for bringing its owner bad luck. It had supposedly belonged to Marie Antoinette, and a later Greek owner was said to have leaped to his death from a cliff. A third owner had gone down with a ship at sea after disposing of the diamond. The Hope Diamond's "fatal power" worried Evalyn McLean only slightly, but she did agree to ask a priest to "lay the curse." The priest, one Monsignor Russell, received Mrs. McLean in his chapel, donned his robes, and placed her "bauble" on a velvet cushion. Just as he was about to begin his blessing, lightning flashed across the sky and there was a giant clap of thunder and a great rush of wind without rain. Still, the Monsignor continued with his incantations, and the curse was pronounced removed.

But was it? At her huge Washington estate, "Friendship," Evalyn Walsh McLean became one of the first great Washington hostesses, in whose footsteps such women as Perle Mesta and Gwendolyn Cafritz have tried to follow. Even though Evalyn rarely rose before five in the afternoon, and was usually too dazed from drink and drugs to recognize her guests, her parties were legendary, and the only qualification needed for an invitation to one of them was that the guest be either rich, famous, or preferably both. Her addiction to morphine became extreme, and she secreted packets of the drug under carpets, behind mirrors, and in slits cut in furniture upholstery. When she tried to withdraw, she suffered agonizing pain and had visions of monsters crawling under her bed and up her wall. For a while, an upper floor of her house became a private sanitarium, with nurses and doctors in attendance, because her husband refused to have her put away. Her escapes from morphine were terrifying, and tragically brief.

Her husband, meanwhile, had a drinking problem even more severe than his wife's, and an associate at the Washington *Post*, Alfred Friendly, has written of McLean's exploits, which, as he has put it, "reached a new high, or low, in ingenious profligacy, inventive wildness, and general hell-raising of a sort that this enfeebled age, thirty or forty years later, simply cannot conceive of, much less match." In bars, Ned McLean enjoyed knocking fedoras off other patrons with his cane, then stamping and crushing them, while his two bodyguards went patiently about taking orders for new hats. Mrs. Harding was understandably irked when McLean urinated into the fireplace of the East Room of the White House, nor was the Belgian Ambassador pleased when Ned McLean urinated down the leg of his striped trousers. A *Post* reporter woke up one morning aboard a transatlantic steamer—drugged and kidnaped because McLean wanted company on the trip. McLean once hired ten prostitutes to pose nude on pedestals in his garden for a party, and at a New Year's Eve gala all the guests were stripped naked and ordered to run around the block to celebrate the New Year. He had a pet seal named Colonel George Harvey which itself consumed a quart of Scotch whisky a day, delivered regularly by a *Post* reporter from McLean's inexhaustible cellars. In his drunkenness, McLean agreed to commit perjury in telling the transparent lie that he, not Ned Doheny, had given the $100,-000 to his good friend Albert Fall, at the time of Teapot Dome. At times, because of his alcoholic tremor, he had to tie a bar towel around his wrist and make it into a pulley around his neck so that he could get his drinking hand and his glass up to his lips.

When Evalyn McLean's son, Vinson, was born in 1909, both she and the baby nearly died. The following year, Tom Walsh painfully died of cancer, driving his daughter to renewed bouts with drugs. Little Vinson, whom the press christened "the hundred-million-dollar baby," was the subject of repeated kidnap threats, and the McLean house bristled with guards and burglar alarms. Although Mrs. McLean often complained that her husband was "spoiled," she did her thorough best to spoil her own children. Because Ned McLean had had a Negro playmate as a child, it was decided that little Vinson should have a black friend too. "We could not buy a colored boy, of course," she commented, "although it was our habit to buy anything we wanted." She did, however, make arrangements with his parents to hire a five-year-old named Julian Winbush to live with the family, and Julian's parents agreed to relinquish all control of him for ten years. The experiment was not a complete success. There were awkward moments with Pullman porters traveling to Palm Beach in those Jim Crow days—even on Ned McLean's private train, which went everywhere with the whistle blowing at full blast. And as for little Vinson, he could not have cared less. "So far as he was concerned," Mrs. McLean wrote, "I would have done as well to have borrowed a playmate from the zoo."

At the age of twenty, Vinson was run down by an automobile and killed. Ned McLean had, meanwhile, taken up with Marion Davies's sister, and the affair went on for months all over the United States and Europe. Evalyn McLean's brother Vinson was also killed in an automobile accident, in which she herself was seriously injured. At the age of twenty, Evalyn McLean's daughter married fifty-seven-year-old Senator Robert Reynolds of North Carolina, and later died of an overdose of sleeping pills. Still, Evalyn Walsh McLean continued to mock the story of the curse of the Hope Diamond, even lending it to Army brides married at her home during World War II. But in the end, her body racked by drink and drugs and malnutrition—her habit completely destroyed her appetite for food—she died with a scream as awful as the sound of the thunderclap that shook Monsignor Russell's church so many years before.

Money, as Grandpa Murray used to point out, can divide a family. It can also destroy one.

Chapter 13

MR. RYAN'S FORTUNE

The Ryan family in America has long considered itself quite superior to such families as the Dohenys of California, as well as to the Murray-McDonnell-Cuddihy family axis in New York. The Ryans, in fact, if asked which was the First Irish Family in the entire United States, would answer that without question it is the Ryans. Their feelings in this matter are based on the fact that there have been Ryans on these shores longer than almost any other Irish-American family. The Ryans did not, as the others did, emigrate to America as a result of the potato famine, nor did they come directly from Ireland. The first American Ryan, Philip, went from Ireland to England during the reign of James II and then, after some unrecorded difficulties with the Crown, made his way to the Colonies, where he first appeared in Virginia around 1690. Philip Ryan married a girl named White-head, whose father is said to have been a ship's captain, and the Ryans settled in Lynchburg, where a number of Ryans—not rich—can be found today.

Those Ryans today who *are* rich very much resent having the founder of the family wealth, the appropriately named Thomas Fortune Ryan (his mother's maiden name was Fortune), described as having started out in life "penniless." Cleveland Amory, for example, in *Who Killed Society?* has stated that Thomas Fortune Ryan "was left orphaned and penniless at fourteen," and that he "walked the streets" as a youth. Not so, counter the Ryans, who point out that an early Lynchburg business directory lists Thomas Fortune Ryan's father's occupation as "tailor," and that the family was probably respectably prosperous—though they may have lost some money at the time of the Civil War. Also, though Thomas Fortune Ryan was indeed an orphan at age fourteen, he did not take to the streets but, rather, went to live with his maternal grandparents, the Fortunes.

But at the age of seventeen, in 1868, Thomas Fortune Ryan did indeed leave home, as Ed Doheny had done, and made his way to Baltimore. Baltimore was even then known as one of America's "Catholic cities"—the others being New Orleans, St. Louis (both French Catholic), San Francisco (Spanish Catholic), and St. Paul, Minnesota (Scotch-Irish). Baltimore alone was of English Catholic origin. The first Lord Baltimore, George Calvert, one of the most powerful of all the colonial governors, had embraced Catholicism early in the seventeenth century, and both he and the city had taken the name from a tiny fishing village of Baltimore on the southern coast of Ireland because it was considered "the Catholic parish closest to America."

When Thomas Fortune Ryan arrived in Baltimore, he was not himself a Catholic. But he did go to work for a dry-goods commission merchant named John S. Barry, who was a Catholic. Ryan promptly fell in love with Mr. Barry's daughter, Ida, and, in Horatio Alger fashion, married her. This undoubtedly was one factor in his conversion to Catholicism, but Ryan himself always claimed that his interest in the Church was first sparked by a man he met who was a line manager on the Southern Railroad and who gave him his missal to read.

From Baltimore, young Ryan and his bride—backed with a small dowry from her father—made their way to New York, where Ryan worked for a while on a newspaper and then as a clerk in a brokerage house. It was here, in the mid-1870's, that Ryan had the good luck to meet William C. Whitney, the transit entrepreneur. Whitney was so impressed by the young man that he eventually made him his partner, and, while still in his twenties, Ryan was able to purchase his own seat on the New York Stock Exchange.

Thomas Fortune Ryan was a strikingly handsome man, tall—over six feet two—and with intense and burning eyes, who could exercise, when he wished, enormous personal charm. The "Ryan charm," in fact, has become a family trait. But he could also be withdrawn and quiet and austere, and when the Irish smile faded from his lips, it was possible to glimpse the strength of the will behind the easygoing façade. He was, according to Whitney, "the most adroit, suave, and noiseless man that American finance has ever known." Others have spoken of the power of Ryan's "silences," which conveyed worlds of meaning, and Bernard Baruch, with whom Ryan also became friendly and with whom he was also soon working on elaborate Wall Street deals, has written of Ryan's imposing presence, combined with "the softest, slowest, gentlest Southern voice you ever heard. When he wanted to be particularly impressive, he would whisper. But he was lightning in action and the most resourceful man I ever knew intimately in Wall Street. Nothing ever seemed to take him by surprise." Baruch concedes that "Many people spoke harshly of him as ruthless and not to be trusted. . . . Still, I found him exact in all his transactions with me."

It wasn't long, working with men like Whitney and Peter A. B. Widener, before T. F. Ryan's affairs were a complicated—but hugely successful—network of railroads and street railroads, lighting systems and coal companies, life insurance companies and diamond mines. With Whitney, he consolidated and soon controlled the New York City transit system, and presently Ryan was ready to invade the tobacco empire of James Duke. Duke was no easy man to tangle with, but, using men like Baruch as his chief lieutenants, Ryan embarked upon what became known on Wall Street as "The Great Tobacco War." Ryan put together a syndicate which purchased the National Cigarette Company. National Cigarette was then artfully merged with the Union Tobacco Company, which, though independently chartered and organized, was actually controlled by Ryan, Whitney, Widener, and Anthony N. Brady. By 1898 Liggett & Myers remained the only tobacco company in the country not controlled by either Mr. Duke or Mr. Ryan. Ryan had ordered Baruch to "get Duke," and at one point became so alarmed at the possibility that he would actually succeed that he rushed into Baruch's office, saying, "I want to annoy them, not ruin them." ("But I knew he was pleased," Baruch commented.) The result of the "Tobacco War," with stocks in the various companies being driven up and down by the two opponents and their hired manipulators, was that both Duke and Ryan ended up making huge profits, and *both* men were pleased. "As hard as I fought the dissolution of the Tobacco Trust," Duke commented cheerfully afterward, "I'd fight even harder any effort to put it back together again. We made more money after we were broken up and had competition." In fact, it was rumored at the time that there had been no real war at all, and that Duke and Ryan had acted in secret collusion to achieve just such a result— more money. If true, it was a successful strategy for both operators.

Ryan's operations went on to extend into coke, coal, oil, lead, and typewriters. His activities spread from New York City to Ohio, Virginia, West Virginia, and Illinois, and into the Belgian Congo, where he was asked to reorganize the diamond mines by none other than King Leopold of Belgium himself. By 1905

Thomas Fortune Ryan, at the age of fifty-four, was worth fifty million dollars. A few years later, he was worth a hundred million. In 1924 he paid $791,851 in income tax—the tenth largest in the country. He built a huge mansion on Fifth Avenue, in which an area equal to one-third of a city block was devoted entirely to statuary—mostly busts of himself, three of them by Rodin—and in which almost as much acreage was given over to his private chapel. He was a heavy contributor to the Democratic Party and to the Catholic Church (giving the Church, all told, some $20,000,000, including New York's Church of St. Jean Baptiste). Like Estelle Doheny, Ida Ryan was made a Countess of the Holy Roman Empire by Pope Pius X.

Not all of his operations, of course, may have been entirely within the law. After William Whitney's death in 1904, and an investigation into the pair's consolidation and complete takeover of New York's rapid transit system, and the accompanying collapse of the Metropolitan Street Railway Company, a grand jury found that with such tactics as stock-watering and franchise-buying Mr. Ryan had done "many things deserving of severe condemnation . . . dishonest and probably criminal." Still, as so often happens after investigations into the affairs of rich American businessmen, no action was taken against Mr. Ryan.

He was less fortunate in his efforts to take over the Equitable Life Assurance Society of the United States, "Protector of the Widow and Orphan," and the largest insurance company in the country. The company became suddenly very much a Wall Street plum in 1908 following the death of its founder, H. B. Hyde, and its inheritance by his son, James Hazen Hyde. Young Hyde found himself, at the age of twenty-three, the custodian of a billion dollars' worth of life insurance policies and the savings of over 600,-000 individuals. At the time of his father's death, Equitable had more than $400 million in its treasury, and James Hazen Hyde received a 51 percent controlling interest of it.

It was quickly apparent that young Hyde cared little and knew less about running an insurance company. An aesthete and a dandy, James Hazen Hyde was more given to extravagant dress and elaborate party-giving. When he drove his private hansom cab down Fifth Avenue, matching bunches of fresh violets were tucked behind his horses' ears, sprouted from his coachman's hat, and bloomed from young Hyde's lapel. He tossed huge costume galas at his Long Island château, and once hosted a *bal masqué* at Sherry's that cost him $200,000. Here, the ballroom was transformed into an exact replica of the Hall of Mirrors at Versailles. Fond of all things French, Hyde imported chefs from the greatest restaurants of Paris and Lyons and stationed them in his favorite Manhattan eating places, where they had nothing at all to do but wait until their employer took a notion to drop by and order some favorite dish. One day, just for the fun of it, Hyde and his friend Alfred Gwynne Vanderbilt I drove a team of seventy-eight drag horses from New York to Philadelphia to see how long the trip would take them. In addition to the horses, a considerable retinue of humans was required, including a carriage expert, a photographer, and a valet. On their return, the young men proudly announced that the journey to Philadelphia had taken exactly nine hours and twenty-five minutes. They had stopped in Philadelphia six minutes, and were back in New York in another ten hours and ten minutes. Seven cases of champagne had been consumed. Such carryings-on made Hyde and his friends the darlings of the press in that golden era, but Wall Street took a more practical view. Hyde, Wall Street decided, needed help running his company to make sure that it "did the right thing" for the widows and the orphans. In their quietly determined way, the giants of the Street moved in to take over Equitable.

The two leading contenders for control were the principal Jewish investment house, Kuhn, Loeb & Company, headed by Jacob H. Schiff, and the leading Protestant banker, J. P. Morgan. Morgan already had a large interest in another insurance company, the

New York Life, and Morgan's plan was to acquire Equitable and merge it with New York Life; Morgan's client and ally, James J. Hill, believed that Equitable's half-billion-dollar treasury would be a handy source of capital for Mr. Hill's railroad ventures. Schiff, and *his* pet client, E. H. Harriman, had much the same thought in mind with regard to Harriman's railroads. What neither Schiff nor Morgan realized was that a Roman Catholic financier was also working quietly behind the scenes, and it was therefore something of a shock to both to learn that James Hazen Hyde had suddenly and without explanation sold all his Equitable stock to "that Irish upstart"—as Morgan put it—Thomas Fortune Ryan.

Perhaps young Hyde had succumbed to Ryan's famous charm. But when the price Ryan had paid—$2.5 million for controlling interest in a half-billion dollar company—was revealed, things looked very fishy indeed. They looked even fishier when it turned out that the dividend income on this amount of stock was only $3,514 a year. The reason for this, Ryan explained, was that the company's charter stipulated that all profits except 7 percent of the $100,000 par value of the stock should go to Equitable policyholders. (The stock could, of course, be used as a massive borrowing tool for whoever controlled it.) All this was too much for Mr. Morgan, who was, in the first decade of the twentieth century, the foremost financial power in America and who ran what amounted to his own Federal Reserve System before a real one was invented. By 1908 the financial community had become so thoroughly "Morganized" that literally nothing could be done that did not meet with Morgan's approval. (The only reason Morgan tolerated Schiff was that he respected Schiff's ability, and found him useful in dealing with other Jewish houses.) A year earlier, Morgan had forced another upstart, John W. "Bet-a-Million" Gates out of the Tennessee Coal & Iron Company, and now, marshaling all the power at his command, Morgan set out to accomplish the same thing with Ryan.

And Ryan, alas, powerful though he was, was no match for

Morgan. As Morgan piously explained, after successfully compelling Ryan to dispose of his controlling interest in Equitable, he had done so to prevent "hands that might prove injurious from manipulating the Society's funds." He had done it for the sake of the widows and the orphans. But there was more to it than that. There was more to it than revenge or reprimand against an upstart who had acted rashly and, perhaps, illegally. Under the rules of Morganization, according to William Miller in *A New History of the United States*, room at the top of American businesses was reserved strictly for "the congenial clubmates, churchmates, and cliques of the ruling oligarchy."

Rich he might be, but Thomas Fortune Ryan was an Irishman and a Roman Catholic. He could never join the club.

Chapter 14

AND FOR MY ELDEST SON,
ONE SET OF PEARL STUDS

By 1910 it was well known among the Thomas Fortune Ryans' friends that Tom and Ida Ryan were having marital difficulties. Ida Barry Ryan complained that her husband spent most of his time on his business dealings, and virtually none on herself or their children; when not doing business, he was working on his sculpture collection and posing for more busts of himself. Tom Ryan complained of his wife's complaints. There were also whispers of another woman. Since both were staunch Catholics, however, there was never a question of divorce. Ida Ryan's health was failing, and she became a virtual invalid. When she died in October, 1917, the rumors of another romance were quickly confirmed when Thomas Fortune Ryan, at the age of sixty-six, married again—just twelve days after his wife's death. His second wife was Mary T. Nicoll, the sister of the late De Lancey Nicoll, and a member of a family that had been socially prominent in New York since the early eighteenth century. She had also been married twice before, to James Brown Lord and Cornelius C. Cuyler. This hasty remarriage did not please any of Ryan's children, but it particularly distressed his eldest son, Allan, who commented at the time, "It is the most disrespectful, disgraceful, and indecent thing I've ever heard of." Allan Ryan's antipathy to his father's marriage, and to his stepmother, created a deep rift between father and son. By 1920 it was known that the two men were not on speaking terms.

Allan A. Ryan was, if anything, even handsomer than his father had been as a young man, and he had inherited a full share of his father's Irish charm. He lacked, however, his father's quiet reserve, and enjoyed talking freely to the press—a thing his father almost never did. He was physically on the weak side, and caught colds easily, but he had his father's stubborn will and knack for financial manipulation. Also, unlike his father, he had had a proper education and had graduated from Georgetown University. He was, in other words, in every way a promising young successor to his father and, until their falling-out, had been his father's favorite son. At the age of thirty-five, Allan had been given his father's seat on the New York Stock Exchange for his birthday, and his father had also brought him under the wing of Charles M. Schwab of United States Steel, who had helped the career of another bright young Irishman, James A. Farrell. "Thomas F. Ryan and I have been friends for many years," Mr. Schwab once said. "When he was retiring from business, he brought his boy Allan to me. Told me Allan was his hope for the future. Would I look after him? I have looked out for Allan ever since."

With such backing as this, plus whatever financial assistance his father may have supplied at the outset (it was always supposed that this was considerable, but members of the family insist that Allan's father staked him to only nine hundred dollars, in order that he would have to prove himself), Allan's firm, Allan A. Ryan & Company, quickly became known as a powerful Wall Street house. His reputation was gained as a "bull operator," a stock optimist, whose particular talent was squeezing short sellers, stock pessimists, or "bear operators." (Selling short is a technique by which a dealer borrows stock, and then sells it for delivery at a future date; the dealer hopes that the price of the stock will drop before the delivery date so that he can buy it back at a lower price, return the stock to the lender, and keep the profit.) In the bull-market year of 1919, Allan Ryan was known as the most powerful bull of all. Word that Ryan was buying was enough to send any stock up in price. That year, Allan Ryan told a friend that he was now worth thirty million dollars—well on his way to matching his father's huge fortune.

Like his father, Allan Ryan operated in a variety of fields. But it was known that his biggest investment was in the Stutz Motor Car Company of America, Inc. He had acquired a controlling interest in Stutz, and made himself its president in 1916. Stutz was one of the glamour issues of the day, and a company that was in splendid shape. Its famous Bearcat ("Knows No Master on the Road") was the glamorous symbol of the Flapper Era, when in its snappy bucket seats, fair-haired youths in raccoon coats with Prohibition flasks in their pockets tore across the landscape and through the pages of Scott Fitzgerald novels. The new president of Stutz was barely thirty-six, part of the nation's Flaming Youth himself, with a beautiful wife, six fine children, a grand house on Murray Hill, and of course a specially styled Stutz Bearcat. With the exception of a certain penchant for gambling—Allan Ryan was often seen out at the racetrack in Jamaica—he seemed like a man who could know no limits.

Projecting ahead for the year 1920, Allan Ryan had announced that he expected Stutz's profits would amount to around five million dollars, and this estimate was considered to be on the conservative side. But in January of that year Allan Ryan came down with influenza and had to enter a hospital. In February, still suffering from the pneumonia that had followed the influenza, Allan Ryan discovered certain facts that caused him immediate concern. Stutz had been selling for around $100 a share, but, throughout January, its price had jumped to around $120. Then, on February 2, the price of Stutz suddenly jumped again for no valid reason from $120 to $134 in a single day's trading, and it seemed clear that manipulators were at work, forcing the stock up beyond its worth, and that organized short selling was taking place; raiders were grabbing up Stutz shares, hoping to trap Stutz in its highly exposed position. These raiders were, Ryan had good reason to believe, members of the Stock Exchange's ruling clique, the Old Guard old-school club to which Allan Ryan, like his father, had never been admitted. In a raid like this the raiders stood a good chance of losing their shirts—if the stock continued upward. If it didn't, the raid could ruin Stutz and Allan Ryan's heavy position in it.

This was just the sort of fight that Allan Ryan enjoyed, and had been good at in the past—though now he was battling the men who really ran the Street, and the Exchange itself. Still ailing, and in the company of a nurse, Ryan went from his Murray Hill house to his downtown office. His strategy was simple: to buy up all the Stutz stock that he could, supporting the inflated price and forcing it even higher, and buying more on a constantly rising scale. The short sellers would be forced to buy stock themselves in order to cover what they had borrowed and sold, and Ryan would have caught them in a viselike squeeze. To carry out his plan successfully, however, Ryan needed sizable amounts of cash. He could no longer turn to his father. But he did turn to friends and to banks, where he obtained large loans, and he even resorted to putting up articles of his own and his wife's personal property as collateral. "We never loaned him more than $1,500,000 on furs," the president of the Chase National Bank once told a reporter. It must have been a chilly winter for Mrs. Allan Ryan.

At first, things looked very bad. Ryan had underestimated the tremendous pressure of the short sellers, who, by early March, had succeeded in pushing the price of Stutz back down to $100. Still, having embarked upon his strategy he could not abandon it—he was in debt too deeply now—and presently his efforts began to take effect. On March 24, Stutz was up to $245, and during that day it rose to $282. A week later it had leaped to a startling $391 and, in the face of this spectacular rise, many shareholders decided to take their profits and sell their shares, which Ryan quickly bought. At the same time, the inflated price of Stutz had become even more attractive to the short sellers, who, convinced that the price *had* to drop, were borrowing Stutz to sell for future delivery wherever they could. By the end of the month of March, a situation had developed where, in order to borrow stock to sell short, the short sellers had to borrow it from Allan Ryan. After all, now no one but Ryan owned any Stutz. In other words, the stock that they were selling *to* Ryan had first to be borrowed *from* him, and in the process Ryan not only got to know the name of every individual in the enemy camp but was also doing lively business with them. Also, in the process and in the clerical confusion surrounding this spiral of mind-reeling activity, Allan Ryan found himself the owner of more shares of Stutz stock than actually existed, and was in the odd position of owning more than 100 percent of his company. Still, confident that he was winning, Ryan went on lending stock and buying it back—borrowing more money to protect his cash position—and, on March 31, when Stutz skyrocketed to $391, he knew that he had won. The short sellers had either to buy back the stock they owed him, at his price, incurring huge losses, or else face professional ruin—or jail sentences for breach of contract if they defaulted on their loans. Allan Ryan had managed a "corner" on Stutz.

But the trouble was that his cornered foe represented the Wall Street Establishment, and included members of several of the

Stock Exchange's key committees. He had taken on not just a handful of brash manipulators, but the New York Stock Exchange itself. And so, on the morning of the day Stutz peaked at $391, Allan Ryan was called before the Exchange's powerful Business Conduct Committee, and asked to explain just what had been going on with Stutz. He might have easily tossed the question right back at the committee, since many of the principal short sellers were seated facing him in the room. That would not, perhaps, have been quite in keeping with the unwritten gentleman's "code" of the Exchange, which, in many ways, was a Mafia-like Code of Silence, but he could have done it, and been within his rights. After all, the short sellers' dilemma was of their own making. Instead, possibly because he was flushed with success and drunk with power, he made a move that was both bold and rash. He offered to sell them all the shares they needed to fulfill their contracts—at $750 per share.

In theory, according to the loose rules and practices of the Stock Exchange at the time, the losers in a battle of this sort had nothing to do but pay the winner's price, as had happened in the famous Northern Pacific Railroad corner of 1901, which had nearly wrecked the economy of the country. Or they could beg Ryan for mercy, as had also happened in the past—anything to avoid a public scandal that might reveal the names of the manipulators, or to avoid a lawsuit, or an investigation, or—most dreaded of all—interference by the U. S. Government in the Exchange's methods and activities. But, perhaps because Ryan was regarded as an "outsider," and perhaps because his price was too high, the Exchange was in no mood either to pay or to ask for pity. That afternoon the Business Conduct Committee called Allan Ryan on the carpet again—again taking the attitude that Ryan was the guilty party. The joint committee sternly told Ryan that it was considering removing Stutz from the trading list—a serious threat since, if this happened, Ryan would have trouble finding a market for Stutz.

But Ryan decided to call the committee's bluff. If they did this, he said, his price per Stutz share would go from $750 to $1,000. With this exchange of warnings, the meeting broke up angrily, and the two Exchange committees went to report the proceedings to the Governing Committee.

The Governing Committee took exactly half an hour to reach a decision. At the close of the day's trading, the New York Stock Exchange announced that, in a unanimous decision of its board of governors, the Exchange had voted to suspend all dealings in Stutz. In the excitement that followed the release of this news, a reporter reminded the Stock Exchange spokesman that no Exchange rule or precedent appeared to support this move. The Exchange spokesman replied, "The Stock Exchange can do anything."

It was a remark that must have struck a chill in the heart of Allan Ryan. Because, in those days, it was absolutely true.

There was no doubt that Ryan was now in deep trouble. He had borrowings hanging over his head, and only a few months before the loans would be called. And yet all was not lost. Stutz, which he now owned completely, was still selling Bearcats at a lively and profitable rate. But rumor, that most intangible and unfightable of Wall Street enemies, was running against him. The identity of the short sellers was still a closely guarded secret within the Exchange, and the story began to circulate that the leader of the band that was out to "get" Allan Ryan was none other than his own father, Thomas Fortune Ryan. It was also said that Allan's old protector, Mr. Schwab, had abandoned him as a result of a slighting comment about Stutz that Schwab had uttered at a dinner party, and that a lady guest had repeated to Ryan. (Actually, Schwab had loaned Ryan a million dollars to help him fight for Stutz, had a heavy stake in Ryan's success, and Ryan had not taken the dinner-table remark all that seriously.)

Then, while Ryan was marshaling advice and legal opinions and planning tactics, he was dealt another blow by the Exchange. Its Law Committee, it announced, had decided that it considered all Ryan's contracts null and void. "The Exchange will not treat failure to deliver Stutz Motor stock, due to the inability of the contracting party to obtain same, as a failure to comply with contract." In order to protect its precious Establishment, the Exchange was therefore ready to overlook the fundamental tenet on which its entire operations were based. Yes, the Exchange could do anything, and its Law Committee could reverse the law. If Ryan didn't like it, the Exchange announced, he could sue. But, it pointed out ominously in its release to the press, in its 128-year history only twice had rulings of the mighty New York Stock Exchange been overthrown in the courts.

But Ryan was not ready to capitulate; indeed, he could not. Too much was at stake now. He decided to ignore the Law Committee's announcement, and simply sent word that he was still willing to negotiate on the price of the stock the short sellers owed him, and that he expected Stutz to be promptly relisted. The Stock Exchange loftily left this message unanswered.

With things at a standstill, lawyers began to enter the picture. The Exchange engaged none other than the august Mr. Charles Evans Hughes, who had narrowly missed being elected President of the United States four years earlier. Ryan obtained the services of a lesser-known firm called Stanchfield and Levy. Then he made a strong move: he tendered his resignation to the Stock Exchange, saying, "So long as your body is responsible only to itself, and so long as you can make your own rules and regulations for their immediate execution . . . I cannot with self-respect continue as a member." This put the Exchange in a serious spot. Once out of the Exchange, Ryan was no longer bound by Exchange rules, and could name the names of the short sellers and otherwise tell all; the secrecy code no longer bound him. And, that evening, he did name names, to a reporter on the New York *World*. Those named immediately issued shrill denials, but there was talk in the press of the urgent need to establish some sort of government investigative or regulatory force to look into the operations of the Exchange, "a development that many earnest friends of the Stock Exchange are extremely anxious to avoid," which was putting it mildly. Ryan announced that he agreed a government commission should be established, which heaped insult upon insult. The Exchange was then made even more nervous when, in a rare interview, Thomas Fortune Ryan announced to the *World* that he "admired the fighting spirit of his son and would back him in his controversy to the limit of his resources." This was indeed bad news for the Exchange, which had been counting on the family feud to keep the senior Ryan out of things. If Thomas Fortune Ryan's wealth and power were brought fully to his son's aid, there was no telling the outcome. Allan Ryan seemed to be inching into front position again. It began to seem that, David-like, he would succeed in felling his Goliath.

To support its position, the Stock Exchange issued an edgy and self-praising statement, taking the stand that everything it was doing was, as always, in the public interest. "There is not a word of truth in the statement that the action [the delisting of Stutz] was dictated by a desire to benefit the short interests," the Exchange announced. "The members of the Governing Committee of the Exchange are firmly convinced that in all actions taken in respect to Stutz Motor stock they have been guided solely by a sense of their duty to the best interests of the Exchange and the public."

Ryan's next move was to call back the Stutz stock he had loaned. Obviously, no stock would come back, since he had already bought it all from the borrowers, but this move permitted him, under Exchange rules, to "buy it in"—in other words, to buy the stock from himself on behalf of those who owed it to him, at whatever price he chose to place on it, and to bill the borrowers for the cost.

This he proposed to do on the morning of April 24, at ten o'clock, on the outdoor Curb Exchange on Broad Street. As for the price he intended to place on his stock, Mr. Ryan would not say, but, if he succeeded with this complicated tactic, it would mean that he had bested the short sellers. In the meantime, the Stutz Affair had become one of the liveliest topics of the financial community, and excitement mounted as the date approached. Would plucky little Allan Ryan really be able to bring some of the mightiest titans of Wall Street to their knees? Even those closest to the titans themselves could not help but relish the thought that he just might. Watching the mighty fall can be fun.

On the morning of the twenty-fourth, clerks up and down Broad Street jockeyed for positions at office windows to watch the proceedings that were due to take place on the street below. When ten o'clock came and went, and nothing happened, the street buzzed with rumors. What had taken place, it turned out, was that a delegation of the Stock Exchange Protective Committee had arrived at Ryan's office at exactly nine-forty. "Did you wish to see anyone?" the receptionist asked. Yes, they did: Mr. Allan Ryan. The committee was ushered into Mr. Ryan's office. They had met, they explained, and each man on the committee had written on a slip of paper a suggested price per share for Stutz to pay back Ryan what was owed him. The figures had been added up, and an average computed. It came to $550. Would Mr. Ryan accept that? Yes, he replied promptly, he would, and all shook hands. Ryan, it seemed, had won. True, he had not got the prices of $750 and $1,000 a share he had originally asked, but he had made a million and a half dollars on his corner, and he was the sole owner of Stutz. "The Stutz matter is settled," the Exchange announced stiffly. "The settlement price is $550. The Stutz controversy is ended." The Stock Exchange retired to its tent to nurse its wounds.

But it wasn't ended—not quite. Allan Ryan had borrowed tens of millions of dollars to wage his fight, and now the banks and friends that had lent him money were pressing for repayment. Also, the battle had earned him bitter and powerful enemies who were now determined to have their revenge. He might appear to be victorious, but he was still the son of an Irish upstart, and there were those of the Establishment who were never going to let him forget it. When he had resigned from the Exchange, he had expected to receive about $100,000 in payment for his seat. Now this money was being held up on some mysterious technicality or other. Then, in June, the Exchange announced that it had not, in fact, accepted Ryan's resignation; instead, it was considering expelling him, and for "misconduct." The Exchange invited Ryan to a hearing on the matter to determine whether or not he had been "guilty of conduct inconsistent with just and equitable principles of trade." Ryan announced that he would not attend such a hearing. In the defendant's absence, the hearing, which lasted five hours, reached a verdict: guilty as charged. The punishment was expulsion from the Exchange, from which he had resigned some months earlier. Learning of the verdict in his office, Ryan said, "It is immaterial to me, and really I do not give a damn." He slammed on his hat and departed for the racetrack at Jamaica.

There were other things, however, that he was required to give a damn about—the banks, for instance, who were increasing their pressure on him to get their money back. And suddenly, in midsummer, a number of other companies in which he was known to have invested heavily suffered sharp and inexplicable losses on the Big Board. His Stromberg Carburetor fell, as did his Hayden Chemical, his Chicago Pneumatic Tool, and his Continental Candy. It seemed more than an unfortunate coincidence that only the stocks in which he had held an interest were suddenly performing poorly; the wolves of Wall Street were after him again. Then, to add to his woes, there was a general collapse of the national economy, and stocks began falling across a broad front. By the end of 1920 stocks generally had gone down a full one-third from their April prices. Then the insidious rumors, by which alone a financier could be killed, started. "I hear Ryan is bust," one would hear across a table at the Stock Exchange Luncheon Club. One story circulated that Allan Ryan owed the banks fourteen million dollars that he couldn't pay. "The banks have got Ryan" became the word, while the Stock Exchange rubbed its hands and waited for the banks to finish him off.

In August, Allan Ryan instituted a one-million-dollar suit against the Stock Exchange, declaring that his honor had been sullied by the "verdict" at his "trial." The suit, however, was as much a serious attempt to raise money as it was to clear his name. The Exchange had still not paid him for his seat, and the matter languished "in committee." The banks, meanwhile, approached Thomas Fortune Ryan in the matter of his son's indebtedness. The senior Ryan replied, through an aide, that, after all, the banks had loaned money to his son, not to him, and he showed no further inclination to help Allan out.

Allan Ryan launched a heated attack against banks and their loan policies, and the banks responded to this with a certain amount of pique. They had supposed Allan Ryan would be *grateful* for all they had done for him. "Why, I could never conceive that a man could be so mean!" declared the president of Chase, indicating that Allan Ryan, if he had ever had one, had lost his friend there. Not only to win political friends but also to help create, in the community, an impression that things were not as bad as they were, Allan Ryan made a well-publicized gift to the Democratic National Committee of $40,000. But nothing seemed to work. On July 21, 1922, he filed a bankruptcy petition listing debts of $32,435,477 against assets of only $643,533.

Perhaps nothing exposes a man more pathetically to public scrutiny than bankruptcy—particularly the bankruptcy of a man who has long been considered rich. There, for the readers of the daily tabloids to see and enjoy, were all the sad and telling details of Allan Ryan's financial and private life. He owed, among other things, $60.36 to the Buckley School for his son's tuition. He owed $207.80 to the Plaza Hotel for theater tickets. Best & Company wanted $157.75 for children's clothing, and Black, Starr & Frost had him down for $3,260.25 for jewelry for his wife. He owed the Montauk Club of Brooklyn $13.75 for dues, E. P. Dutton & Company $134.08 for books and stationery, Charles & Company $768.68 for groceries. Among the more impressive debts were $66,000 to T. Coleman du Pont of Wilmington, $8.66 million to the Guaranty Trust and $3.5 million to the Chase Bank. His old friend Schwab, who had stuck by him, had him down for only $300,000. Ryan had either paid back, or Schwab had forgiven him, the balance of the million Schwab had loaned him.

One hope for a way out of this morass lay in his Stutz stock— 135,000 shares of which he had put up for collateral. If he could realize at least $50 a share on this, his lawyers figured, he might escape total ruin. But Stutz, which had been around $100 at the beginning of Allan Ryan's fight, had tumbled as a result of it to as low as $5 by the middle of 1921. When the stock went up for auction on August 2, 1922, the highest any bidder would go was $20 a share, and the $3,700,000 realized from the sale was barely enough to pay off one of the smaller of the big bank loans. The bidder, it turned out, was acting as an agent for Charles M. Schwab. It was apparently the best Schwab could do for his friend. With his purchase, of course, Schwab became the head of Stutz.

Allan Ryan's father would be seventy-one in October, and might be expected to leave him something in his will. But Thomas Fortune Ryan did not die for six more years, and when he did die, in November, 1928, his estate of $135 million was divided into fifty-four parts. Twelve each went to his widow and two of his surviving sons, John Barry Ryan and Clendenin Ryan, eight went to Allan's six children, and five to the children of his two deceased sons. There were no bequests for charity "for the reason that in my lifetime I have contributed largely to religious, charitable and educational causes." He added a codicil which stated that if any of his bequests were questioned, or if anyone in the family complained about his or her share, he or she would lose that share.

His son Allan's name was mentioned only twice in Thomas Fortune Ryan's will. Allan was given a third option, if two other survivors didn't want it, to purchase any object he wished from the deceased's art and sculpture collection—Allan could not by then have scraped enough money together for one of his father's Rodin busts. The will also stated, "I give and bequeath my white pearl shirt studs to my son Allan A. Ryan."

The Ryan family today insists that the old man's will was not intended to be rancorous or vindictive—merely practical. Any money he had left to his eldest son would simply have been gobbled up by creditors. It would have been like flushing money down a drain. They are probably right.

Allan Ryan's daughter Miriam still has Grandpa Ryan's studs.

Chapter 15

THE TROUBLES OF ONE HOUSE

ew rich Irish-American families have endured more second-generation problems than the Ryans. One thinks of the Kennedys, but consider the House of Ryan. One is reminded of the doomed Greek House of Atreus. Drink, divorce, multiple marriage, and lapsing from the Catholic Church are only a few of the furies that have beset the heirs of Thomas Fortune. After Allan Ryan's bankruptcy, Charles M. Schwab was asked whether he thought there was a chance that Allan might get back on his feet. Schwab replied, "I hope he does—I think he will." But he never did, and after his father's death his two brothers, John Barry and Clendenin, got together and agreed to share in an allowance for their brother of $50,000 a year. On this he was required to live.

Nor did bankruptcy end his woes. In 1922 Allan Ryan had a court battle with a man named George Maxwell, president of the American Society of Composers, Authors, and Publishers, over the affections of the latter's wife, the former Sally Tuck of Philadelphia. Allan Ryan and his wife were divorced in 1925, and that same year he married a girl from Montreal named Irene McKenna. In 1933 he was unsuccessfully sued for $100,000 by his housemaid, on whom, or so she claimed, he had forced his attentions. Allan Ryan died quietly in 1940.

His children, by contrast, did fairly well, even though they received a smaller share of Grandpa Ryan's estate. Two of Allan's sons, Allan, Jr. and Fortune Peter Ryan, joined Grandpa Ryan's Royal Typewriter Company, and did well, and a third son, Theodore, made a name for himself as a breeder of prize Black Angus cattle on his Connecticut farm, where he also became active in local politics. A fourth son, Barry, not only owned race horses but became celebrated as a trainer of them. But multiple marriages marked this generation too—led by Allan, Jr., who married no less than four times, all to society ladies. His first wife was the beautiful Janet Newbold (who later became Mrs. William Rhinelander Stewart and, later than that, dated Randolph Churchill). His second was Eleanor Barry (no kin), his third was Priscilla St. George, and his fourth was Grace Amory, to whom he is currently married.

The second of Thomas Fortune Ryan's sons, John Barry, was a dreamy young man whose chief talent seemed to be spending his inheritance, though he did write undistinguished poetry from time to time which he published under the name "Barrie Vail." He and his wife, the former Nan Morgan, had a total of fifteen children, of whom ten lived. Their daughters made generally proper society marriages, but they were not immune from scandal —Adele Ryan, in 1930, becoming involved in a sensational breach-of-promise suit. As for the boys, all of whom had the Ryan good looks and charm to a pronounced degree, only one became famous, and then briefly, when, after a night of carousing, he drove his car up and down the streets of Stamford, Connecticut, tossing rocks in the windows of every store in sight. He concluded this escapade by driving up the courthouse steps, and into the court as far as his car would fit, which made his apprehension and arrest for vandalism somewhat easier for the police, though somewhat more expensive for his father. One of his brothers, the late Thomas Fortune Ryan II, was first married to a Pittsburgh divorcee named Margaret Moorhead Rea and then, after a divorce from her, married another divorcee, Mayme Cook Masters, of Sheridan, Wyoming. He died in 1955 after a life in which, according to the family, his greatest difficulty was that "he just couldn't seem to keep off the front page." Still another of these brothers, John Barry Ryan, Jr.—the most socially prominent of this generation—worked for a while as a reporter, and then married the former Margaret Kahn, daughter of the German-Jewish banker Otto Kahn, who had been Jacob Schiff's partner at Kuhn, Loeb. This union must have caused both the old adversaries in the Equitable Life battle to spin violently in their graves. Their son, John Barry Ryan III, is presently at Kuhn, Loeb, and his wife, the former Dorinda Dixon (the exotic-looking "D.D." Ryan), was voted one of America's best-dressed women in 1959, and frequently decorates the pages of such publications as *Vogue* and *Women's Wear Daily*.

Suicide is another specter that has stalked the latter-day Ryans. Joseph Ryan's son, Joseph, Jr., who ran Mount Tremblant Lodge in Canada, married a girl named Nannie Moore of Washington, D.C. He was separated from his wife at the time of his sudden death in 1921. In his will, he left one hundred dollars to his wife, and the balance of his estate to an actress named Lucille Waterford. He died "under circumstances suspicious of suicide." The Clendenin Ryan branch of the family fared even worse, in terms of tragedy. Clendenin, who was named after a town in West Virginia, had been a partner in his brother's ill-fated Allan A. Ryan & Company, and, in 1923, shortly after the firm's collapse, Clendenin Ryan was in the tabloids when he was sued for five hundred dollars' "room rent" by a New York showgirl. In 1939, in the library of the great Manhattan mansion that had been the Ryan family home since the days of Thomas Fortune, he quietly placed his head in a gas fireplace and turned on the gas. Eighteen years later, in the same house, his son, also named Clendenin, also committed suicide. He had promised to donate the famous rose window to St. Patrick's Cathedral. His widow had to finish paying for it. His sister, Caroline, lives today in Florida, in a completely shuttered and sealed-off house.

And the fate of Stutz was no more cheerful than the fate of its once-head, Allan Ryan. Mr. Schwab, it seemed, was not as clever in the automobile industry as he had been in steel. Though Stutz cars went on breaking speed records in road tests, the company's books began showing deficits nearly every year after Schwab's takeover. Its famous bucket-seated Bearcat—which, though infinitely glamorous, was never really practical, or even comfortable—had been discontinued in 1920, and the company never managed to share in the great 1920's automotive boom. In 1938, a year before Mr. Schwab's death, Stutz quietly went broke. Its corporate obituary, tucked in the back of the financial pages, noted that the last Stutz products had been an unsuccessful line of grocery wagons. *Sic transit gloria mundi.*

Chapter 16

WHY DON'T THE
NICE PEOPLE LIKE US?

One current reason for the pronounced antipathy, among such families as the Murrays and the McDonnells, toward the entire Kennedy clan is the family's pompous habit of referring always to the late John F. Kennedy as "The President," as though he were the only one. But another has been that the older-established families considered the founder of the Kennedy fortune, Joseph Patrick Kennedy, a rogue and a scoundrel and, in his business dealings, a double-crosser. Born in East Boston in 1887, the son of a saloon keeper who had elevated himself— though just barely—from the "shanty" Irish status of his immigrant father to where he might have been considered, by Boston's Protestant elite, "lace curtain," young Joe Kennedy early showed himself to be a man of restless drive, energy, and ambition, for whom business scruples came second. From a relatively humble position in the Boston office of Hayden, Stone & Company, Joe Kennedy had been able, by 1922, to go into business for himself behind an office door that proclaimed somewhat grandly—and pretentiously—"JOSEPH P. KENNEDY, BANKER." He rapidly gained a reputation as an aggressive stock manipulator and, two years later, he was ready for New York, "where the real money was."

On Wall Street, Joseph P. Kennedy, Banker, was at first placed in the category of such other Irish upstarts as Mike Meehan and Bernard E. Smith. Like others of his generation, who had little education, no social background, but no end of determination to succeed, Mike Meehan got his start by becoming the helpful friend and useful errand boy to Old Guard members of the Establishment. Meehan had started out as a theater-ticket broker, and by wangling aisle seats at Broadway hits for the partners and their wives of such eminent firms as Morgan & Company, Lehman Brothers, and Goldman, Sachs. The partners would not have entertained a Mike Meehan at their dinner tables, but they rather liked his brash and spirited ways, and clearly the lad was smart. When Meehan expressed an interest in becoming a stock trader, several of these men were willing to help him out and to set him up on the Curb Exchange. Meehan turned out to be as clever at cornering stocks as he had been at securing tickets to musicals, and, within two years, he had a seat on the New York Stock Exchange alongside the Morgans, Whitneys, Rockefellers, and Lehmans. Meehan originated the idea of placing brokerage offices on the decks of ocean liners, and his firm established them on the *Bremen*, the *Leviathan*, and the *Berengaria*. By 1929 Mike Meehan was living in a floor-through apartment at the Sherry-Netherland, owned no less than eight Stock Exchange seats and—though he was barely literate—operated from a downtown office whose walls were lined with volumes of Shakespeare bound in calf. Mike Meehan became known as "the mastermind of the Radio pools," and, in 1929, succeeded in bull-trading RCA up from a 1928 low of 85¼ to an unprecedented high of 549—even though RCA had paid no dividends whatever in the period. It was the most spectacular, and perhaps the most shameful, stock manipulation of the decade. In the process, Meehan became the darling of "little men" investors who, in the wake of such feats, began plunging heavily into the market throughout the twenties—the cab drivers, barbers, and shoeshine men who tossed their savings into RCA may have felt differently about Meehan after the stock plummeted in the Crash (and after Meehan had got himself out).

Bernard E. ("Ben") Smith was an even tougher character than Meehan. Ben Smith grew up, around the turn of the century, in a tough Irish neighborhood in New York's far-west fifties, near the docks, left school without graduating, and for a while bummed around the country selling newspapers, working for a used-car dealer, and finally winding up with a job in a brokerage house. Here he managed to become friendly with some of the firm's richer customers, who fondly regarded young Ben Smith as "a diamond in the rough." Rough he certainly was, addicted to simple-minded practical jokes, bathroom humor, and foul language. And yet, in 1926, when Smith was barely thirty, he had none other than such old-line aristocrats as Percy Rockefeller and Stuyvesant Fish to sponsor him for a seat on the Stock Exchange. Throughout the late twenties, Smith was behind some of the biggest bull pools of the day, and made enormous profits—enough for a country estate in Bedford Village and a swimming pool. He became so arrogant and inaccessible that one of his clients, none other than the British Lord Rothermere, was kept waiting, hat in hand, outside his office. Reporters, seeking to interview the financial wizard, often had to wait a week or more before Mr. Smith deigned to return their calls, and, when the calls were returned, they did not come from Mr. Smith or even his secretary but from his personal public-relations person. He had been staunchly on the bull side of the market during the summer of 1929, and was hurt badly in the first wave of the Crash. Then he suddenly reversed himself and became bearish. At one point—it has never been clear quite when—he rushed into his brokerage office and shouted, "Sell 'em all! They're not worth anything," earning him the life-long nickname of "Sell-'em Ben" Smith. His huge short sales, and enormous profits in the process, earned Ben Smith a reputation for villainy almost unequaled on the Street as, in the process, he helped the plunge of prices and the destruction of the American economy. As for his old friends who had helped him along a few years earlier, he announced, "To hell with them," or possibly something even stronger. He had never given a damn for the Wall Street Establishment, or its code, and, furthermore, did not give a damn what the Establishment or the world thought of him or his trading methods. He had been in the stock game to make money for Ben Smith, and no one else. As for America, to hell with that too. What had America ever done for him?

Joseph P. Kennedy, however, was to turn out to be of not quite the same breed as Meehan and Smith, who were roughly his contemporaries. Kennedy wanted to make money, yes, but money to him appears to have been only an incidental item, a tool. He also wanted power, which, according to an old Chinese proverb, has been defined as "ancient wealth." Kennedy wanted his money magically to acquire the patina of age as quickly as possible. He wanted prestige also, and to be liked and well thought of by the men he intended to make his peers. Inside him, an Establishmentarian was trying to get out; his ambition, or at least a good part of it, was to be instant Old Guard. In this, he was assisted by his personality—an affable surface good nature and reserve, a charm equal to that of a Thomas Fortune Ryan, poise, good looks, a clubman's good manners, and a speaking voice which he did his best to rid of its East Boston accent. On the surface, Joseph P. Kennedy appeared to be, of all things, a gentleman, or at least a man trying very hard to be one.

Kennedy's first big New York assignment, in 1924, was to defend John D. Hertz's Chicago-based Yellow Cab Company against a raid from the bears that was seriously threatening the company's owners. Hertz himself offered to raise the money for a bull pool, and Joe Kennedy was thereby relieved of the terrible burden of raising his own money, which had undone Allan Ryan a few years earlier. Kennedy hurried down to New York from Boston, and set himself up in a suite at the Waldorf-Astoria, where a battery of telephones and a ticker-tape machine were hastily installed. He managed his bull counterattack so skillfully that he was able to collect an important commission for himself as well. To be sure, a few months later Yellow Cab stock dropped again, and this time Hertz suspected that Joe Kennedy himself was the principal bear behind the raid. Hertz was so enraged at Kennedy that he threatened to "punch the s.o.b. in the nose" if he ever encountered him. The punch in the nose was never administered, nor has the Kennedy double-cross ever been definitely proved, though Kennedy's biographer, Richard J. Whalen, has said in *The Founding Father*, "It would not have been unthinkable." Kennedy was that sort of trader. In any case, in 1926 Kennedy moved his family—including his sons, John F., aged nine, and Robert F., less than a year old—to New York, where they settled in a large house in the fashionable Riverdale section of the Bronx (and later in even more fashionable Bronxville, in Westchester County). Throughout the rest of the decade, Joseph P. Kennedy was known as one of Wall Street's ablest and most agile wheeler-dealers—bullish or bearish as suited his purposes—specializing in the then glamorous and lucrative motion picture company stocks.

By 1929 Kennedy was rich and, with his hail-fellow personality, was able to do business not only with the likes of Meehan and Smith (often referred to as "The Underworld of Wall Street") but also with the Street's upper crust, including such *Social Register*-ites as Jeremiah Milbank and the patrician Owen D. Young of General Electric. But there was one man whose shell Kennedy could not crack. Early that year, he strolled casually into the redoubtable offices at 23 Wall Street and asked to see Mr. J. P. Morgan. Kennedy must have expected that Morgan, by now, would be curious enough about the Street's new genius to receive him, for Kennedy was not a man to risk being snubbed unnecessarily. But he had miscalculated. He got no further than the receptionist. After telephoning her boss, she told Kennedy that Mr. Morgan was too busy to see him.

Unlike his friend Ben Smith, Joe Kennedy did not make extra millions through selling short during the 1929 Crash, but there is no evidence that he lost any substantial amount either. In September, according to his biographer, Kennedy was "standing at a safe distance" from the market, and had commented, "Only a fool holds out for top dollar." He himself wrote later, "In those days I felt and said I would be willing to part with half of what I had if I could be sure of keeping, under law and order, the other half." But there is no evidence that he lost anything even close to half in the Crash, and, in fact, during that winter of Wall Street's greatest discontent Joe Kennedy casually removed himself from the financial community entirely and retired to the pleasant purlieus of Palm Beach, where his thoughts seem to have turned from the making of money to the uses of it—to acquire power. A few months later, through the good offices of his friend Henry Morgenthau, Jr., Kennedy arranged an invitation to lunch at the Governor's Mansion in Albany, New York. He emerged from that meeting with the announcement that he believed Franklin D. Roosevelt would be an excellent Democratic candidate for President, and that he, Kennedy, would do everything in his power to see that Roosevelt was nominated and, in due course, elected.

Roosevelt's reward to Kennedy, after his election in 1932, was to name Kennedy Chairman of his newly created Securities and Exchange Commission, designed to regulate and control just such speculators as Kennedy had himself been. At first, Roosevelt's New

Deal supporters were dismayed with the appointment; it struck them as a complete sellout to Wall Street. Here was a man no better than the notorious Smith and Meehan; could he possibly be expected to "regulate" such villains? Wall Street, on the other hand, was delighted with the appointment, deeming it "wise and just." Kennedy, after all, was known as a wily trader, and the Street was certain that any control he attempted to apply would be minimal. What happened, of course, amounted to another Kennedy double-cross because Kennedy did an about-face, turned his back on his old Wall Street cronies, and proceeded to initiate a long series of stiff and much-needed reforms. He began by requiring the registration of the country's 24 stock exchanges, their 2,400 members and their 5,000 listed securities. He then tackled the biggest exchange of them all—the New York—instigating the first of many legal actions by the SEC against manipulators who would not hew to the hard SEC line. "Traitor to your class!" Wall Street cried, as even such sacred figures as Morgan began to feel the force of the Kennedy pinch. Instead of the "friend in government" Wall Street had hoped to find in Kennedy, it found a dreaded enemy, a "henchman" of "that Man in the White House." None of these activities endeared the Kennedys to such Wall Street families as the McDonnells.

Kennedy, meanwhile, with his new friends in the White House and Cabinet, was able, quietly, to be of service to his old friends in the motion picture industry in ways small and large. Early in the Roosevelt administration, Joseph M. Schenck, head of Twentieth Century-Fox in New York, was able to report to his friend Sam Goldwyn in Hollywood that, through State Department channels —and in coded cablegrams (which Kennedy let Mr. Schenck see) —Kennedy was working out a formula by which the movie industry could withdraw, and transfer out of England, all the money that it was likely to earn there. The money would come out of England in dollars, not in pounds, which was important since at the time the pound was in a weakened state. Originally, a five-million-dollar ceiling had been in force for such withdrawals. Kennedy, however, had assured Schenck that this limit could be raised to between twenty and thirty million. Schenck also warned Goldwyn not to interfere with Kennedy, since Kennedy was a testy customer and resented anyone who attempted to go over his head, or that of the State Department. Kennedy, in his ambassadorial role, would deal directly with the British Chancellor of the Exchequer, Sir John Simon.

In terms of his personal morality, Joseph Kennedy also managed to offend such First Irish Families as the Murrays and the McDonnells. While the F.I.F.'s were determined to create an aura of the strictest moral rectitude around their activities and private lives, Joe Kennedy's private life did not meet their standards. There was, to begin with, his much publicized association with the actress Gloria Swanson, the leading glamour figure of her day, whom Kennedy had met on one of his jaunts to Hollywood. He and Miss Swanson became the talk of both coasts, and appeared together at parties in both New York and California. Joe Kennedy became Miss Swanson's banker and adviser. Her husband, the French Marquis de la Falaise de la Coudray, was often in Europe on some project for Pathé Pictures.

Kennedy loaned large sums of money to Miss Swanson's Gloria Productions, Inc., and financed a number of her motion pictures. The first was called *Queen Kelly*, a legendary flop, and a revealing study of the character of the producer. Erich Von Stroheim had been hired to direct, and both Kennedy and the Hays Office had approved the script, but, during the shooting, Miss Swanson became alarmed. The mercurial Von Stroheim was improvising scenes, adding new material, and changing the story line entirely. She telephoned Kennedy in Palm Beach in an agitated state and said, "There's a madman in charge here. The scenes he's shooting will never get past Will Hays." Kennedy hurried to Hollywood and asked to see the rushes. What he saw horrified him. One scene portrayed a young priest administering the Last Rites to a dying madam in a bordello in Dar es Salaam. Another showed a young convent girl being seduced. All this was to be offered under the banner, "Joseph P. Kennedy Presents." Kennedy hastily consulted Sam Goldwyn and Irving Thalberg, who suggested that Edmund Goulding be brought in to try to save the film. But Von Stroheim had shot over twenty thousand feet of celluloid, and very little could be done to tame *Queen Kelly*. In the end, though he had invested some $800,000 in the picture, Kennedy did not dare release it in the United States, though it was distributed in Europe.

For months afterward, Kennedy told everyone who would listen how he had "lost a million" on *Queen Kelly*. It is often as much fun for a rich man to lose money as it is to make it. Actually, Mr. Kennedy had lost little or nothing on the venture. He might admire Miss Swanson personally, but his contract with her was strictly businesslike and stipulated that losses on *Queen Kelly* be offset by profits on future films. At length, Miss Swanson grew tired of hearing her friend talk about his "failure," and announced the actual state of affairs to the press.

Kennedy next sponsored Miss Swanson in her first "talkie," *The Trespasser*, and personally hired Hollywood's leading dramatic coach, Laura Hope Crews, to guide the star through every syllable of Edmund Goulding's script. *The Trespasser* was a huge box office success, handily repaying the losses on *Queen Kelly*, and Kennedy went on to produce a second sound film for Swanson called *What a Widow!* Critics were disdainful ("A comedy of sorts," sniffed the *New York Times*), but crowds, as they usually did for a Swanson film, formed long queues outside the box office, and again Kennedy made money. *What a Widow!* marked the end of Joseph Kennedy's career as a Hollywood angel, and his relationship with its star came to an abrupt end shortly afterward. "I questioned his judgment," Miss Swanson commented. "He did not like to be questioned."

The association with Gloria Swanson might be over, but not Joe Kennedy's reputation as a rake. In Catholic circles in New York, it was inevitable that the Kennedy children should meet and mingle with the children of the older-established Murrays and McDonnells, and pretty Charlotte McDonnell became a close school friend of the Kennedys' daughter, Kathleen "Kick" Kennedy. In the days when both girls were of debutante age, Charlotte McDonnell Harris recalls (Kathleen was later killed in an airplane crash) an instance when Mr. Kennedy was staying in his Waldorf-Astoria apartment and Mrs. Kennedy was ensconced in a suite at the Plaza. One evening before a party, Charlotte called for her friend at the Waldorf apartment and was met by Mr. Kennedy. After a few pleasantries, Mr. Kennedy jogged her arm, winked mischievously, and said, "Leave your coat here. Will Hays is coming by in a little while, and I want him to think I've got a girl in the bedroom." At around the same time, Kick Kennedy fell madly in love with a young man of whom her father disapproved. The senior Kennedy got columnists like Walter Winchell to dig up "dirt" about the young man and print it, thus stifling the romance.

But perhaps the fact that irked families like the Murrays and McDonnells most about the Kennedys was their social pretensions. It was patently clear that both Mr. and Mrs. Kennedy wanted places in New York society for themselves and for their children, and the McDonnells have always felt, and resented, the Kennedys' attempts to "copy" them. "They copied us by coming to New York in the first place," one of the McDonnells says. "In New York, they tried to copy every move we made." In New York, Murrays and McDonnells and Cuddihys had not only made it to the top of Irish Catholic society, through such institutions as the Catholic Big Sisters and the Gotham Ball, but were also receiving society-page attention in connection with Protestant affairs, and were listed in the *Social Register*. Quite obviously, the Kennedys were striving for the same sort of recognition.

In Boston, "high Irish" like the Kennedys who had made it out of the cellars and attics of the East End, and out of the tiny maids' rooms of Beacon Hill, had never been accepted by the Brahmin group who ruled the city's social seas. They still have not, and few names beginning with *O'* or *Mc* decorate the rosters of such clubs as the Somerset, the Chilton, and the Myopia Hunt, although more than a few are listed in the *Social Register*. Faced with this state of affairs, Boston's new-rich Irish had formed their own, and pathetically imitative, social institutions. In Boston, Rose Kennedy had been a member of the Cecilian Guild, the Irish answer to the exclusive Junior League, and had helped organize the Ace of Clubs, a group of "better" Irish girls (an ability to speak French was a requirement for admission, indicating that Boston's Irish families were already beginning to draw lines within their own ranks) that had an annual ball at the Somerset Hotel (not Club) which was a thin echo of the no-Irish-allowed debutante parties on the Hill. In her own Irish Catholic group, Rose Kennedy was something of a social leader; after all, her father had been Mayor of Boston. But the second-rateness of it all could not have escaped Rose Kennedy's notice, and it probably rankled within her. She wanted something better.

The Kennedys had spent several summers at the Massachusetts beach resort of Nantasket, which was predominantly rich Irish Catholic. Moving on, they then took a large house at Cohasset, predominantly Old Guard Protestant, where they suddenly discovered that they had unfriendly neighbors. When Joseph P. Kennedy applied for a family membership in the Cohasset Country Club, he was blackballed.

"It was petty and cruel," admitted Brahmin Ralph Lowell. "The women of Cohasset looked down on the daughter of 'Honey

Fitz,' and who was Joe Kennedy but the son of Pat, the bar-keeper?"

The same thing happened in Palm Beach, where the family attempted to establish a social base. The old families of Palm Beach came to the Kennedys' parties, mostly out of curiosity when there was nothing better to do, but they did not invite the Kennedys to theirs. The Kennedys applied for membership to the Everglades Club, and were turned down. In order to play golf, they were obliged to apply to the Jewish Palm Beach Country Club, where they were accepted. McDonnells and Murrays snickered at the Kennedys' social striving, not least when, as Ambassador to the Court of St. James's, Joseph P. Kennedy succeeded in having all his daughters, including the tragic Rosemary, presented at Court.

Long after the family had moved to New York, the wounds from the snubs of Boston had not healed in Rose Kennedy. Once, on the eve of a holiday when he was a student at Harvard, John F. Kennedy was picked up by his family in the big limousine for the drive down to New York. He brought with him a friend and classmate who was a member of one of Boston's topmost families. When he introduced his friend to his mother, and she heard his name, Rose Kennedy reacted with nervousness. She was tense during the drive, and at one point she turned suddenly to her son's friend and, "with a note of desperation in her voice," according to Richard Whalen, asked the young man, "Tell me, when are the nice people of Boston going to accept us?"

The answer, from the "nice" people of Boston even today, is: not yet.

Part Three

HIGH
SOCIETY

Chapter 17

THE DUCHESS BRADY

In Rome in the 1920's, one of the loveliest villas in the city was the Casa del Sole, perched on the Janiculum Hill at 16 Via Aurelia Antica, the winter home of an American couple, Mr. and Mrs. Nicholas F. Brady. Its view took in a breathtaking panorama of the Eternal City, with St. Peter's in the distance, and the house was surrounded by beautiful gardens and terraces, groves of lemon trees, and hushed avenues of tall cedars designed for meditative strolls. There were fountains and statues and tennis courts, and one tiny garden created just for tea. Servants in slippered feet waited on the Bradys, who were the Roman equivalent, in that sunlit era, of Gerald and Sara Murphy, the Americans who entertained with similar elegance slightly to the north, on the French Riviera. There was one difference. The Murphys' guests were largely artistic, from the worlds of letters, the theater, and dance. The Bradys' guests were ecclesiastical, consisting predominantly of Princes of the Church. Three particularly good friends were Cardinal Bonzano, Cardinal Gasparri, and Cardinal Pacelli.

Nicholas Brady had inherited a fortune from his father, the utilities emperor Anthony N. Brady (who had been the first to spy and promote the inventing talents of Grandpa Thomas E. Murray), and his wife was the former Genevieve Garvan, a sister of the celebrated detective, Francis P. Garvan, who headed the Bureau of Investigation of the United States Attorney General's office (to confuse things somewhat, Nicholas Brady's sister, Mabel, was married to Mr. Garvan). Nick Brady, a lapsed Catholic, had, under the influence of his wife's dynamic personality, returned to the Church. One of the reasons for the Brady's winter residence in the city was Mrs. Brady's strong affinity to the Roman Church, particularly the Jesuit Order. She had selected the site of Casa del Sole largely because of its unimpeded view of St. Peter's.

In the autumn of 1925, a young priest in his middle thirties named Francis J. Spellman had arrived in Rome, where he had been assigned to duty with the Papal Secretariat of State, something of an honor for an American priest. Born in the little town of Whitman, Massachusetts, the son of a grocer and the grandson of an immigrant cobbler from Limerick who had made shoes for the rich of Boston, Francis Spellman had, on his graduation from Fordham and his decision to enter the priesthood, been told by his father, "Always go with people who are smarter than you are—and in your case it won't be difficult." In Rome, where his title was the modest one of "playground director," Father Spellman was actually working closely with the Papal Secretariat of State and the important Cardinals who were the nucleus of the Brady circle. One day at St. Peter's, Spellman noticed Mr. and Mrs. Brady sitting a few pews behind him. There were two much better seats up front, which had been reserved for the Ambassador of Portugal, who had not shown up, and Spellman suggested to Cardinal Bonzano that the Bradys might prefer these seats. The Bradys were delighted to be moved up front, and so was Cardinal Bonzano, an old friend of the Bradys and an important star in the Brady set. Cardinal Bonzano jotted down the name and address of the young priest who had been so helpful and gave it to the Bradys, and presently Father Spellman was joining the red-hatted guests at the little lunches and dinners at Casa del Sole. The Bradys were charmed by the young priest from Boston, and when a chaplain was needed for the Bradys' private chapel, the Bradys asked Father Spellman if he would like the job. He eagerly accepted.

From then on, his letters home were full of the doings of his new and enormously rich friends. "Yesterday was Monsignor Bernardini's feast day, the feast of St. Philip," he wrote. "Mrs. Brady gave a dinner in his honor. Cardinal Gasparri, Monsignor Borgongini, Monsignor Pizzardo, Monsignor Bernardini and I were the guests." He was in heady company. A few months later, he wrote, "Yesterday Cardinal Gasparri, Monsignor Borgongini, Monsignor Pizzardo and Mr. Brady and I had a one hundred and fifty mile ride in the country. We brought our lunch and had it in the old Monastery of Subiaco. . . ." There were other pleasant picnics and excursions with the Bradys and their high-placed Vatican friends, and after saying morning Mass for the family Father Spellman enjoyed tennis games with Mr. Brady on the private courts of Casa del Sole. While helping, and being helped by, the Bradys, Father Spellman was also able to help the Brady money help the Vatican. He suggested to Mr. Brady that Cardinal Gasparri needed a new automobile, and particularly admired the new Chrysler Limousine 82. Mr. Brady said, "Sure." The Cardinal was delighted with his new car. Through the Bradys, Father Spellman quickly got to know virtually everyone of importance in Rome, including the most important Cardinal of all, Eugenio Cardinal Pacelli. In 1928, Father Spellman noted in his diary, "October 19: Heard indirectly that I am to be made a Monsignor." And a few days later, "October 30: Monsignor Borgongini told me I was made a Monsignor on October the fourth."

His next elevation, to the rank of domestic prelate, was not long in coming and, in 1931, Monsignor Spellman was named Auxiliary Bishop of Boston and, seven years later, he was appointed Archbishop of New York. In the process, he was able to reward his friends and sponsors, the Bradys. In 1927, through his offices, Mr. Brady was given the Grand Cross of St. Gregory, and Mrs. Brady and Mrs. James A. Farrell were named two of the three Dames of Malta in the entire United States. Thus Genevieve Garvan Brady became the Duchess Brady.

The Bradys also maintained a huge estate called "Inisfada" on the North Shore of Long Island near Manhasset. The road on which "Inisfada" was situated had been nicknamed "The Irish Channel" because so many wealthy Irishmen had large estates along its length. In addition to "Inisfada," there was the big place belonging to Nicholas F. Brady's nephew, James Cox Brady, Jr. James Cox Brady had inherited $25 million and directorships in fifty corporations from his father, though he had started out "shoveling coal by the side of Polish and Italian immigrants" at the Consolidated Gas Company in the Bronx—which his uncle happened to own, so his rise was not too slow. It was James Cox Brady who "bailed out" Walter Chrysler when his company was in difficulties. James Cox Brady put substantial money into the Chrysler Corporation, and went on its board. In addition to his place on the Channel, James Cox Brady owned a racing stable in Ireland and the lovely old Cashel Palace Hotel.

Next door to "Inisfada" was the Joseph P. Grace estate. Joseph Grace was one of the sons of the Irish-born William Russell Grace who, with his brother Michael, founded W. R. Grace & Company, the Grace Steamship Line, and the Grace National Bank. W. R. Grace & Company was founded in Peru in the 1850's, and old William R. had married a Yankee skipper's daughter and, in the 1860's moved to New York, where he built up a substantial business and became the first Irish-born Mayor of New York. His son, Joseph P. Grace, divided his time comfortably between the Long

Island place, a grouse-shooting moor in Scotland, a big house in Northeast Harbor, Maine, and another big place in Aiken, South Carolina. On the other side of "Inisfada" was the estate of Cornelius F. Kelly, the Anaconda Copper king.

But "Inisfada" was the greatest showplace on the Channel, even though, after Nicholas Brady's death in 1930, the Duchess rarely visited it, and the estate was looked after by gardeners and caretakers. Late in the summer of 1936, however, the Duchess arrived in New York from Rome and confided to a few close friends what she described as her "secret." The secret was that her friend Cardinal Pacelli was coming to America in October to spend his vacation with her "in seclusion" at "Inisfada," which she would open for the occasion. One of the first people she told was Bishop Spellman.

The Bishop was not entirely pleased with the news. A visit from the Cardinal Secretary of State, who had already been mentioned as a leading candidate for the Papacy (Pacelli would become Pope Pius XII three years later), was an event of international importance, with vast religious and political implications. Franklin D. Roosevelt was just concluding his first term as President, and, as part of his appeal to combined minority groups in the country, he had already suggested the need for United States diplomatic representation at the Vatican, where there had never before been an American ambassador. Discreet feelers on the subject had gone out from the White House to Rome, and the right moment for some sort of agreement seemed close at hand. But, at this delicate stage, and to the President's distinct annoyance, a Catholic priest from Detroit, Charles E. Coughlin, had stepped into the proceedings and was thoroughly muddying the diplomatic waters. Father Coughlin had, in addition to his parish, a highly popular and controversial radio program—a single Coughlin broadcast once drew as many as 350,000 letters—and, earlier that year, Coughlin had entered the Presidential campaign, concentrating his attack on Roosevelt. On the air, he had referred to "Franklin Double-Crossing Roosevelt," and he had called the President "a liar." He had also referred to him as "a scab President," "anti-God," and "an upstart dictator," and said that Roosevelt's chief supporters were Communists. He had publicly recommended the use of bullets "when any upstart dictator in the White House succeeds in making a one-party Government and when the ballot is useless." The situation had, of course, been noted in Rome, and the *Osservatore Romano* had called Coughlin's statements "improper." But Coughlin's Archbishop, Michael James Gallagher, who supported him, had announced to the Associated Press that "The Vatican never interfered in the Coughlin matter." In light of all this, the Duchess Brady's notion of having Cardinal Pacelli spend three weeks "in seclusion" at "Inisfada" struck Bishop Spellman as grotesque, and even impossible to carry out. The press would make much of the visit, and there would be endless speculation about its true nature—particularly if His Eminence were to be kept in mysterious, even ominous, sequestration in Manhasset. Spellman, on the other hand, owed much to the Duchess and knew her to be a woman of fierce determination and will. His notation in his diary the day he received her news was understandably terse: "Had telephone call from Mrs. Brady in Paris about proposed visit to America."

A month later—with the visit still a month off—the Spellman diary noted: "Labor Day. Luncheon with Mrs. Brady . . . We spent the whole afternoon talking. I did not contradict her, but I shall have to oppose some of her plans. . . ."

Following this luncheon, Spellman sent off four lengthy dispatches to Rome, explaining the situation. He received a cable a few days later, saying that his suggestions would be followed. Mrs. Brady was not at all happy when Bishop Spellman showed her the cable, but, since it was a directive from the Vatican, there was nothing she could do. She had had her heart set, she said, on "seclusion" for His Eminence, for a very private visit during which she and he would while away their days discussing high ecclesiastical matters.

On September 30 the news was released from the Vatican that Eugenio Cardinal Pacelli would sail for New York the following day on the *Conte di Savoia*. A statement was issued from the Cardinal which said, "I am going to America simply on a vacation. I have a great longing to see the United States. There is no political aspect to my trip whatever." But these words did not satisfy the American press, and immediately there were stories claiming that the real reason for the Cardinal's visit was the Pope's concern over Roosevelt's Communist supporters; or that he was coming to try to establish diplomatic relations between the United States and the Holy City. All the newspapers brought in the Coughlin matter.

The Church, meanwhile—the three American Cardinals, the Apostolic Delegate, and the hierarchy below—was thrown into a frantic state of worry over how to treat and handle, and how to interpret, the signal honor that the Duchess Brady had arranged to have paid to the United States. A plan to have the Cardinal taken off the liner by tug before it entered the harbor was abandoned when it was remembered that Queen Victoria of Spain had taken the same short cut with unpleasant consequences. While the ship was still twenty hours away from New York, Bishop Spellman telephoned the Cardinal in his stateroom to prepare him for his first American press conference. Managing the Cardinal's visit had naturally become Francis Spellman's job.

On his arrival in New York, Cardinal Pacelli handled the throng of reporters waiting to interview him with considerable agility, wittily fielding their questions without, in the process, really saying anything at all. He read a short prepared statement which said, in part, "Despite the private character of my visit I know well that I am expected to make my little contribution to the representatives of the press as a sort of 'journalistic tax of entry' into the United States." The press was charmed by the Cardinal and, from then on, would see to it that his visit was hardly "private," and his every move about the country was enthusiastically chronicled.

After a few days' rest at "Inisfada," there began a heavy schedule of public and semipublic appearances. There was a motor trip to Boston, with a stop en route to visit the Knights of Columbus headquarters in New Haven, and a visit to Bishop Spellman's parish in Newton Center, where the Cardinal said Mass twice. There were trips to Philadelphia and Washington, which included numerous stops at various Catholic churches, schools, colleges, and orphanages, and endless lunches, dinners, and speeches, and honorary degrees conferred. There was an extended trip to the West Coast, with stops along the way in Cleveland, Cincinnati, Chicago, St. Louis, and South Bend, during which the Cardinal's plane made detours so that His Eminence could have aerial views of such sights as Niagara Falls, the Grand Canyon, and Boulder Dam. There were only a few tense moments, such as one in Washington where it turned out that Bishop Spellman had not received an invitation for a Press Club luncheon at which the Cardinal was to speak. The Cardinal insisted on the Bishop's being included. In Philadelphia, the Bishop and the Duchess crossed swords briefly over a businessmen's luncheon which the Duchess wanted the Cardinal to attend, and which the Bishop did not (the Bishop prevailed). In Washington, Joseph P. Kennedy had arranged a lunch with Roosevelt at Hyde Park, but Spellman insisted that the invitation come directly from the President, and not through Kennedy as an intermediary.

The glittering capstone to the future Pontiff's visit was the huge reception, on October 24, which the Duchess Brady gave at "Inisfada." As the guests arrived at twilight, the long and winding driveways of the estate were lined with thousands of tallow lights like those used for solemn illumination in the Vatican. Inside, the great house was filled with flowers, with vases of long-stemmed roses banked in every corner, and lighted candles everywhere, and the leaders of American society in furs and feathers and jewels mingled with the beribboned dignitaries of the government and Church—the Cardinals and Bishops in their brilliant cinctures and silk *ferraiuoli*. While Pietro Yon played softly in the background on "Inisfada's" famous pipe organ, the Duchess Brady and her guest of honor received in the great hall in front of a blazing fire. For pomp and sumptuousness, it was said, the Duchess's mid-Depression party had been matched in American social history only by the famous dinner and ball given in 1924 by Clarence Mackay at "Harbor Hill" for the Prince of Wales. As for privacy and seclusion with her guest, however, the Duchess complained that the only way she had been able to have any conversation with Pacelli at all had been to get him into "Inisfada's" private elevator with her, and have the car stopped between floors.

It would be the last great party in the lavish house Nicholas Brady had built for his wife twenty years earlier. The Duchess had already completed arrangements to sell its furnishings, and to turn "Inisfada" over to the Jesuits for use as a Catholic retreat. (Her neighbor, Michael Grace, was less gracious when his family sold the Grace estate on the Irish Channel to a local country club; something of an eccentric, he regarded the house as still his and refused to move out, and, when the country club moved in, he enjoyed annoying the golfers by walking around the golf course in bathing trunks, swinging at members with a golf club.)

It had been deemed improper to have the Cardinal meet with the President during the election campaign, but when, in November, Roosevelt was re-elected by an overwhelming majority, the Hyde Park luncheon was quickly set up. The Cardinal was received by both the President and Mrs. Roosevelt, and those Roosevelt servants who were Catholics received His Eminence's blessing. Mrs. Roosevelt, though not a Catholic, knelt with her servants during it. In the conversation that followed, the subject of a United States minister to the Vatican came up, and the President virtually promised that the Vatican would receive such recognition. In the negotiations toward this end that followed, Bishop Spellman—the future Cardinal Spellman—would act as the chief liaison between the White House and the Vatican. But the true heroine behind the establishment of such a mission was, of course, the Duchess Brady.

When Anthony N. Brady died, he had left an estate of over $100 million—the largest of its day. Grandpa Murray had been the estate's executor. When Brady's son Nicholas died in 1930, his widow inherited some $60 million. Not long after her great party at "Inisfada" the Duchess met in Rome a man named William Babbington Macauley. Macauley was the son of an Irish trawler captain, and was serving as Minister to the Vatican from the Irish Free State. In 1937 the Duchess married Mr. Macauley in a small private ceremony at St. Ignatius Loyola Church in Manhattan. One of the few witnesses was Bishop Spellman. Bishop Spellman was also at the pier to see the couple off on their wedding trip on the *Conte di Savoia*. Relations between the Duchess and the Bishop had become somewhat strained, however, because Mr. Macauley was not as enamored of the Jesuits as his bride was, and had privately vowed to terminate the Duchess's long romance with them. For several months, the Bishop and the Duchess—who still liked to be known as "the Duchess Brady," though she was sometimes referred to as "the widow Brady"—were out of touch.

In 1938, Bishop Spellman received a cablegram from Rome which said simply: "GENEVIEVE DIED AT NOON." After scarcely more than a year of marriage, the Duchess had succumbed to complications following a routine visit to the dentist. Mr. Macauley's feelings in the matter aside, the Duchess was buried beside Mr. Brady in the Jesuit novitiate which they had built in Wernersville, Pennsylvania. As Bishop Spellman wrote to one of his nieces in college at the time:

I am glad, Mary, that there is to be a Mass celebrated at Manhattanville for Mrs. Brady. She was a marvelous woman and in several respects one of the most wonderful persons I have ever met. . . . Of course she may have made some mistakes but they were fewer than most of us make. Fundamentally she had a wonderful heart and a good brain, and she believed, I am thoroughly convinced, that everything she did was right. Certainly everything that she did was done with the right motive. She tried to be guided by supernatural considerations, and I know that even in her social activities she had religious motives. She was a daily communicant, and whenever possible she passed an hour each day in adoration before the Blessed Sacrament.

She did not live to see her friend Cardinal Pacelli become Pope Pius XII in 1939.

After the Duchess's death, William Babbington Macauley found himself in very comfortable circumstances indeed. The bulk of her great fortune was left outright to him. Macauley traveled between New York and Rome and Florida, accompanied by his personal chef-butler, a man named Woods. Eventually, Macauley elevated Woods to the post of private secretary. When Macauley died, eyebrows went up on both continents when it was revealed that he had left all *his* money to Mr. Woods. Thus a great portion of Anthony N. Brady's fortune passed out of the Brady family, a development that did not exactly please the other Bradys, who fell to wrangling over what was left.

When Grandpa Murray used to remind his children and grandchildren that "Money can divide a family," he might have been anticipating the fate of the Bradys.

Chapter 18

"ATOMIC TOM"

roper and pious Uncle Thomas E. Murray, Jr., who was often criticized within the family for the way, after Grandpa Murray's death, he more or less appointed himself the conscience of the Murrays, McDonnells, and Cuddihys— the family's moral and religious watchdog—could also be a man of urbanity and gentle humor. For example, when his nephew, Jack Cuddihy, was a student at Portsmouth Priory in 1937, he wrote to Uncle Tom to ask whether the latter would be interested in buying an ad in the school yearbook, *The Raven*. Young Cuddihy gently reminded his uncle that he himself was a stockholder in certain of the Murray companies and therefore, speaking as a stockholder, he recommended his uncle's using *The Raven* as an advertising medium. Writing on the letterhead of his Metropolitan Device Corporation, which manufactured industrial electric switches, Uncle Tom replied with tongue firmly in cheek:

Your recent communication calling attention to the advertising possibilities of the Portsmouth "Raven" has been duly received and referred to our Advertising Manager for a complete report. . . . It may take several days to get all of the necessary data to enable us to reach a final decision. . . . In the meantime, we are enclosing herewith an order for a full page "ad" from the Metropolitan and we are very anxious to know when this publication will reach the public, as we wish to be prepared, with extra help, to adequately meet the switch demand that is bound to result from this publicity. Will you therefore be good enough to give us some idea as to when we will have to prepare for the rush of orders?

His nephew had asked him if Metropolitan was listed on the New York Stock Exchange, and in the same vein Uncle Tom replied:

In answer to your question, permit me to say that it is not, as the facilities of that Exchange are not nearly adequate enough to absorb the additional load that would be placed upon it if our stock was listed. It is quite evident to us that the whole mechanism of the Exchange would jam, resulting in confusion and possibly discharge of employees, and it would seem to us, from the philanthropic standpoint, we should put aside all selfish motive and refrain from permitting our stock to be used as a gambling medium. I feel sure, when you consider this matter you will agree with our conclusions.

He was also a public-spirited man, and was to become easily the most distinguished Murray of the second generation. He himself held two hundred patents for electrical and welding devices, and, after a brief bout with politics—as an unsuccessful Democratic candidate for Mayor of New York—Uncle Tom spent a number of years devoted to the family businesses. During World War I, under a commission from the government, he helped to apply his father's welding process to munitions-making, and he designed and manufactured welding equipment for the Army's trench warfare division. After the war, he devised a new and improved type of rear-axle housing for automobiles.

During the Second World War, Uncle Tom converted his plants to the production of mortar shells for the government, and for his wartime inventions in this field he received a citation for distinguished service and a personal letter of thanks from President Franklin D. Roosevelt. In 1947, Tom Murray was named presiding trustee of a three-man board to administer the $15 million health and welfare fund of the United Mine Workers of America.

But he found his thoughts turning again to government service of some sort, and when President Harry S. Truman asked him in 1950 if he would be interested in serving as a member of Truman's five-man Atomic Energy Commission, Uncle Tom eagerly said yes. He was appointed to fill the unexpired term of David A. Lilienthal, who had resigned.

Uncle Tom Murray—or "Atomic Tom" as he was soon being called—was a man of strong principles. And, on the AEC, it was not long before he found himself locking horns with the Commission's Chairman, Lewis L. Strauss. Part of their differences was political—Strauss being a Republican, Murray a Democrat. But it went much deeper than that. A lot had to do with the difference in the two men's personalities. Tall, slender, and handsome Tom Murray was quietly conservative in manner, a gentle persuader when attempting to convey his beliefs and express his opinions. Strauss was tough, assertive, pugnacious, and autocratic, a man who liked getting his own way and who reacted stormily when he didn't. "Humility" was one quality Strauss had little of, and his tenure as Chairman of the AEC was marked by a series of stormy confrontations, among them his ousting of the physicist J. Robert Oppenheimer from the handling of classified research. Strauss liked to take full personal credit for the development of the hydrogen bomb, while his detractors insisted that he really had very little to do with it. With his toplofty manner, Strauss did not make many friends in Washington, and those who disliked him mocked his excessively precise speech—he insisted that his name be pronounced "Straws"—and the impeccably manicured tailoring of his clothes.

Tom Murray objected to what he called Strauss's "one-man rule" of the Atomic Energy Commission. But the basic difference between the two men was over matters of atomic policy. Murray wanted "rational limits" on nuclear warfare. Lewis Strauss wanted more and more big bombs. Strauss was for nuclear testing, Murray was opposed. Strauss wanted private industry to produce atomic energy, while Murray favored a government program. Strauss was a hawk, Murray a dove. Tom Murray argued that hydrogen bomb tests should be stopped because the atomic bombs were already powerful enough to destroy civilization, and there seemed to be no sane reason for building bigger ones. He said that, instead, the United States should equip its armed forces with tens of thousands of smaller atomic weapons as protection against the danger of limited wars. He also argued that the federal government could produce peacetime atomic power better and more quickly than if the task were left to private companies, as Strauss advocated. The government should produce atomic power, Murray believed, for use in areas where ordinary fuel was scarce and power was costly.

Murray's chief objection to Strauss's management of the AEC was the tight lid of secrecy which Strauss imposed on the activities of the Commission, even bypassing and ignoring Congressional inquiries into what the AEC was up to. The public needed more information about, for example, the hazards of nuclear testing. "The world actually learned about radioactive fallout from twenty-seven Japanese fishermen, and I think that was the wrong way to have learned it," as Tom Murray put it.

On the AEC Murray later wrote that he was dismayed to discover that "It is not easy to say precisely who makes atomic energy policy in the United States or how it is made," and that if one were "to try to trace the making of a basic nuclear policy decision, he would have to go through a tortuous maze of governmental agencies that initiate or suggest policies, draft position papers on proposed policies, advise, dilute, compromise, and modify policy proposals. He would probably get lost or give up before he had completed his quest through the State Department, the Department of Defense, the Joint Committee, the National Security Council, the Operations Coordinating Board, the President's special staff assistants on scientific affairs, disarmament and other matters, and the Atomic Energy Commission itself." It was a maze of lethargy and confusion, created, he implied, by the Commission's cantankerous Chairman.

Murray was startled to discover, from General Douglas Mac-Arthur's testimony to Congress upon his return from the Far East in 1951, that those charged with executing American nuclear policy were also kept in the dark and not given access to the full facts, and that the General himself "had not been fully briefed on our atomic strength." At the time, Murray was determined to convey information about America's nuclear stockpile to members of the National Security Council, including the Secretary of State. It was ruled, however, by Chairman Strauss, that neither the Secretary of State nor the Security Council had any "need to know" these facts. This struck Murray as absurd, since the National Security Council was the highest policy-making body in the country, and had been principally created by Secretary of State John Foster Dulles—the celebrated advocate of America's "massive retaliation" policy. How could one retaliate massively without some glimmer of an idea of what wherewithal there was for retaliation at all?

Murray believed in "dismantling the Era of Terror," an accomplishment, he felt, that would be as desirable to the Kremlin as it would be to the rest of the world. And, a moralist, he urged the Commission to consider what he called "the forgotten equation"— the connection between morality and national strategy, and he argued that the policy dominating American thought since the end of World War II, of retaliation with giant thermonuclear weapons, was, in the final analysis, insane. Finally, he stressed that "the future welfare of humanity at large must not become exclusively dependent upon the decisions of a very small group of people. We were not brought up to believe that democracy was a form of government under which the people decide all issues that are trivial, or even moderately important, but not those of the highest importance."

With ideas like these, he battled with Lewis Strauss for fully seven years. At one point, in 1953, Murray noted that Admiral Hyman Rickover had been turned down on a plan for a 60,000-kilowatt reactor for an atom-powered aircraft carrier. Murray went to Rickover and suggested that an industrial reactor be built by Westinghouse, through government subsidy. The immediate problem was the tight Eisenhower budget, and so Murray went to the chief Eisenhower economist, Secretary of the Treasury George Humphrey, and presented his case. Though Humphrey favored the idea, Defense Secretary Charles Wilson was opposed to spending the money. "Money down the drain" was Wilson's comment. But, in the end—because the President usually tended to take George Humphrey's advice more readily than anyone else's when it came to money matters—Eisenhower approved Murray's plan, and an atomic reactor was built in Shippingport, Pennsylvania. Despite Eisenhower's famous and well-publicized "Atoms for Peace" speech, this was the only peacetime reactor built in the United States during his administration. England, at the time, already had five.

Atomic Tom Murray was also the first to warn of the danger of Strontium 90, which was finally—many years later—recognized by Eisenhower in his ordering suspension of atomic tests. When, within the AEC, Murray strongly urged that the perils of Strontium 90 be recognized and publicized, he was bitterly opposed by Strauss. When Murray insisted on going to New York to deliver a speech on the subject in 1954, Strauss went so far as to have another of his commissioners, Willard Libby, issue a statement just prior to his speech refuting him on the issue and calling his fellow commissioner, in effect, a liar and an alarmist. In the end, of course, Murray—not Strauss or Libby—was proven right.

In 1957, when Murray's term on the Commission was scheduled

to expire, rumors circulated in Washington that he would not be reappointed, and that Eisenhower planned to appoint a Republican commissioner in his stead. As a result, a majority of the Congressional Joint Committee on Atomic Energy—the majority consisting of nine Democrats and one Republican—publicly urged the President to reappoint him. The ten Congressmen wrote a letter to Eisenhower, citing Murray's many accomplishments on the Commission—pointing out how he had led the way to opening up American uranium resources, calling attention to Murray's stand on hydrogen bomb tests and his having been singlehandedly responsible for the building of the first big industrial atomic power plant. Newspaper editorials all across the country, led by the *New York Times*, backed the Congressmen and urged the President to keep Murray. As it became increasingly clear that Eisenhower intended to listen to none of these pleas, Tom Murray's niece, Mary Jane Cuddihy, wrote to her cousin-in-law in Detroit, Henry Ford II—an influential Republican—asking Ford to intercede for her uncle. Ford replied, in a somewhat chilly tone, that he would not do this, since he was certain that the President intended to appoint a man from his own party. And, in the end, that is what happened, and Atomic Tom was not reappointed.

After leaving the AEC, Tom Murray was made a part-time consultant to the Congressional committee that had tried to intercede for him. Still, though he did his best not to show it, he was privately bitter about Eisenhower's refusal to acknowledge his work by keeping him on the job. He even wrote a book, entitled *Nuclear Policy for War and Peace*, in which he gracefully and lucidly told of his AEC experiences, outlined his beliefs, and attempted to play down his differences with Lewis Strauss. Of this book, the *Times Book Review* commented, "It sheds important light for the first time on an area that has been shrouded in darkness and confusion and should serve as an important guide to public understanding of one of the most crucial issues of our generation, and thus greatly aid in the formulation of a sane nuclear policy upon which may depend the future of all of us." Editorially, the *Daily News* commented, "Read a book, Ike!" But the Eisenhower snub may have helped shorten Tom Murray's life. He died three years later, in May, 1961, at the age of sixty-nine.

Despite his soaringly liberal views on American atomic policy and world affairs, Uncle Tom had remained staunchly conservative in terms of his Church and family. In 1945 his niece, the beautiful Jeanne Murray, met and eloped to Philadelphia with the millionaire sportsman-playboy, Alfred Gwynne Vanderbilt. Jeanne had been working as a publicist for Sherman Billingsley's Stork Club, and the two had met there. For days afterward the tabloids were filled with photographs of the handsome pair. Though many an American family might be delighted to have a daughter marry a Vanderbilt, the Murrays were not. Not only was Alfred Gwynne Vanderbilt not a Catholic, but he had been married before, and divorced, and had a child by his former wife. Vanderbilt men, furthermore, had already acquired a poor record when it came to keeping their wives. Jeanne's mother, Mrs. Jack Murray, was aghast when her daughter telephoned the news of the elopement, and it was weeks before she could bring herself to mail out a very few restrained wedding announcements. Most scandalized of all by Jeanne's behavior was Uncle Tom. At the time, he called on Jeanne's mother at her Park Avenue apartment, and told her, "You must never receive her again. She is not your daughter any longer."

Chapter 19

THE BUCKLEYS OF "GREAT ELM"

he Buckley family has always preferred to think of itself as in a somewhat special category, set apart from such families as the Murrays and the McDonnells. They are, of course, "connected." New York Senator James L. Buckley is married to the former Ann Cooley, whose brother, Richard, was married to the former Sheila McDonnell, though the latter couple is now divorced. "We've never had the interest in High Society that they've had," says Carol Buckley Learsy. "Our interests, as a family, have turned in other directions."

It is true that only a few of the Buckleys have regularly maintained a listing in the New York *Social Register*. The others have chosen not to be listed. And, in the 1920's, when a social publicist approached William F. Buckley, Sr., the founder of the family fortune, and said to him, "Mr. Buckley, for a fee of three hundred dollars a month I'll guarantee that you and your wife and children will appear once a week in society columns, and at least monthly in social magazines," the senior Buckley replied icily, "Young man, I'll pay you the same amount to keep me and my family out of the press." Instead of social position, the Buckleys have devoted themselves to their *principles*, and such publicity as the family has had has resulted from their public expression of these principles—principles which have led the family to be labeled "America's First Family of Conservatism."

The Buckleys, it sometimes seems, have *always* been conservative, and almost militantly so, defending their beliefs with more than a touch of steamy Irish temper. In 1793 a William Buckley of Clonmel, County Tipperary, marched to the guillotine, head held arrogantly high, for his leading role in the Royalist counterrevolution. The first Buckley to come to America had been an Orangeman—a member of the secret society organized in the North of Ireland in 1795 to defend the laws and rule of the reigning King of England, and to support the Protestant religion, but he showed his independent nature by marrying a Catholic girl from County Cork. His political stance had put him somewhat at odds with his England-hating Catholic neighbors near Killarney in the South, who took to crossing Buckley's fields in order to reach their potato farms and pastures. He formally requested them to stop, but they stubbornly refused to comply. One day, after an argument on this subject, Buckley lifted up a plowshare and hit one of his neighbors over the head with it. He was trucked off to jail, where he languished for several weeks while the village waited to see whether the man would die. When he did not, Buckley was released and permitted to emigrate to Canada as a felon. There he took up farming again.

His son, John Buckley, was an equally stubborn sort. He married an Irish Catholic girl named Mary Lee and then announced to her mother, "I'm taking Mary Lee to Texas." Her mother cried, "I'd rather see her in the local graveyard than in that savage country!" But, her mother's wishes notwithstanding, he took

Mary Lee to Texas, where they settled in the border town of Washington de los Brazos. This turned out to be a fortunate move for future Buckleys. John Buckley was a great bear of a man who, in those freewheeling post-Reconstruction days, set himself up as sheriff of Duval County, and, armed with a nickel-plated Colt .45 Peacemaker, would strut into saloons to break up fights, ordering gunslinging cowboys to turn over their firearms. He prospered sufficiently to send his son, William F. Buckley, to the University of Texas, where he graduated with a law degree. With two other brothers, Edmund and Claude, William F. Buckley set up the law firm of Buckley, Buckley, & Buckley. This firm prospered, and presently was specializing in legal counsel for the various oil companies that were rapidly springing up on both sides of the Texas-Mexico border. Before long, the Buckleys were looking for—and finding—oil.

Will Buckley was every bit as tough-minded as his father. In an era and in a part of the world where every man, including his father, carried a gun, William Buckley chose to emphasize his strength of character by going about the streets of the tiny Texas towns and Mexican villages unarmed. Unlike his contemporary, Mr. Doheny, Buckley refused to bribe Mexican officials in order to acquire oil leases, but he was nonetheless able to get his hands on a good deal of choice land. His moralistic stand on bribery did not endear him to the Mexican Government, and for a while he was stalked by an armed assassin named Monty Michael, who already had a considerable reputation as a killer and bank robber. Will Buckley's approach to Monty Michael was typical of his approach to other problems: he disarmed Michael with his straightforward-ness. Buckley knew the gunslinger was under orders to kill him, and so he went out of his way to make Michael's assignment easier and pleasanter. Once, when he noticed Michael shadowing him down the street, he stepped over to the fellow and said, "Monty, I'm having lunch in this restaurant with a couple of friends. Why don't you and your boys pick up something to eat in the mean-time?" The baffled outlaw stammered, "But, Mr. Buckley—don't you realize that I've been hired to scare you out of Mexico, and—if that doesn't work—to kill you?" Buckley said gently, "Well, never mind about that, Monty. Meanwhile, you'll have about an hour before I leave here."

Mr. Buckley began making it a point to keep Monty Michael informed of his schedule and intended whereabouts. On chilly nights, while Buckley worked late in his office and while the bad men waited outside for him in an unheated vestibule, Buckley sent out for hot sandwiches, chili, and coffee for them. One very late night, Monty and his men came crashing into Buckley's office, their faces flushed from tequila. Each carried a Colt revolver at the hip, a cartridge-studded bandoleer over the shoulder, and all bran-dished sawed-off shotguns. Buckley was startled, but did not lose his composure. "Yes, Monty—what is it?" he inquired politely. Monty said, "We've been talking it over, Mr. Buckley. Look, the men who hired us to kill you are in the casino. They're drunk. Now, if it's all right by you, my friends and I'll amble down there and blast them to kingdom come. How's that, Mr. Buckley? We'd rather work for you." Mr. Buckley said, "Good heavens, Monty—you can't do that!" The bewildered outlaw shook his head and said, "Mr. Buckley, I don't understand you. Pass up a chance like this. I just don't understand you." He departed with his friends, and that was the last Will Buckley ever saw of Monty Michael.

Still, there was something about Southwestern lawlessness that rather appealed to Will Buckley. One of the stories of those days that he liked to tell involved a trip to Mexico City on a railway flatcar with his brother Edmund. There was a revolution going on and, according to Buckley, "Corpses were strung from every tele-phone pole for miles along the way!" Gazing with awe at the scene, the two brothers agreed, "This is a wonderful country!"

Wonderful or not, Will Buckley's most formidable enemy became General Obregón, the revolutionary President of Mexico, but still Buckley would not pay the expected bribes. Obregón once swore, "If I don't live to kill Will Buckley and his sons, my sons will live to do it." Finally, the pressure from Obregón's government became too much for him, and in 1921 Buckley was banished from Mexico as a "pernicious foreigner" and ordered never to return under penalty of death. Later, Buckley liked to explain to his children and friends that he could have paid the price to avoid expulsion, but that to do so would have meant sacrificing his principles, and this he would not do. Instead, he sacrificed about a million dollars' worth of oil properties which the Mexican Government expropriated. In any question of money versus principles, he explained, a man's principles must be served first. In 1922 he came to New York nearly penniless and proud of it. But, in the great boom market of the twenties, he plunged aggressively into Wall Street, specializing in the stocks of oil companies, which he knew best, and presently he was flat broke no longer. In fact, before he was through, he would amass another fortune in the neighborhood of $110 million.

In 1923, for $22,000, he bought a forty-acre farm and farmhouse in Sharon, Connecticut, which he named, expansively, "Great Elm." He added onto the house at "Great Elm" until it became the huge Georgian showplace that it is today, filled with antiques, porcelains, crystal, and silver, and presently he acquired a second winter home in Camden, South Carolina. As his tastes grew patrician, he took to sporting a fresh carnation in his buttonhole, pince-nez, and high formal collars. His became a commanding presence in New York and as he strode about the grounds of his two country estates, which he dappled with prize livestock—Merino sheep, Irish hogs, and Jersey cattle.

He and his wife, Aloise, had ten children, and, as a parent, Mr. Buckley was both a classicist and a perfectionist. The children were tutored in French, Latin, Greek, Spanish, mathematics, history, grammar, poetry, and music. As a former Texan, he insisted that his children be able to sit a horse, and so they had a private riding instructor. Once, fearful that his sons were becoming too effetely Eastern, he imported an entire boxcarful of broncos from the West. The horses proved to be unridable by anyone but a rodeo champion, and so they eventually had to be shipped back again. And there was one Christmas morning when the senior Buckley, dressed as Santa Claus and listening to the babble of children's voices, turned to his wife and said, "Aloise, has it occurred to you that it's been years since we understood a word our children say?" Promptly, speech instructors were added to the international retinue of tutors in the Buckley household.

Politically, he was, like his ancestors, every inch a royalist, standing somewhere to the right of William McKinley, and he lectured to his children endlessly on his suspicions of any kind of compromise, of government in general, and of liberals without exception. Though his relations with the Mexican Government were not cordial, he objected strenuously when President Wilson dispatched Marines to invade Veracruz. This was carrying government too far. He dispatched himself to Washington, where, as an expert on Mexican affairs, he testified before the United States Senate against the invasion, calling Wilson's decision "typical of the provincial American, who in need of civilization himself, seeks to civilize the rest of the world."

He was a vociferous writer of memoranda to the various members of his family, and these dispatches might be directed to one person in particular or to all Buckleys in general. His directives advocated a continuous effort to develop the virtues of self-reliance and self-control, ambition, independence, good sportsmanship and good manners, honor, dependability, and steadfast devotion to the Roman Catholic Faith. They inveighed against smoking, slovenliness in any form, and all manifestations of indolence. A memo might take to task his daughter Maureen's diction (which was never quite to her father's satisfaction, despite the instructors), or it might praise his son Jim's punctiliousness in paying back a ten-dollar loan. He particularly remonstrated against what he considered the overwhelmingly bad American habit of not listening to other people. He inveighed against divorce, overuse of alcohol, and reliance on the automobile for a journey that could be accomplished by shank's mare.

His memos—usually signed "W.F.B."—overlooked few areas of his children's lives, and were issued from wherever Mr. Buckley's business might have taken him. Often they were touched with gentle humor. Writing to his son Bill on the subject of his younger brother, Reid, at Yale, he wrote:

Memorandum to William F. Buckley, Jr.:
Jane tells me that Reid has quite extensive sideburns. When he started growing them I mentioned them to him very casually and he said that that was required of the Glee Club—which sounds rather extraordinary. If you could gently suggest to him that he remove them, it would be a great relief to the family. I would rather he not belong to the Glee Club.

And, in another, he wrote:

Memorandum to the Buckley children:
I have been much concerned of late with the apparent inability of any of you, at any time, to go anywhere on foot, although I am sure your mother would have informed me if any of you had been born without the walking capacity of a normal human being.

A few of the older children, notably Priscilla, occasionally walk a few hundred yards behind a golf ball, but all the others "exercise" exclusively by sitting on a horse or a sailboat.

Concurrently, I have noticed that the roads around Sharon are crowded with Buckley cars at all hours of the day and night, and it has been years since any of you has been able to get as far as the Town Clock, much less the Post Office, without a car, or if under 16, a car and a chauffeur.

All the cars are left out every night in all kinds of weather, undoubtedly because of the dangerous fatigue involved in walking from the garage to the house.

I think that each of you should consider a course of therapy designed to prevent atrophy of the leg muscles if only for aesthetic reasons, or you might even go to the extreme of attempting to regain the art of walking, by easy stages of course. The cars might then be reserved for errands covering distances of over 50 yards or so.

Affectionately,
FATHER

In his penchant for memo-writing, Will Buckley was matched only by his contemporary, John B. Kelly of Philadelphia, whose grandfather had emigrated to Vermont, where he had been arrested for stuffing a ballot box. (He had been the only registered Democrat in town, but when the votes were counted there were two Democratic ballots.) Kelly, who had started out as a bricklayer, and had built his business to what was eventually the largest bricklaying concern in the United States, left a will when he died in 1960 that was close to a Buckley memo in both wit and paternal sentiment. To his chauffeur, Kelly bequeathed $1,000 with instructions that the man was to be kept on the family payroll "so long as he behaves himself well, making due allowances for minor errors of the flesh." His unusual will continued:

For years I have been reading last wills and testaments and I have never been able to clearly understand any of them at one reading. Therefore I will attempt to write my own will with the hope that it will be understandable and legal.

Kids will be called "kids" and not "issue," and it will not be cluttered up with "parties of the first part" or "per stirpes," "perpetuities," "quasijudicial," "to wit" and a lot of other terms that I am sure are used only to confuse those for whose benefit it was written.

Some lawyers will question this when they read my will; however, I have my opinion of some of them, so that makes it even. . . .

I don't want to give the impression that I am against sons-in-law. If they are the right type, they will provide for their families and what I am able to give my daughters will help pay the dress shop bills which, if they continue as they have started out, under the able tutelage of their mother, will be quite considerable. . . .

I can think of nothing more ghastly than the heirs sitting around, listening to some representative reading a will. They always remind me of buzzards and vultures awaiting the last breath of the stricken. Therefore, I will try to spare you that ordeal and let you read the will before I go to my reward. . . .

As for me, just shed a respectful tear if you think I merit it, but I am sure that you are all intelligent enough not to weep all over the place. I have watched a few emotional scenes at graves, such as trying to jump into same, fainting, etc., but the thoroughbred grieves in the heart.

Not that my passing should occasion any "scenes," for the simple reason that life owes me nothing. I have ranged far and wide, have really run the gamut of life. I have known great sorrow and great joy. I have had more than my share of success.

In this document I can only give you things, but if I had the choice to give you worldly goods or character, I would give you character. The reason I say this is that, with character, you will get worldly goods, because character is loyalty, honesty, ability, sportsmanship and, I hope, a sense of humor. . . .

After ticking off the various bequests to his wife and children, in which he made it clear that Prince Rainier of Monaco was not to get his hands on any funds inherited by the daughter Kelly mischievously referred to as "Her Serene Highness, Princess Grace," he added:

If I don't stop soon this will be as long as "Gone With the Wind." So just remember, when I shove off for greener pastures or whatever it is on the other side of the curtain, that I do it unafraid and, if you must know, a little curious.

He signed his will in green ink. It was all perfectly legal.

Because he had waited until the age of thirty-six to marry, Will Buckley was regarded, particularly by the younger children, more as a grandfather than a father, and this fact contributed to the awe he was able to inspire among them. The words "I'd like to see you in the Empire Room after lunch" were sufficient to strike cold terror in the heart of an errant child. The meeting in the Empire

Room at "Great Elm" would inevitably begin, behind closed doors, with a few general questions: "How are you doing at school?" and so on. Then the senior Buckley would get right to the point: "Reid, I've called you in for this talk because I was very sorry to hear that you lost your temper again last week and hit Maureen over the head with a golf club. Did you?" "It was a croquet mallet, Father." "I am not going to put up with that kind of behavior," he would begin, and continue with a long, stern lecture on the inadvisability of boys hitting girls, and the importance of manly self-control. At dinner that night, the chastised child would sit in shamefaced silence, so deeply felt was a Buckley's guilt at having offended the patriarch. But the children loved their father. Within a few days after one of these sessions in the Empire Room, there usually came in the mail, addressed to the errant child, a large check.

In order to avoid huge inheritance taxes, Will Buckley had managed, over his final years, to distribute nearly all of his wealth among his wife and children. From their father's actual estate, in fact, which was said to be well over $100 million, each Buckley child received exactly seventeen dollars. After his death in 1958, at the age of seventy-seven, the children got together and prepared a charming book called *W.F.B.—An Appreciation*, which was privately printed and distributed to some fifteen hundred of his friends and relatives and business associates. The book is full of warm anecdotes about his early adventures, but most of all it bears witness to his devotion to his family. His family came before anything else, and this was one of his strongest principles. The chapter on Father Buckley's memos begins, "There was nothing complicated about Father's theory of child rearing. He brought up his sons and daughters with the quite simple objective that they become absolutely perfect."

The Buckley sons and daughters have been famously true to the principles which their father implanted within them, and to his right-of-center political beliefs. Most famous of all has been William F. Buckley, Jr., whose book *God and Man at Yale* caused a great flurry of controversy in the academic community when it was published in 1951. That book, as many recall, mounted an attack against the liberal politics and the all but socialist economics being propagandized, the author felt, and advocated at Yale a renewed emphasis on the virtues of the American free-enterprise system. William Buckley has gone on to become a controversial author, political essayist, lecturer, and television personality. Since 1955 he has edited the conservative-minded *National Review*, and his sister Priscilla Buckley serves as the magazine's managing editor. Another sister, Carol Buckley Learsy, also works for *National Review*. Not long ago, at a family party honoring the joint birthdays of their mother and brother Reid, a two-decker London bus was hired to carry the guests to dinner at New York's "21" restaurant, Carol looked at the vehicle and said, "There goes my year's salary at N.R."

With his brother-in-law, L. Brent Bozell—who, in turn, edits a right-wing Catholic publication in Virginia called *Triumph*—William F. Buckley, Jr. wrote a book called *McCarthy and His Enemies*, defending the ideas and tactics of the late Communist-hunting Senator from Wisconsin. The younger Buckley has also inherited his share of the Buckley Irish temper, as was demonstrated dramatically in a celebrated exchange between himself and writer Gore Vidal before millions of television viewers in 1968. Vidal had called Buckley a "crypto-Nazi," to which Buckley replied, "Shut up or I'll smash you in the mouth, you queer!" This was followed by a vituperative and extended exchange of insults in *Esquire*, which in turn led to Buckley's suing Vidal and *Esquire* magazine, and to Vidal's filing a countersuit.

Equally hot-tempered is brother-in-law Brent Bozell, a zealous Catholic convert and the husband of Patricia Buckley, who is the managing editor of *Triumph*. In 1970, when a number of Buckleys—there were by then forty-nine grandchildren of old Will Buckley—were gathering at "Great Elm" for one of their periodic reunions, Bozell was arrested in Washington for his vehement role in a demonstration protesting abortions in a local clinic.

Bozell and Bill Buckley used to be the best of friends (they were classmates at Yale), but recently there has been a falling-out. Their differences have been political as well as religious. Bozell feels that Buckley's *National Review* is, of all things, too liberal. Buckley feels that Bozell's Catholicism is too strict. Family friends, while conceding the Buckleys' charm and intelligence and wit, often get annoyed with *all* the Buckleys for their right-wing political attitudes and opinions. "They're all right as long as they're on Mozart," says one friend.

Oddly enough, though James Buckley has become New York's Conservative U. S. Senator, the only one of his sons whom William Buckley, Sr. encouraged to enter politics was Bill. "I have the feeling that you will inevitably be drawn into politics, or alternatively catapult yourself into this field," the father wrote in one of his famous memos after *God and Man at Yale* was published. "What this country needs is a politician who has an education, and I don't know of *one*. There hasn't been an educated man in the Senate or House of Representatives since Sumner of Texas quit in disgust three or four years ago."

Since his father's death, his eldest son, John Buckley, has been president of Cawtawba (named after a river near the Buckley winter estate in Camden), the family corporation which runs the Buckley holdings. Cawtawba owns large blocks of stock in seven oil companies all over the world, and these companies lease drilling contracts to other companies. Cawtawba takes care of what the Buckleys call "what little we have," and what little they have permits all the Buckleys to live in considerable comfort.

Aloise Buckley still divides her year between her two large places. When, in 1967, she and Rose Kennedy were honored by

Harper's Bazaar as America's foremost Catholic matriarchs, Mrs. Kennedy commented, "My greatest accomplishment has been bringing up our children to make full use of their talents and resources for a notable purpose: benefiting the community, not themselves." Aloise Buckley is reported to have said, "My great accomplishment is not having one single child who has been a failure." Presumably she meant that her children had held fast to their Catholicism.

But, as with the Kennedys, there have been deeply disturbing personal problems in the Buckley family, none of which their father lived to see. Two of his daughters, Maureen and Aloise, died young of similar causes—an aneurysm—within two years of each other. John Buckley was the first of the children to be divorced *and* remarried, and when his second wife suddenly died of a heart attack, he suffered a deep emotional crisis. "I underwent two years of the most severe unhappiness," he told the *New York Times*. "I even lost my faith in God." But, he says, "I finally realized if I was ever going to see Ann again, I had to make my peace with the Church, which I did."

"Four out of the nine marriages were unhappy," says Carol Buckley Learsy. Carol herself has been divorced, after suffering a nervous breakdown. "She was very Catholic," a friend has said, "and she just couldn't face the fact that she might be unhappily married." She has since remarried Raymond Learsy—"He's a broker, an operator"— who is Jewish. (His uncommon name is a variant backward spelling of "Israel.") Her sister Jane has also been divorced, and lives alone just a mile down the road from "Great Elm" in Sharon. In 1972 the Reid Buckleys were divorced. Of the ten children, only the oldest daughter, Priscilla, has never married.

The four divorces and the two remarriages must have given the Buckleys almost as much pain, perhaps, as the deaths of the two girls, since, to a believing Catholic, death is not just a loss but a removal of the loved person to a more peaceful, ordered place. It is perhaps significant, too, that three of the family divorces took place within a year of William Buckley, Sr.'s death. If he had been able to live forever—as everyone had always taken for granted that he would—might the marriages have stuck? It is possible that if one has had an overpowering father like Will Buckley, who saw to it that the strands of family remained securely knotted, and if then one loses him abruptly, the whole family fabric begins to come apart.

Chapter 20

THE UPWARD CLIMB

ne reason the emergent Irish families placed so much
emphasis on their sons' and daughters' getting into society, asked to the best parties and dances, and invited into
the best clubs was based on their special feelings about their
faith. The "nice" people of Boston, by whom Rose Kennedy so
desperately wanted to be accepted, might be Protestant, but in
her opinion, and in the opinion of others like her, the Irish Catholic families were every bit as nice, or even nicer, because they
were more pious and more strict about their religion. Their piety
made them more moral, more stable and secure, and didn't this
add up to niceness? It was easy for the Irish Catholic rich to see
that their Protestant counterparts were much more casual about
their religion, going to church whenever they felt like it and,
presumably, seldom receiving Communion. Nor were the wealthy
Jews, on the whole, particularly observant. As the Jews became
Americanized and affluent, they tended to abandon the strict

orthodoxy of their parents and grandparents, and to visit their synagogues and temples only on certain High Holy Days.

Those who considered themselves the First Irish Families were determined to see to it that this sort of thing should not happen to them. Furthermore, the tenacity with which the Irish clung to the letter of their faith set them, they believed, above all other Catholics. To be an Irish Catholic (or, as some preferred, "Catholic Irish") was in itself a mark of social and religious superiority. Second in importance to the Irish Catholics came the German Catholics, and after the Germans came the English, though there were not too many of them. Much further down the ladder came the French, Italian, Belgian, Spanish, Portuguese, and all other kinds of Catholics—simply because the Catholics of these countries were not as conscientious about their religion. In the North Central states, Wisconsin, Minnesota, and the Dakotas, where so many Scandinavian families settled, the Swedish and Norwegian Catholics are regarded as decidedly lower-class. This is particularly apparent in the pronounced rivalry between Minnesota's Twin Cities—Irish Catholic St. Paul and Scandinavian Minneapolis. F. Scott Fitzgerald (Irish Catholic) was always proud that his family had been from St. Paul, and not from socially inferior Minneapolis across the river.

It was considered "best" for an Irish Catholic to marry another Irish Catholic, but marriage to a German Catholic was acceptable and a number of such marriages took place. William F. Buckley, Sr.'s marriage to the former Aloise Steiner joined him with a German Catholic family from the south. Horace Flanigan's son John, whose sister Peggy married Murray McDonnell, married Carlota Busch, of the long-prominent Anheuser-Busch brewing family in St. Louis, and Robert F. Kennedy married Ethel Skakel, German Catholic. Uncle Tom Murray might have been aghast when his niece Jeanne eloped and was married—not by a priest but by a justice of the peace—to a divorced Protestant. But he would have not been much happier if she had married an Italian Catholic, because the Italians were not "good Catholics."

When Uncle Tom Murray instructed his family never to receive Jeanne Murray after her marriage to Alfred Gwynne Vanderbilt, it was simply because, to him, no marriage existed. Jeanne might call herself "Mrs. Vanderbilt," but she was in fact living in sin. When young Bob Cuddihy married a divorced woman out of the Church, his sister Mary Jane MacGuire, who loved him more than any of her brothers, tearfully told him over the telephone that she could not invite him to a large family Thanksgiving gathering at her house in Rye. What kind of an example would it set for her children if, by including him, she appeared to approve of his sinful relationship? Bob, who had a famous temper, did not lose it, but merely said quietly, "I understand."

Because of the purity of their faith, the wealthy Irish Catholics saw no reason why they should not be accepted by the highest of high Protestant society, particularly when they had no intention of going so far as to marry into it. And such social institutions as the *Social Register* seem to have agreed with them. Early in their rise to affluence, the little black and red book began listing such New York families as the Murrays, McDonnells, Cuddihys, and Graces, and, in San Francisco, the Mackays, Fairs, and Floods (though the first San Francisco Flood had been a bartender, and his wife a chambermaid). At the same time, there are very few Italian names in the *Social Register*s of American cities, and even fewer Jewish ones. But this may be because the Jewish upper crust has tended to regard non-Jewish society as frivolous and self-indulgent. Not so the Irish Catholics.

Perhaps another reason why the First Irish Families have cared so deeply about society is that, in the early days following their arrival in the United States, the Irish were so widely employed as servants in the households of the rich and well-placed. The Irish cook or parlor maid could observe and learn at firsthand the manners, inflections, and tastes of her mistress, and the Irish chauffeur, gardener, or valet could observe his master's ways. The Irish were quick studies in these matters, and were determined that, if perhaps not they, then at least their children should acquire every attribute of the American upper classes. Even back home in Ireland, though they had not been able to rise, the poorest Irish tenant farmer and his wife could watch—and someday hope to imitate—the ways of the gentry and the manners of their English landlords. In Ireland today, the upper-class Irish accent (not a brogue) is considered the purest spoken English in the world. Hence Will Buckley's preoccupation with his children's diction (it had to be perfect), and Anna Murray McDonnell's daily inspection of her children's clothes before they set off to school. Hence James Francis McDonnell's motto: "Always go First Class." The map of the world that hung in the McDonnell dining room was not so much to teach the children geography as it was a reminder that travel is a social tool. When one traveled, one stayed at the best hotels. The grand manner, the children learned, got one wherever one wanted to go. The H. Lester Cuddihys, scheduled to travel to Europe on a North German Lloyd liner, discovered on their day of departure that labor trouble at the pier would mean that they would not be permitted to board the ship. Mr. Cuddihy drew himself up and announced to the passenger agent, "I am Mr. North German Lloyd." The party was ushered aboard. Not that some of the Irish families weren't naïve when they traveled. Uncle Ennis McQuail, who was married to Auntie Katherine Murray, arrived in Paris for his first visit and exclaimed wonderingly, "Even the children here speak French!"

Clothes came from the best shops in Paris and London. If one bought antique furniture or silver, it had to be of the very best. China was Royal Crown Derby, Rockingham, or *old* Spode. There were George III tea sets and Meissen baskets, linen sheets with hand-embroidered monograms above insets of French lace.

Table manners had to be faultless. The McDonnells had the reputation of setting the most perfect table of all the families, even for a simple lunch. A McDonnell cousin, now married with children of her own, remembers vividly her first meal with the McDonnells as a child. She had been accustomed to taking meals in her family's third-floor nursery dining room, the food sent up on a dumb-waiter, but this was to be a formal lunch with grownups. The first course was grapefruit, and, after spooning out the sections, she picked up the grapefruit and squeezed it. A deathly silence fell across the length of gleaming mahogany as her relatives gazed in horror at what she was doing. To this day, she teaches her children, "It's all right to squeeze grapefruit when you are home, and to pick up a lamb chop with your fingers at the end—but *never* when you are out."

Perfection was the constant rule. The Murray and McDonnell houses were decorated by McMillen because McMillen was the best society decorator in New York. John Murray Cuddihy's portrait was painted by Robert Henri because he was the best society portraitist around. Cleanliness was stressed almost as much as godliness. Houses were kept scrubbed and polished, and so were bodies. Uncle Joe Murray had a constant fear of germs, and at family birthday parties a separate cake was used for blowing out the candles; then a fresh one was brought in to eat. Uncle Joe dosed himself with drops and pills and remedies so often to ward off colds that when, one winter, he actually came down with pneumonia, one of his sisters commented dryly, "It's about time."

The rather special social position that the First Irish Families have been able to achieve was demonstrated not long ago by an episode that occurred on the staff of that good gray lady of American publishing, the *New York Times*. The editor of the woman's and society pages, Charlotte Curtis, a graduate of Vassar, had written in a story, "The McDonnells are like the Kennedys. They are rich Irish Catholics, and there are lots of them." These sentences caught the eye of Theodore Bernstein, who, as editor of the "bull-pen," acts as the *Times*'s official watchdog and arbiter of taste, style, and decorum, and who is Jewish. Bernstein was offended by the sentences, and in his interoffice bulletin, "Winners & Sinners," he cited them as an example of impropriety, and warned the staff:

Omit racial, religious, or national designations unless they have some relevance to the news or are part of the biographical aggregate, as in an obit or a "Man in the News." Perhaps it is a tribute to the Irish that "Irish Catholic" does not seem offensive, but would you write "rich Russian Jews"?

A few days later, Bernstein received a memorandum from his superior, Clifton Daniel, the *Times* managing editor:

I agree with you that it is a tribute to the Irish that "Irish Catholic" does not seem offensive, and I also agree that "rich Russian Jew" might be offensive. But it seems to me that we can certainly say that a family is rich, that it is Russian, and that it is Jewish, if those things are relevant to the news. In fact, I myself have written about such families, and nobody ever questioned the relevance of doing so. But the trick is not to put these facts together in one bunch so that they have a cumulative pejorative aroma.

In a postscript Daniel added, "Since this note was dictated, we have published an obituary of Sean O'Casey, calling him a poor Irish Protestant." In other words, "bunching" adjectives is vulgar when speaking or writing about Jews, but it is not in the case of the Irish.

Certainly, the McDonnells raised no objections to being called rich Irish Catholics. But what they do rather mind is the curious habit of society reporters on the *Times* and other newspapers of dwelling, to excess, on the *size* of their families. Reports of weddings, debuts, and other social activities of the rich Irish are given subtly different treatment in the press, it often seems. In covering a Protestant wedding, for example, it is customary to list the bride's and bridegroom's parents and perhaps grandparents—and, if there is a distinguished ancestor further back than that, perhaps his name as well. In writing up Catholic weddings, however, society editors seem to enjoy listing not only the couple's direct antecedents, but their aunts, uncles, brothers, sisters, and cousins by the dozens. This has been going on for some time, as in this 1938 report from the old New York *World-Telegram* on social doings in Southampton:

"Look out for children" signs along the elm-shaded, oiled streets of Southampton might be the clew to the family life that characterizes this peaceful society resort. . . .

Junior activity could fill a social column, what with James F. MacDonald's [*sic*—editors of 1938 seem not yet to have learned the correct spelling of the McDonnell name] fourteen children (Mrs. MacDonald was Anna Murray), the seven children, including post debutantes Rosamund and Therese [*sic*], of the Joseph Bradley Murray's; the eleven children of the Thomas E. Murray, Jr.'s; the H. Lester Cuddihys' attractive offspring—Mary Jane—who makes her debut this season; H. Lester, Jr. and John M. Cuddihy, to mention a few. Mrs. Cuddihy is the former Julia Murray. Pat and Jean [*sic*] are the daughters of Mrs. John F. Murray. . . .

As if the number of Murrays wasn't enough to tax a society editor, there are two Catherines—one, daughter of Mrs. John F. Murray, of Lighthouse Farm; the other, daughter of the James F. MacDonalds, of East Wickapogue Cottage.

Thomas E. Murray 3rd is the son of the Thomas E. Jr.'s, while Thomas E. Murray 2nd, is the son of Mrs. John F. Murray.

There are enough Murray children for a gymkhana all their own. . . . There are always Murray children taking part in these events at local and national horse shows. . . .

Reports like this, with their somewhat mocking tone, seem to be making the point that to have many children, which is part of being a good Catholic, is rather vulgar. And, though the above article never says so, the implication is clear enough: These are rich, Irish, baby-having Catholics.

Interestingly enough, in Catholic High Society in New York, at least two of the grandest *grandes dames* have not been Irish. One was the late Mrs. Robert Louis Hoguet, a woman of imposing social importance in Catholic affairs, and the Hoguets today are still extremely prominent. Mrs. Hoguet had a rather shrill speaking voice, and one day when she telephoned Mrs. H. Lester Cuddihy on some matter, Mrs. Cuddihy assumed that it was one of her friends trying to be funny, and she imitated the shrill voice back to her caller. When she realized that it *was* Louise Hoguet, she knew that she had committed a sizable social gaffe. The other lady, still very much around, is Mrs. Christopher Billopp Wyatt, the mother of actress Jane Wyatt. Mrs. Wyatt's full name—Euphemia Van Rensselaer Waddington Wyatt—is the longest name in the *Social Register*. Families like the Hoguets and the Wyatts may consider themselves a little "better" than the Irish families, but they do their best not to let their feelings show.

There are a number of Catholic social institutions in New York. One of these is the annual Alfred E. Smith Memorial Dinner, usually held at the Waldorf-Astoria. A glance at any one of the souvenir programs and seating plans for this event tells an interesting story, and reveals the nature of the Catholic hierarchy in the city. Among the thousands of guests seated in relative anonymity on the main floor of the ballroom at the 1945 event were, for example, people named De Arango, Jacobi, Algase, Calderazzo, Valente, Di Lorenzo, Costelli, Nigro, Bardia, La Rotunda, Mecca, Quaranta, and Borgia. Up on the dais, seated front and center, along with such dignitaries as John D. Rockefeller, Jr. and James V. Forrestal and Archbishop Spellman, were Mrs. James F. Mc-Donnell, Philip A. Murray, Basil Harris (married to a Murray), Thomas E. Murray, Joseph P. Ryan, Joseph P. Kennedy, and John F. Kennedy. Perhaps because they were not Irish, Mr. and Mrs. Robert L. Hoguet were *not* placed on the dais.

Then there is New York's Gotham Ball, an annual event that evolved out of the Gotham Dances, first organized in 1912 for subdebutantes and preparatory-school boys of "good" Catholic families. The Gotham Ball, usually held at the Plaza, is now New York's leading Catholic debutante affair. The Ball benefits the New York Foundling Hospital, which, though a Catholic charity, cares for abandoned and neglected infants of all religions and races until they can be placed in proper homes. A feature of the Ball has always been the formal presentation of the young ladies to the leading prelate of the New York Archdiocese, currently Terence Cardinal Cooke.

Though members of New York's First Irish Families support the Gotham Ball, and present many of their daughters there, they tend to regard the Gotham as a somewhat second-rate social event, and if a girl comes out *only* at the Gotham, and nowhere else, she is not really considered "out" at all. Mary Jane Cuddihy Mac-Guire recalls going to her first Gotham Ball and says, "My impression was one of just poor taste—a lot of Italians and foreigners and it seems to me a lot of doctors' children coming out in front of a lot of drunks. I felt sorry for the girls, they looked so innocent." Later, she says, "We wouldn't be caught dead going to the Gothams. I don't think this was a social thing so much as that it was just a punk, stupid party." Much more exclusive and fashionable— and fun—were the Junior Assemblies and the Baltimore Cotillon (which clings aristocratically to the archaic single-*i* spelling of the word), neither of which is Catholic, and if an Irish Catholic girl is invited to come out at one of these, she has really entered society in an important way.

Mrs. MacGuire remembers the family excitement at the time of her presentation at the latter event. This was in the 1940's, and fashionable girls had begun wearing their hair "up." She had been wearing her hair up for several months—she had had it expensively styled in Paris—and yet, as the date of the party approached, her mother fretted nervously for fear the other girls at the ball would not be wearing theirs up. Mrs. Cuddihy made several anxious telephone calls to friends to ask their opinions on what would be the correct hair-do for her daughter, and the consensus was that Mary Jane's hair should be *down*. On the night of the party—after all hairdressing salons had closed—Mrs. Cuddihy not only personally scrubbed all the make-up off her daughter's face but also took a hairbrush and tried to brush the hair down. It had been swept upward for so long that "the result was something like a Ubangi— not up or down, but straight out." She entered the ballroom in a dress of pale-pink tulle with violets at the throat, where her escort presented her with a clashing bouquet of orange and yellow flowers (which she chucked under a coat rack), and was furious to see that all the other girls were wearing their hair up, "but with bobby pins showing, and not properly as mine had been done in Paris." During the procession, her escort, one Roswell P. Russell ("Who could forget the name?"), stepped on her dress five times, and ripped the hem. When she was being presented at the Junior Assemblies, Mary Jane Cuddihy was in such a high state of nervousness—with her own and all the other mothers gathered on the balcony looking down at the dancers—that she whispered three Hail Marys during the first dance. And yet this was the same girl who, some time later, was seen teaching Errol Flynn to rhumba at the Hamptons' Canoe Place Inn. "The only reason I dared to date him—he was married to Lili Damita at the time—was because my mother was out of town."

Still, though all the best people may not be presented at it, the Gotham Ball confers status of a certain sort. In 1963 the ball's traditional honoree, Francis Cardinal Spellman, who was also board chairman of the Foundling Hospital, could not attend because he was in Rome for the Ecumenical Council. It was decided, instead, to honor four prominent lay Catholic women. Those selected were Mrs. Thomas E. Murray, Jr., Mrs. Joseph Bradley Murray, Mrs. James F. McDonnell, and Mrs. H. Lester Cuddihy. Instead of the usual cardinal-red roses that are presented to the

Cardinal, pink carnations were selected for presentation to the ladies. Among the thirty-two debutantes—which included girls named Caballero, Monte-Sano, and Pallavicini—were four great-granddaughters of Thomas E. Murray.

Though the *Social Register* may have adopted a liberal attitude toward the Irish rich, there are still some clubs and resorts where Catholics are not really welcome. The New York Athletic Club, for example, which is notoriously anti-Semitic, is said to have an unwritten "quota" for Catholic members, though many F.I.F.'s belong to it. The exclusive Links Club in New York also has only a handful of Irish Catholic members, though Nicholas F. Brady, Judge Morgan J. O'Brien, John B. Ryan, and William R. Grace—who had worked as a singing waiter and then as a long-shoreman before developing W. R. Grace & Company and the Grace Steamship Line—were all members in their day, and there are Bradys, Graces, and Ryans in the club's present membership, along with Murray McDonnell. It has often been noted that no Catholic has ever been elected to the Yale Corporation, though Jews and even blacks have been. In the 1930's Nicholas Brady, Sr. was put up for the Yale Corporation, but was not elected.

As for resorts, the First Irish Families have tended to cluster in places where they have established sturdy beachheads—the most fashionable being, of course, Southampton. The "Irish Channel" in Manhasset, on Long Island's opposite shore, is no longer what it used to be when James Cox Brady, Nicholas Brady, Joseph P. Grace, and copper king Cornelius Kelly all had huge houses on vast acreage there. Now Joe Martino has a house on the Channel, and so does William Paley, who is Jewish. There are other resort areas that are largely Irish in character—Saltaire, on the western end of Fire Island, and in sections of the New Jersey shore, around Spring Lake—but these, like the Gotham Ball, are considered to cater mostly to the second-rate. Significantly, Grace Kelly first entertained her Prince on the Jersey shore, in Margate. She may have risen to where she is now, as Her Serene Highness of Monaco, but these Kellys have never been regarded as one of the F.I.F.'s.

For years, the First Irish Families took winter skiing vacations at the Lake Placid Club in the Adirondacks, which has, from its earliest days, excluded Jews. Lake Placid was then followed by a week or two of spring golf in Pinehurst, North Carolina, although Pinehurst's Bostonian genesis (it was first developed by Boston's Protestant Tufts family) was responsible for a detectable chill in the social air. But now the New York F.I.F.'s, not to be put down by anybody, have a ski mountain of their very own. In the early 1960's the family of Thomas I. Sheridan, who is married to the former Jane Murray, Atomic Tom's daughter, bought Windham Mountain, an 800-acre tract with a 3,100-foot peak near the Catskill village of Windham, New York, just north of the Borscht Belt. For several years, the Sheridans operated Windham as a public ski area. But, as the popularity of skiing soared—it is now one of the world's most popular winter participation sports—the Sheridans and their skiing friends grew irked with the long lines that had to be endured before getting on the lifts. In 1967, with $175,-000 chipped in from some fifty-four friends and relatives, Sheridan turned the place into the Windham Mountain Club. During weekdays Windham is open to the public, but on weekends it is strictly private and can be skiied by members only.

Founding members—who each paid $2,000 to join—include Jane Murray Sheridan's brother, the Rev. D. Bradley Murray, a Jesuit priest; her cousin, Thomas E. Murray II; another cousin, Mrs. John F. Hennessy, Jr., the former Barbara McDonnell; and Basil Harris, Jr., whose brother is married to the former Charlotte McDonnell. Others are the Rushton W. Skakels—he is Mrs. Robert F. Kennedy's brother—and Dan W. Lufkin, whose aunt was Marie Murray (her first husband was a McDonnell). Ethel Kennedy often skis there, as do the Stephen Smiths, the Sargent Shrivers, the Edward M. Kennedys, and Patricia Kennedy Law-ford. The mountain has three lifts, Argentinian ski instructors, a handsome lodge with a sauna, a discothèque with strobe lights, banquettes upholstered in zebra-printed plush, flamenco music, and lots of parties. A number of the founders of the club have built their own $20,000-to-$80,000 chalets in the area, and no one but members is permitted to build there.

On winter weekends at Windham, it's much the same crowd one finds in summer in Southampton. "It's the same people each weekend, so we can organize anything we want," says one member. "We know each other, so we get no surprises." There are, of course, the usual throngs of children. Thomas Sheridan, the club's president, likes to point out that his own six children have ninety first cousins. Does the Windham Mountain Club manage, with $750-a-year family dues, to stay in the black? "Millionaires don't mind if they lose money," Mr. Sheridan says. "The main thing is, there's no waiting in lines."

Chapter 21

SONS OF THE PRIORY,
DAUGHTERS OF THE SACRED HEART

One of the great bulwarks, emotionally and theologically, of the Roman Catholic Church has been its establishment of what sociologists call "parallel structures"—Catholic charities, social organizations, and schools, all designed to keep the Catholic snugly within the confines of his faith, to enwrap him perpetually in his Catholicism. Catholic families feel strongly that their children need constant, daily reminders of their Catholicism, and hence the elaborate network of parochial schools and Catholic colleges and universities. Jewish families may send their children to Hebrew school on Sundays, or to one of a handful of Jewish colleges, but, for the most part, upper-class Jews have tended to educate their sons and daughters at fashionable Eastern and nondenominational boarding schools and even at such schools as St. Paul's and Kent, which are primarily oriented toward the Episcopal Church. A wealthy Jewish father would rather send his son to Harvard than Brandeis. Something of an exception to this rule was, for a while, the Sachs Collegiate Institute in New York, established in 1871 by Dr. Julius Sachs, which was for many years the favored private day school for the sons of the German-Jewish upper crust. But Dr. Sachs's school was not a "Jewish" school in the sense that it taught Judaism or employed Judaic ritual, nor was Dr. Sachs a rabbi, and a number of non-Jewish parents sent their sons to Sachs because they admired Herr Doktor Sachs's stern and Teutonic sense of discipline. After Dr. Sachs's death, the school changed, and the Sachs Collegiate Institute no longer exists.

The First Irish Families, on the other hand, have had strong feelings about their children being educated in Catholic schools by Catholic monks and nuns. The first New England boarding school for Catholic boys was Canterbury, in New Milford, Connecticut, established in 1915 "to give Catholic boys sound college preparation, as offered by the best non-sectarian boarding schools, together with thorough training in the doctrines and practices of the Catholic Church." Classes were conducted by Catholic laymen, there was a resident chaplain, and the school was organized under the patronage of the Archbishop of Hartford. Very quickly, Canterbury became the "fashionable" school for wealthy Irish Catholic families.

Then, in 1926, Portsmouth Priory was founded in Portsmouth, Rhode Island. Portsmouth Priory, now called Portsmouth Abbey (its official name is the Benedictine Monastery of St. Gregory the Great), has had an altogether unusual history. The Rev. J. Hugh Diman had been the rugged, ruddy Episcopalian minister of a fashionable Rhode Island summer church. Very much a "society minister," he was the Arthur Lee Kinsolving of his day, and in 1896 he decided to become a schoolmaster. He had one teacher and eleven pupils when he opened his "Diman's School for Small Boys" in Newport, but gradually his wealthy Newport neighbors began sending him their sons, and, within twenty years, he had

120 students and a considerable social and academic reputation. Renamed St. George's, Hugh Diman's school educated any number of Newport Belmonts and Vanderbilts. St. George's, Diman thought, came close to providing the ideal of a general education, but, because it taught slowly, and tried to teach character and gentlemanliness and not job skills, it was, as he put it, "clearly and necessarily a school for rich boys," many of whom would never look for a job in their lives.

As a schoolmaster, Diman was no Mr. Chips, and preferred respect to affection from his students. His friendliest gesture to a boy was a poke in the ribs with the heavy walking stick he always carried, and he once complained that a photograph of him did not make him look strict enough. Few jokes were told about him, and those that were pertained to his notoriously bad driving (he repeatedly scarred a big maple along a driveway at St. George's with his car), his general absent-mindedness, and his dislike of office routine (his letters and memos were always worded so that no reply was required). Students and faculty held him in deepest awe, and few got to know him well. Like two other famous Episcopal headmasters—Peabody of Groton and Coit of St. Paul's—Dr. Diman admired the aristocratic British public (which is to say, private) school system, which stressed the three C's—character-building, classics, and Christianity—more than the three R's. He was an intensely private person, a bachelor who believed that Episcopalian ministers should remain celibate, and he spent long hours in quiet meditation.

As a High Church Episcopalian, Dr. Diman was, as they say, "very close" to being a Catholic anyway, and, in his fifties, he underwent a religious crisis and began exploring Catholicism. An attack of appendicitis decided him, and he summoned a priest and told him, "If I'm going to die, I'd rather die in the Catholic Church than out of it." He headed for Rome and the priesthood. At the age of sixty-three, Father Diman entered a Benedictine abbey in Scotland, where he swept corridors, dug ditches, and performed penances with novices in their teens. In 1926 the Benedictines sent Father Diman back to Rhode Island to do for Catholic education what he had done for the Protestants. The result was Portsmouth Priory, just nine miles down the road from St. George's. By 1946 the Priory had 120 boys and 20 masters (more than half of them Benedictine monks), and, though he retired as headmaster in 1942, Father Diman continued to teach the course in "Christian Doctrine." In his flowing black Benedictine habit, clipped tonsure, and swinging his ever-present cane, he strolled about the lovely Portsmouth campus overlooking Narragansett Bay. In the process, and probably because of Father Diman's original Episcopalianism, Portsmouth Priory became the most fashionable Catholic boys' school in America, outranking Canterbury, and the favored school of such families as the Murrays, Cuddihys, Kennedys, Hoguets, and Wyatts along with a number of titled European families. (The Duke d'Uzès, premier Duke of France, is a Priory alumnus.)

Father Diman once told *Time* magazine: "Religion as a living force in deepening and enriching personality has been almost eliminated from the public schools, and with it the most powerful instrument for the development of character. . . . The greatest disappointment of my school career has been that my schools are 'expensive schools.' I have never ceased to hope that they might become schools for the rank and file." The First Irish Families, however, were quite satisfied with not having their sons schooled with the rank and file.

After Portsmouth Priory, a proper Catholic boy was "supposed" to go to Georgetown University in Washington, run by the Jesuits. Of all the Catholic colleges, Georgetown ranks the highest, socially. It has often been said that an Irish Catholic father, who may have gone to a socially inferior college like Fordham, Holy Cross, or Notre Dame, looks forward to having his sons accepted at

Georgetown. Fordham and the others are regarded as colleges for "lace curtain Irish," just one step above "shanty Irish." Georgetown is the college for *"real* lace," or, as it has been called, "re-embroidered lace." Members of the Windham Mountain Club have said that one reason for the club's congeniality is the fact that so many of the members are Georgetown alumni. The principal benefactors of Georgetown, like those of Portsmouth Priory, include all the members of the F.I.F.'s.

In the Murray family, with Uncle Tom as its spiritual head, there was always a crisis when a son wanted to go to a college other than Georgetown, or to a college in the Ivy League. When young Jake Murray wanted to go to Yale, Uncle Tom was seriously upset and inveighed against the young man's choice. "It's canon law that he should get a Catholic education!" he insisted. "Encyclical Number 6,978. *Canon law!"* Jake, however, finally won, and went to Yale. This branch of the family—the Jack Murrays—were, in Uncle Tom's opinion, heading for damnation, what with Jake Murray's sister Jeanne having married a divorced Vanderbilt. The Cuddihys were more liberal, and the children were always aware that Harvard, Yale, and Princeton were academically better than the Catholic colleges. And yet, when the time came, Catholic colleges were chosen for them. Tom Cuddihy had done extremely well at Portsmouth, and had been accepted at Harvard, but his father still had misgivings. Late in the summer before he was to enter Harvard, his father invited two priests to dinner, Father Gerald Phelan, head of the Pontifical Institute of the University of Toronto, and a Monsignor Hartigan, and Mr. Cuddihy asked these men what they thought of Tom's Harvard plans. Both priests said, "No—don't send him there. Send him to St. Michael's College in Toronto." Not even Georgetown would do. And so Tom Cuddihy was shipped off to Toronto. He stayed two days before running away—to enter Harvard.

As for girls, the right schools were those operated by nuns of the

Order of the Sacred Heart. If a Catholic girl of good family decided to become a nun herself, the most fashionable order was Sacred Heart. In every city, the Sacred Heart school is usually considered the "snob" Catholic school, and in many ways it is. Sacred Heart nuns are rather special people. Unlike the nuns in ordinary parochial schools, for example, who hide their original identity under the veil of saints' names—Sister Joseph, Sister Theresa, Sister Ignatius—Sacred Heart nuns are permitted to keep their own names, as Mother Byrnes, Mother O'Malley, or Mother Shea, and they often come from the wealthiest Catholic families in town. They are also allowed to dine out in mufti, and to go to cocktail parties. Their schools, in addition to academic subjects, teach upper-class values, morals, and manners.

The Sacred Heart girl is taught how to hold a fork, how to pierce the breast of a chicken Kiev with the tip of a knife, how to fold a napkin, how to speak to servants, how to sit and how to rise from a chair, how to turn the dinner conversation at the conclusion of a course, and how to curtsy. She is taught, in other words, how to be an elegant lady, a gracious hostess, and a proper guest. French is stressed because French is the second language that every well-bred English-speaking girl should have, and when Reverend Mother enters the classroom at a Sacred Heart school, she is greeted with a chorus of *"Bonjour, Réverende Mère,"* to which she responds, *"Bonjour, mes enfants,"* and then, *"Au nom du Père, et du Fils, et du Saint-Esprit. Ainsi soit-il."* Sacred Heart girls sometimes argue with the nuns about certain of the rules of behavior, but the nuns, who are usually gently bred ladies themselves, will argue pleasantly back, explaining what it means to be a Sacred Heart girl. A Sacred Heart girl should sit erect, with her knees together and her feet flat on the floor, or else crossed gracefully at the ankles—never with knees crossed. When asked what is wrong with knee-crossing, the Sacred Heart nun will reply, "My dear, there is nothing wrong with it. It is just something that a Sacred Heart girl does not do."

To her pupils, the Reverend Mother reads this doctrine:

The child of the Sacred Heart understands that her role is central to the design of creation. If she is not among those few called to the perfect life of religion, it will be her task to guide the souls of her own children. Her special influence depends upon her distinctively feminine qualities: tact, quiet courage, and the willingness to subordinate her will to another's gracefully and even gaily. Filled with the tranquility of inner certitude, she does not disperse her energies in pointless curiosity, in capricious espousal of new theories, in the spirit of contention. Long years of silence, of attention to manners and forms, have instilled in her that self-control without which order and beauty are impossible. Her bearing is the outward shape of that perfect purity which is her greatest beauty, and which models itself on the ideal womanhood found in the Mother of God. She who can bear the small trials of daily discipline will not falter at those crises in life which require firmness and fortitude.

The child of the Sacred Heart frequently emerges from her education with the inner certainty that she is a distinctly special and superior person. In New York, the Murray, McDonnell, and Cuddihy girls went to the Convent of the Sacred Heart, which was originally at the fashionable address of Fifty-fourth Street and Madison Avenue, and later moved to an even more fashionable location at Ninety-first Street and Fifth Avenue, where the school occupied the Italian Renaissance mansion originally built by Otto H. Kahn. (Kahn, the Jewish philanthropist and banker, toyed with Catholicism in his later years, though he never converted, and this is how his house came to become the property of the order, and to be humorously called "The Otto H. Kahn-vent.") There are some New York parents who do not think that the New York convent is quite what it used to be academically—Jacqueline Kennedy Onassis withdrew Caroline Kennedy from the convent several years ago and enrolled her in the nonsectarian Brearley School—and yet it remains the "best" Catholic school for New York girls.

After her secondary schooling, the *real* Sacred Heart girl goes either to Barat, in Lake Forest, Illinois, or to Manhattanville, in Purchase, New York, both fashionable addresses. Oddly enough, a third Catholic college, Marymount—even though it is more or less right in the family, with James Butler as its chief benefactor, and his cousin, Mother Butler, as its many-years Mother Superior—is rated socially below the other two. "Perhaps," says Mary Jane Cuddihy MacGuire, who married James Butler's grandson and who went to Manhattanville, "it was because we didn't think that Marymount was academically as good as Manhattanville. But I do know that we considered the Marymount girls— well, 'not much.' "

Chapter 22

ROYALTY

nce, one of Uncle Tom Murray's nephews, irked at his uncle's proprietary manner—in matters of faith, education, marriage, the spending of money, to name just a few areas of family life over which Uncle Tom assumed authority and had strong opinions—muttered to a friend, "I'm going to spread rumors about him that will get him kicked out of the Knights of Malta and the Knights of St. Gregory. In fact, I'll make it so bad that he won't even be able to get into the Knights of Columbus!"

The point is, of course, that belonging to the Knights of Columbus carries with it about as much social prestige as joining the Rotary Club or the Oddfellows. There are any number of Rotary-style Church organizations. There are others that carry genuine prestige, memberships to which are not given out lightly by the Vatican, including the Knights of St. Gregory, the Grand Knights of the Holy Sepulchre, and the Knights of the Grand Cross. But to be chosen for the Papal order of the Knights of Malta is the highest Catholic honor of all. Those Irish elected to it can consider themselves true "Irishtocracy," or, as they have also been labeled, "silk curtain Irish." Both Uncle Tom and his father were Knights of Malta, and the Duchess Brady was a Dame. The Knights of Malta comprise what is perhaps the most exclusive club on earth. They are more than the Catholic aristocracy; they are the nobility, royalty. Of the more than six hundred million Roman Catholics in the world, only eight thousand are Knights of Malta or, to use the full title, the Sovereign and Military Order of the Knights Hospitaller of St. John of Jerusalem of Rhodes and of Malta. Their list stands next in importance only to the Calendar of Saints. While the Knights of Columbus are associated with lodge meetings and bingo, the Knights of Malta can pick up a telephone and chat with the Pope.

The organization was founded in the eleventh century as an order of nursing monks, and, for over nine hundred years, the order has striven to preserve at least a certain amount of the grandeur and elegant trappings of ancient aristocracy. Ever since the Knights captured the island of Rhodes from the Byzantine Empire in 1309, the Holy See has recognized the "sovereign" character of the order, a designation that permits it to have an unusual degree of independence from local officials of the Church. At the Knights' headquarters on the Via Condotti in Rome, the Knights' scarlet-and-white banner flies over a huge palazzo which the Italian police regard as having extraterritorial rights—a nation of its own, like Vatican City—and some thirty-five foreign nations maintain full diplomatic relations with the order.

Over the centuries, countless Catholic kings and queens have been Knights and Dames of Malta. Today, the membership of the Knights is something of an amalgam of ancient European nobility and newly rich North and South Americans. Among the most prominent members are King Baudouin of Belgium and Henri

244

d'Orléans, Pretender to the throne of France, along with Irishman J. Peter Grace, the Honorable John D. J. Moore, United States Ambassador to Ireland, and Danny Thomas, the entertainer, who, in 1940, discouraged about the state of his career, began praying to St. Jude, the patron saint of the lost and hopeless, promising to build a shrine to the saint if he got a job. He got one within days, and later built the two-million-dollar St. Jude Children's hospital in Memphis, Tennessee, as his end of the bargain.

For years the Knights of Malta maintained a semisecrecy about their membership and activities, displaying a lordly disdain of publicity, rarely permitting photographs of their annual meetings when the Knights put on hats festooned with ostrich plumes, golden spurs, uniforms with gold epaulets, sashes, ribbons, medals, and decorations. This attitude also kept the Knights somewhat at arm's length from the hierarchy of the Church, even though, in the United States, the Knights became well known to the hierarchy through their fund-raising activities. The Knights kept their sights focused firmly on the order's ancient military past. After Suleiman the Magnificent and his Turkish fleet drove the Knights from Rhodes in 1522, the Knights took over the island of Malta and fended off, almost singlehandedly, the advance of Islam into Christian Europe. But the Reformation and the rise of European nationalism eventually stripped the order of its temporal power, and the Papacy was more or less forced to take its bold defenders back under the shelter of its wing. "Rhodes formed the character of our order," its Grand Chancellor, Quintin Jermy Gwyn, has said, "but Malta was its splendor. It was a glorious period." Still, that was all a very long time ago.

Today, the Knights of Malta may appear to be something of an anachronism, a bit of ancient tradition and ritual that survives in history-conscious Rome, and the advantages of being a Knight may seem no more substantial than whatever can be got from the opportunity of rubbing shoulders with Cardinals (New York's Ter-

245

ence Cardinal Cooke and the late Richard Cardinal Cushing of Boston). And so, despite the eminence and affluence of the organization, the Knights decided several years ago that they—and their good works—needed more exposure, lest the Knights be regarded as no more important than "kings" and "queens" dressed up for Mardi Gras.

Thereupon the Knights of Malta called the first press conference in their nine-hundred-year history, in order to bring to the attention of the public the nature of their world-wide ministry to the poor and ailing. Next, they went so far as to engage the Italian motion picture director, Vittorio De Sica, to film a television documentary on the Knights' good works. "This film can help our fund-raising," Grand Chancellor Gwyn explained. "What we need are more supporters willing to give their money, brains, and time."

De Sica and his producer, Peter Dragadze, went to London to film British nobles of the order doing menial work, even emptying bedpans in St. John's Hospital, and from there flew to Belfast to follow the Knights' ambulance unit as it tended casualties of Northern Ireland's riots. Providing such medical assistance is still the Knights' main activity. In Germany, the Knights sponsor a nationwide ambulance corps with 24,000 aristocratic and unpaid volunteers, and in South Vietnam, throughout the war, they administered a team of fifty-two doctors. Although many of the Knights and Dames of the order are elderly and infirm, they are all expected to lend a personal hand in the operation of the 150 hospitals and other medical services the order maintains. "When you put a rich man to work for five days in an ambulance, it transforms him," says Count Wolfgang von Bellestrem, the German jurist who oversees the order's medical work, succinctly expressing the order's feelings of *noblesse oblige*.

Even Vittorio De Sica, who had not expected to be, was impressed. "I had thought of it as a purely social group of nobles in uniforms, with ceremonies and lots of pomp," he said at the time. But, after observing the noble gentlemen at work with lepers, earthquake victims, and mentally retarded children, he changed his mind. "They are doing real works of charity," he said, "Christian charity."

In the United States, meanwhile, the First Irish Families are often criticized for limiting their philanthropy to the Catholic Church, Church-connected projects, and the Democratic Party. It is true that, when it comes to charity, Catholics have tended to favor Catholic charities, just as Jews have lent their main support to Jewish philanthropies with a "Let's take care of our own first" philosophy. And, just as the Zionist cause was not a "fashionable" one among upper-class American Jews, the Irish cause at the time of the "trouble" was not popular among the F.I.F.'s, who did little to support it. President Eamon de Valera's comment that such money as had come from the United States to support the Irish Revolution came from housemaids and laborers was not entirely an exaggeration. Grandpa R. J. Cuddihy was one of the few wealthy New Yorkers who gave money to the Irish cause, but when his mother found out about it, she was furious.

There are certain Catholic charities that are more fashionable than others. In New York, in addition to the Foundling Hospital, families like the Murrays, McDonnells, and Cuddihys have helped make the Catholic Big Sisters more or less the Catholic answer to the Junior League. The Big Sisters counsel and place in foster homes young girls in trouble with their families or referred to them by Family Court. Then there is the Guild of the Infant Saviour, founded in 1901 to "give sanctuary to the destitute young girl, friendless, alone, and facing motherhood." At one point, the Guild had among its fourteen directors Mr. Robert J. Cuddihy; his daughter-in-law, Mrs. H. Lester Cuddihy; her sister, Mrs. J. Ennis McQuail; and Mrs. Cuddihy's daughter's aunt-in-law, Mrs. Walter E. Travers, the former Genevieve Butler. Another "social" Catholic charity that is equally inbred is St. Vincent's Hospital. For a 1959 benefit fashion show on behalf of the Cardinal Spellman Wing of St. Vincent's Hospital in Westchester, the seven models—all size ten—were Mary Jane Cuddihy MacGuire; her daughter, Judith Ann; her sister, Anne Marie Cuddihy; their mother, Mrs. H. Lester Cuddihy; and three cousins, Mrs. Basil Harris, Mrs. Thomas Sheridan, and Mrs. Murray Roche. Just as chic—and just as full of the same people as its leading benefactors —is the Catholic Center for the Blind. All these organizations, the F.I.F.'s are quick to point out, may be Catholic-sponsored, but they serve all creeds.

Just as there are fashionable charities, there are also fashionable churches. One might suppose that the "Power House," St. Patrick's Cathedral on Fifth Avenue, would be one of these, but it is not. St. Patrick's is regarded as "lace curtain," and for tourists. Most of the First Families worship at St. Thomas More, St. Ignatius Loyola, or at St. Jean Baptiste, "the Thomas Fortune Ryan church." "The reason for this is mostly geographic, not snobbish," says one of the Murrays. "They're located more convenient to where we live"—on the Upper East Side, on or off Park Avenue. Still, as a result of their addresses (and because they are smaller, more elegant and restrained in their decor), these three have become known as New York's "snob churches" among other Catholics. One, indeed, has been humorously christened "Our Lady of the Cadillac."

Though the Democratic Party might not, strictly speaking, be considered a charity, there are ways in which it can be treated as one. If, say, one wishes to contribute $10,000 to the Democratic Party, which is not tax-deductible, he can make a gift of $100,000 to the Church, which is. The Church then, quietly and without fanfare, can transfer $10,000 to the party, keeping the $90,000 for itself.

Non-Catholics often assume, of course, that the Church itself is immensely rich, and therefore hugely powerful. It is indeed rich, but in many archdioceses, including the largest ones, it is land-rich and cash-poor. In New York, for example, the nonparochial real estate owned directly by the Archbishopric is worth about $105 million, with the high school properties alone worth about $51.9 million. It is true that the Chancery's cash accounts receivable and securities holdings amount to an additional $97.4 million, but these "liquid assets" are actually somewhat less liquid than they appear to be. Of the $97.4 million, $76.4 million is in the form of cash mortgage loans made over the years to individual parishes, and because only a small fraction of this sum would be collectible in any one year, to call the whole $76.4 million a liquid asset is, to say the least, optimistic.

The total parish and nonparish assets of the New York Archdiocese have been estimated at $750 million, a goodly sum indeed, and a full list of the Chancery's real-estate holdings would be a lengthy one. And yet, with a single exception, these holdings are institutional properties used entirely for religious, educational, and charitable purposes. The exception is the Sperry & Hutchinson Building at 330 Madison Avenue, which the Archdiocese bought in 1967 and now wishes it had not. It has not been a successful venture. Harry Helmsley of the Helmsley-Spear real-estate firm in Manhattan has been quoted as saying, "There is no way for the Church to come out in good shape" on the S-H sale and lease-back. And another real-estate man has said, "John Reynolds [the Archdiocesan real-estate broker] better see to it that the Cardinal gets lots of Green Stamps."

Perhaps the charge that disturbs the Irish the most is that, in not supporting the arts, sciences, and non-Catholic education to the extent that Jews do, they are "nonintellectual." The picture is often drawn of the Jew going out to concerts, operas, theater, and ballet, acquiring paintings and giving them away to museums, and buying books, while the Irish Catholic sits home watching football games on television, drinking beer. A Catholic sociologist, Father Andrew M. Greeley, has even lent support to this. The Irish, he insists, are not really "dumb Micks," but while Jewish intellectuals have boldly asserted themselves and imposed their vision upon the rest of America, the Irish have sat back passively, immobilized by their sense of inferiority. Irish intellectuals capable of publishing often don't, he says, because they fear making themselves vulnerable to criticism.

Their fear, he says, comes about from the repressive way in which the children of the Irish are often reared. Too many Irish, Father Greeley feels, fear that to be "different" risks loss of the "respectability" that took them such hard work, over so many generations, to achieve. As a result, he says, the vast majority of brilliant young American Irishmen are doomed to "lead lives of noisy desperation, availing themselves of all the mechanisms of self-destruction that the Irish have traditionally made available for themselves—drink, obesity, temper tantrums, unending quarrels." Their preoccupation with being accepted by the "nice" people accounts for the fact, he implies, that there are no Irish Einsteins.

Well, people like the Murrays would take rather strong exception to Father Greeley's generalizations. Grandpa Murray and Uncle "Atomic Tom" Murray may not have been intellectuals exactly, but they were certainly smart. Nor did they drink much. They were a handsome lot, and kept their figures, and they did not encourage quarrels—though there was a bit of that. The Murrays also have a published author in the family, John F. ("Jake") Murray, Jr., whose novel *The Devil Walks on Water* (Little, Brown), about a rich Irish Catholic family in Southampton, caused a bit of a stir in the family when it was published in 1969. In Jake Murray's book, a number of the family recognized themselves, while others preferred not to, and quite a few Murrays found the title blasphemous.

Then, consider Patent Number 3,038,030, recently awarded to the Jesuit priest in the family, Father D. Bradley Murray, who teaches mathematics at the Georgetown Preparatory School in Garrett Park, Maryland. He is one of Grandpa Murray's grandsons, and his patent is for an electronic translator designed to convert the dots and dashes of Morse code into the binary code, the common language of modern computers. His invention's primary usefulness will be in naval and military communications. Once a radio message is translated into the binary code, it is a quick step from there to the teletypewriter. This is the first Murray patent in the third generation, but clearly young Father Murray is following in the footsteps of his grandfather and his father, Atomic Tom. Clearly, the family feels, there is good cause to speak in the same breath of Einsteins, Oppenheimers, Salks, Freuds, *and* Murrays.

Part Four

WHAT DID
HAPPEN

Chapter 23

PROBLEMS IN THE BACK OFFICE

rom the end of World War II on, the stock market was going pretty much straight up. It was easy for bankers and stockbrokers to believe that it would glide steadily upward forever. Everybody, it seemed, wanted to invest, and at firms like McDonnell & Company there seemed to be no serious problems. The McDonnells continued to live lavishly, with their fourteen children, in their vast apartment at 910 Fifth Avenue, and at "East Wickapogue Cottage" in Southampton. In those days, brokerage firms were making money almost in spite of themselves, and, when James Francis McDonnell died in 1958 at the age of seventy-nine, control of his firm was taken over by his second oldest son, Murray McDonnell, and the company's future seemed secure.

Murray McDonnell is a slightly built, amiable, easy-to-please fellow, who looks rather like a college English professor as cast by Hollywood. He loves horses, and has also inherited his father's taste for splendid living. He and his wife, the daughter of New York banker Horace Flanigan, and their nine children were widely written about in the society columns, where he was frequently mentioned as the "second father" of Mrs. Jacqueline Kennedy's children, often entertaining the Kennedys at his horse farm in New Jersey, and inviting Mrs. Kennedy to his castle in Ireland. True, Murray seemed to spend more time with his horses and his social life than with his business, but that was all right. After all, wasn't that what a rich man was supposed to do? Murray had been placed in charge of the firm's day-to-day operations as early as 1945, when he was only twenty-three. But his real preference was selling, and he maintained a number of large accounts, including several for the Church, which yielded between one and two million dollars in annual commissions. After his father's death, Murray McDonnell announced grandiose plans for McDonnell & Company. It would become, he said, "another Merrill Lynch," a Cadillac among stockbrokerage houses. He opened more new offices and, as usual, had them lavishly furnished and decorated. Even the chairs for the secretaries cost three hundred dollars apiece.

There were a few problems, but they seemed minor. The third brother, Charles—nicknamed "Bish" because he had been named after the Bishop of Brooklyn—resigned from McDonnell & Company as a result of a disagreement over Murray McDonnell's business methods, and joined another Wall Street firm. One of the two men's sisters has described the differences in Murray's and Bish's personalities by saying, "Bish would take two strokes away from a golfer's handicap. Murray would add two." But one of the firm's greatest assets—in terms of both prestige and credit—was the presence in the family of Henry Ford. It was an intangible asset, to be sure, but it had become a general assumption on Wall Street that if ever Murray McDonnell needed money he could always tap the almost limitless resources of his brother-in-law. In fact, there is evidence that Ford did lend McDonnell & Company something in the neighborhood of a million dollars at one point to help the firm consummate some deal. If this is true, it is unlikely that this loan has been repaid.

The importance of the Ford name and "connection" with the family was brought home dramatically to one of the McDonnell cousins, young John Murray Cuddihy, when he and another cousin were junketing around Europe one summer. "We were just college kids," he recalls, "and traveling on a very limited budget, but the minute the word got out that one of my cousins was Mrs. Henry Ford, we got treated like royalty. Naturally, we made the most of this, wherever we went."

Henry Ford II is a burly, roly-poly, extremely sociable man who loves to give and go to parties. He tossed an extravagant coming-out party in 1959 for his oldest daughter, Charlotte. The party, which featured a Middle Ages decor, was held at the Detroit Country Club and was billed as "The Party of the Century." There were twelve hundred guests ranging from the Gary Coopers to Lord Charles Spencer-Churchill, and the whole thing cost $250,000, a record for a debutante affair. Two years later, Henry Ford threw another "Party of the Century" for his second daughter, Anne, which cost just as much. The fact that Ford would give such publicity-ridden parties was an indication that he did not have the aristocratic social inhibitions that would prevent, say, a Thomas J. Watson or a Rockefeller from indulging in such gaudiness. Anne McDonnell Ford, meanwhile, was a coolly blonde thin-lipped beauty who had some of the iciness and reserve of her father, whom the family called "Little Caesar." She saw to it that her daughters went to strict Catholic schools, and were raised as "perfect convent girls." She taught them to do the proper things and to go to the proper places. At their mother's urging, the girls went to Paris to study, Gstaad to ski. The girls traveled to Europe often, frequently with their father, while their mother stayed behind quietly in the Ford mansion in Grosse Pointe on the shore of Lake St. Clair. Henry Ford bought a yacht and took Mediterranean cruises regularly, entertaining friends on board and throwing parties whenever the boat came into port—again, often while his wife stayed home. When Anne Ford went to Europe, she was usually alone.

By early 1960 there were rumors that all was not well with the Fords' marriage, which Monsignor Sheen had proclaimed to be "unbreakable" and "for all eternity." There was talk that Henry Ford was being seen in the company of a mysterious "contessa." He even appeared with the "contessa" at a New York restaurant. The headwaiter refused to seat them, and, when Ford protested, the headwaiter whispered that Ford's daughter Charlotte was dining at a table inside. Presently, the "contessa" turned out to be an untitled and lively Italian-born divorcee named Christina Austin, whom Ford had met in Paris at a party given by Princess Grace. Again, Ford showed no particular reticence about escorting his new lady friend to and from fashionable parties, while his wife kept a stiff and silent upper lip.

While the Fords were having their marital difficulties in Detroit, 1960 was also the beginning of trouble for McDonnell & Company in New York. Suddenly there was a greater volume of stock being transacted on the New York Stock Exchange than anyone had ever imagined there could be. In the quieter days before the war, for the Exchange to have a "million-share day" was something of an event. By 1960 as many as twelve million shares were being traded in a single day. Soon, trading volume would climb to fifteen million shares a day, and then twenty million. There were more individual shareholders than ever before in history, and there had developed the big institutional buyers—mutual funds, bank trust accounts, insurance companies. It was becoming impossible for the back office—the accounting areas of brokerage firms—manually to handle the large numbers of orders that were daily coming in. In the old days, it had been simple. A firm might have a hundred different orders in a day, or even two or three hundred. Tickets were written up, confirmations were sent out, and each transaction was entered in the books according to normal book-keeping procedures. But when orders leaped to tens of thousands a day, human hands became incapable of handling them, and many firms in the 1960's began to computerize their accounting systems in an effort to cope with the deluge of paper work.

In 1962—perhaps a little later than other firms—McDonnell installed National Cash Register computers in order to deal with the situation. But what the firm didn't realize was that the situation was far worse than they had thought, and that the computers they had put in—at enormous cost—were hopelessly unequipped to handle the steadily increasing volume of trades that were taking place. McDonnell & Company now had two thousand employees in twenty-six offices around the country and one in Paris on the elegant rue Cambon, and yet the firm still did not have any real business management. Murray might be an effective salesman, but it was doubtful that he was a strong operations head. McDonnell & Company was still a family-run concern, and at the time Murray, his wife, his mother, his brother Morgan, and his sister Anne Ford were the principal owners of the firm.

Many of the then currently successful brokerage firms were able to realize, quickly enough, that the computer systems they had installed simply were not up to handling the loads of orders that were pouring in. But McDonnell & Company was not one of these, and it continued limping along with its National Cash Register system. In 1964, Anne McDonnell Ford, to the distress of others in the family, divorced Henry Ford in Sun Valley, and a year later Henry married his beautiful Christina. Earlier, the McDonnells are said to have approached Ford for another million-dollar loan, but, with his marriage to Anne disintegrating, they were turned down.

Lemming-like, the company now seemed to be heading inexorably toward self-destruction. Early in 1968 the firm had $18 million in equity and subordinated capital, and was doing a business of about $35 million a year in commissions and fees. And yet, at the same time, the back office was so hopelessly entangled that a feeling of panic had begun to set in. The accounting system was so inefficient that no one knew for sure whether trades were being made for the correct customers, whether stock certificates were being sent to the right people, or who was owed what. To this day, at least one member of the family, John Murray Cuddihy, is not entirely sure whether he really owns shares of stock credited to his account. In that grim summer of 1968, while the stock market was being coincidentally battered by the storm warnings of recession, the firm was forced to admit that out of 47,000 customer accounts there were at least 4,000 that showed errors. There were, furthermore, some $872,000 worth of uncollected dividends for McDonnell customers. The firm had some $9 million worth of securities of which it didn't know the owners. It also owed $1.3 million worth of securities to individuals and other brokerage houses that it couldn't seem to locate. Perhaps the most staggering error of all was the firm's overestimation, by $91.8 million, of the amount of fully-paid-for securities that its customers had on deposit. Meanwhile, it was $87.4 million *short* in other securities which, by law, must be segregated. In 1968, McDonnell & Company was ranked thirty-fifth in efficiency out of thirty-eight top Big Board firms.

Record-keeping procedures were simply a disaster. For example, a customer might order 1,000 shares of Standard Oil of New Jersey at $64 a share, and get a bill for 1,000 shares of Standard Oil of Ohio at $34 a share. The customer would pay the bill—$34,000— and then, when he went to sell his stock, say, "I don't own Standard of Ohio. I paid for Standard of New Jersey." The company would be out some $40,000 as a result of that sort of back-office mistake.

Day-to-day existence within the McDonnell & Company offices had become chaotic. "Every day there was some sort of flap," one employee recalls. Switchboards were jammed with incoming calls from customers wanting to know what had happened to their orders, their certificates, their dividends. McDonnell brokers were often more than a week late returning their customers' calls and, even then, couldn't give them satisfactory answers. Salesmen, instructed to buy and sell only for the biggest, most lucrative accounts, disobeyed orders and bought and sold as they chose. As one of them said, "I want my commissions, and to hell with the company." Clerks complained that they had to work standing up, since there was no place for them to sit. There were no three-hundred-dollar chairs this time, but stools were brought in. Meanwhile, weekly orders fell from 17,000 to 4,000.

At one point during this hectic period, the McDonnells brought in Murray's friend and fellow Irishman ex-Postmaster General Lawrence F. O'Brien to head the firm as president. There were some who considered O'Brien—who had been in the official entourages at the time of the shooting of both John F. Kennedy and Robert F. Kennedy—an ominous choice, as though O'Brien carried with him some mysterious kiss of death. At any rate, O'Brien left after seven months, saying only that the job had not fulfilled his expectations. A curious footnote to the brief O'Brien interlude was that, though O'Brien had brought a certain sum of money into the firm, that sum exactly equaled the cost of an apartment that the company purchased for his use at the luxurious United Nations Plaza. When O'Brien resigned, an arrangement was made whereby the apartment became his property, indicating that O'Brien may have been a better politician than a banker.

One ray of hope glimmered. Sean McDonnell, the youngest son of the McDonnell clan, was a handsome, athletic man who lived elegantly with his pretty wife in a big house in Greenwich, Connecticut. He had graduated from Fordham in 1954, and spent two years with the Wall Street firm of Blyth & Company. After Naval Officers' Candidate School, he had spent three years in the Navy and entered Harvard Business School, graduating in 1961. He then came "home" to McDonnell & Company, joining the firm first as a senior vice president. He was made executive vice president in 1967, when he was thirty-two. Sean McDonnell was something of a family pet, and many felt that he was his mother's favorite son. He, not his brother Murray, was considered the real financial genius in the family, and Anna Murray McDonnell, who had a large personal stake in the company, considered Sean to be her husband's true successor, the young white knight who would lead the family company to further riches and glory. In its present difficulties, Sean might be the only man to help the company out. Murray McDonnell, meanwhile, was perfectly happy to let Sean handle the day-to-day operations of the company, while he, Murray, concentrated on trading for his accounts, including those of the Church (Murray was chairman of the financial committee of the Archdiocese of New York), and his horses. Sean, a stickler for physical fitness, was often seen on weekends, in sweat pants, jogging up and down the shaded lanes of Greenwich near his house on Round Hill Road.

Sean McDonnell had been responsible for the firm's acquisition of F. P. Ristine & Company, a distinguished Philadelphia house. He also had undertaken to unscramble the company's accounting department, and to revamp the entire back-office procedure. To do this, a firm had two choices. One could either install one's own computers and programmers to develop an entire "in-house" computer system. Or one could simply mark the trades initially, and send everything over at the end of a business day to an outside computer house. McDonnell & Company decided on this latter course. At the time, in 1968, there were many firms that were specializing in doing accounting for brokerage firms. Sean Mc-

Donnell chose one called Data Architects, Inc., of Waltham, Massachusetts. At the time, his choice was hailed by the *Wall Street Journal* as a "sophisticated" one. Then, on June 4, 1968, the McDonnell family received terrible news. Sean McDonnell had had a heart attack while jogging in Greenwich, and was dead at the age of thirty-three. The golden promise was gone. On top of bad management, the firm had encountered terrible bad luck.

For a time, the firm became, and behaved like, a riderless horse. No one seemed to be in control. The Data Architects computer system to handle the McDonnell accounts was still unfinished, and it suddenly seemed to be unfinishable. McDonnell & Company bitterly blamed Data Architects, saying that the computer firm "just didn't understand the brokerage business." Data Architects blamed McDonnell, saying that it had become impossible to get anyone at McDonnell to make a decision, as proposals were shunted from one desk to another with no one doing anything. Sean's death was blamed for the entire situation. In retrospect, however, the choice of Data Architects may not have been as sophisticated as was at first assumed. Data Architects was a firm that the McDonnells had been very close to. It was underwritten in the heyday of underwritings in the early 1960's—when any company with the words "Data" or "Computer" or "Scientific Measurement" in its name created excitement in the marketplace—by the Wall Street firm of D. H. Blair & Company. D. H. Blair & Company were very friendly with McDonnell & Company, and the McDonnells and their partners had ended up owning approximately 50 percent of Data Architects.

Normally, it might seem, a firm like McDonnell & Company would investigate all the available computer firms before making a choice, and might have found that only one or two were equipped to handle their problems. Instead, the McDonnells went immediately to Data Architects, which was, so to speak "in the family." The capability of Data Architects left a lot to be desired (the firm has since gone bankrupt). McDonnell & Company had a fiduciary responsibility to its customers; one could argue that the company was unwise to select a firm in which there was so great a potential conflict of interest.

Nineteen sixty-eight continued to be a year of disasters. For the eight-month period ending August, 1968, McDonnell & Company had reported a profit of $1.8 million. By December of that year that profit was entirely wiped out. The printing and stationery bill alone was one million dollars for the year. The firm seemed on the brink of collapse. Murray McDonnell, in a desperation move, brought in Paul D. MacDonald, another friend, to head up his operations, and, under MacDonald, a drastic program of retrenchment was begun. Early in 1969 the firm closed and sold twenty-three of its twenty-six offices, leaving only the three "showcase" ones at 250 Park Avenue, 120 Broadway, and Paris. All McDonnell salesmen who were not producing at least $50,000 a year in commissions were fired. Salaries of all employees in the $30,000-to-$50,000 range were slashed by 10 percent. The sumptuous executive dining room was closed. The limousines which had carried McDonnell executives here and there about town were sold—except Murray's own, which, he explained, he personally paid for. The firm sold one of its three seats on the New York Stock Exchange for $413,000. As a result, by mid-1969 McDonnell & Company was worth half what it had been worth two years earlier.

The cuts, sales, and firings were intended to cut the company's overhead, and get it back on its feet. By November, 1969, Murray McDonnell, who admitted "I've been through hell," was confident that things would work out for his company, and that there was at last light at the end of the tunnel. To a financial reporter from the *Wall Street Journal*, visiting Murray in his comfortable downtown office, Murray McDonnell presented a cheerful, confident front. The reporter caught his mood of optimism and headlined his story: "Riches to Rags—How Bad Management, Bad Luck, *Nearly* Ruined a Big Brokerage House."

With a little smile, Murray said to the reporter, "I've *got* to be optimistic," and he pointed to the photographs of his wife and nine children arrayed on his big desk. No one drew the parallel, but it was a little like the early optimism about the scope of the potato blight in 1845.

Murray also seems to have displayed a certain lack of sensitivity, or public-relations sense. In 1969, when the firm was going through its most agonizing throes, with mass firings and salary reductions taking place, his employees and associates cannot have been pleased to read that Murray McDonnell was off in Saratoga, paying nearly a quarter of a million dollars for a thoroughbred race horse.

Chapter 24

TO THE BITTER END

urray McDonnell was not a stupid man. He was, and is, a shrewd and inventive trader, a good salesman, and has drawn praise for the ability with which he has handled the accounts of the Archdiocese of New York. He had also done his best to manage and preserve the family's money and properties. For example, his "Water Mill Farms" is a horse-breeding farm on Flying Point Road, on the ocean, in Southampton Township, and for a number of years Murray was able to operate "Water Mill Farms" at a tax-deductible loss. Until 1969 the tax laws read that if losses on such things as horse-breeding farms were more than $50,000 a year for five years, the amount in excess of $50,000 was considered as a hobby, not a business, and was not subject to tax relief. In order to circumvent this, Murray worked out a little gimmick—perfectly legal—with his sister, Anne Ford. Murray would own the farm for a period somewhat less than five years, and then he would sell it to Anne. Anne

266

would then own it for a little less than five years before selling it back to Murray. Back and forth "Water Mill Farms" would go, and all its losses were always tax-deductible. In 1970, however, the law was changed to read that if an activity, such as a horse farm, shows any taxable profit, no matter how small, in any two out of five years, it is presumed to be a business, so Murray's gimmick is no longer quite so useful.

In 1969, Anne Ford—by then remarried, to Deane Johnson—attempted to sell some of the acreage at "Water Mill Farms" to a developer, perhaps partially to recoup the losses she was experiencing at McDonnell & Company. There was, however, a considerable furor in the resort community over this proposal, and the land sale was quietly canceled.

As of June, 1969, Murray McDonnell himself had approximately $1,500,000 in his company. His brother Morgan had about $250,000, his mother had roughly $1,500,000, and his wife had some $2,000,000. Anne Ford Johnson had a share worth about $2,700,000, and other officers in the firm had shares worth approximately $650,000. Added to this were half a million dollars in profit-sharing, $5,300,000 in equity, making the company's net worth in mid-1969 roughly $15,000,000. Of Murray McDonnell's share, however, Wall Street rumor had it that $1,600,000 had been recently lent to him by the First National City Bank as an unsecured loan. And, since August of the year before, the company had been running heavily in the red. It was a fact that Murray McDonnell was doing his desperate best to hide.

Prior to June, 1969, McDonnell & Company had had no corporate finance department. By the fall of 1968 the management of the firm thought it would be wise to establish such a department, and to bring in money experts from other firms, hopefully to help untangle the company from its mare's nest of woes. At the time, it was said that Murray McDonnell had personally committed a million dollars of his own funds to start this department, and a number of people were approached for contributions. They were all told that they, and the new corporate finance department, would have a major role in the policy decisions of the firm. The corporate finance group came in on January 1, 1969. Although Murray in no way indicated that the firm was losing money, he did tell the group, when they asked him why he was so willing to split the profit of the group equally with its members, that he would rather have 5 percent of a viable enterprise than 100 percent of no enterprise at all.

A month later, in February, 1969—again at a time when the firm was experiencing large losses—the corporate finance group itself was told that it would be permitted to buy 1,000 shares of McDonnell & Company stock in the form of 750 shares of voting stock and 250 shares of nonvoting stock. When members of the group asked—as well they might—to see the latest figures on the firm, in order to justify the quite substantial investment they were about to make in it, they were told that the auditors were in the process of making an audit, and that no figures were available. The price at which the stock was to be offered, the group was assured, was based upon calculations made by chief financial officer Thomas McKay, and the personal accountants of Murray McDonnell.

The stock offer was, of course, another frantic attempt to raise money for the company. At about the same time, a memorandum, drafted by the then ailing Mr. McKay, was distributed to all McDonnell employees, suggesting that they, too, purchase stock in the company—and promptly. The memorandum indicated that the value of McDonnell stock was going to be increasing, and that therefore it would be to the employees' benefit to get in on the ground floor, before the price of the stock went up. According to SEC regulations, if a stock is offered to more than twenty-five people, it becomes an offering, and if the information presented to prospective buyers in that offering is untrue, the buyers can sue.

The memorandum did not disclose the fact that in the last quarter of 1968 alone McDonnell & Company had lost $1.8 million.

There were other complications. According to the rules of the New York Stock Exchange, the ratio of a firm's liabilities to its capital cannot ever exceed twenty to one. McDonnell & Company had commissioned the accounting firm of Lybrand, Ross Brothers & Montgomery to do an audit of its books, and Lybrand, Ross had come up with the alarming discovery that the firm's ratio of liabilities to capital was actually more than thirty to one. Discussions were also initiated with Lybrand, Ross to see whether that firm might be able to determine how seriously the mess in the back office was affecting McDonnell & Company's dealings. This idea, however, was never pursued.

Meanwhile, the computer system for the firm was still being worked on by Data Architects, and was still not finished. Again, the senior members of the firm must have realized that needed strides were not being made—certainly not being made quickly enough to clear up the mounting spiral of error and confusion in the back office. But Murray and his executives assured their associates and customers that Data Architects had only a few minor "bugs" to work out, and that soon all would be well and running smoothly. And yet an indication of the company's mixed-up accounting system was its "fail-to-deliver" situation. A fail-to-deliver is, quite simply, a situation in which a brokerage house sells securities to a customer and fails to deliver them. Because of the complexity of exchanging thousands of shares of stock from sellers to buyers, it is considered normal for a firm the size of McDonnell & Company to have fails-to-deliver in the amount of two to three million dollars a day. At McDonnell & Company by 1969 fails-to-deliver were already amounting to between eight and nine million dollars a day.

Interestingly enough, the lower echelon of employees in the company seems to have been much more aware of the firm's perilous state than its officers. Many of McDonnell & Company's customers' men, feeling that it was their responsibility to protect their customers, were already taking steps, in 1969, to see to it that they kept these customers in the event that the firm went out of business and the men themselves had to move on to other brokerage firms. There was a great deal of talk about interfirm stealing, whereby a salesman manages to get hold of stock registered in one company's name, and bring it with him, in his customer's behalf, to another company. How much of that was actually going on is anyone's guess, but one thing is sure: a lot of McDonnell & Company salesmen in the summer of 1969 were spending their lunch hours looking for other jobs. Murray McDonnell's family and friends, meanwhile, had become concerned about the number of hours Murray spent at the New York Athletic Club, his favorite watering place.

In July, 1969, Mr. Harry Lindh was made executive vice president of McDonnell & Company, to replace the late Mr. McKay as chief financial officer. Lindh had come from the firm of Faulkner, Dawkins & Sullivan, where he had also been chief financial officer. "Dreadful" was Mr. Lindh's only comment after examining the back-office situation. Rumors were by now circulating in Wall Street to the effect that the New York Stock Exchange was interested in what was happening at McDonnell, and it was at this point that Murray had to put up his additional $1.6 million in order to bring the company up to its capital requirements according to Rule Number 325 of the Stock Exchange.

While Murray and his partners were trying to placate the Stock Exchange, they fell to arguing among themselves, and with members of the McDonnell family who had interests in the company, over who was to blame and what was to be done. Some blamed Murray, and Murray blamed Data Architects and one of his partners, Thomas Cassidy. Others blamed Lawrence O'Brien, who, though he may have been a passable Postmaster General, seems to have been a bizarre choice to head a brokerage house. His reign, though brief, spanned several of the most disastrous months. In July, 1969, the subordinated debt holders—including Anne Ford Johnson and Murray's mother—met, and decided to bring in Paul MacDonald to effectively assume control of the firm. MacDonald had been with W. R. Grace & Company, and had managed money for the Church, but his stockbrokerage background was virtually nil. He was known, however, as a "hatchet man" who was good in turn-around situations. MacDonald's two chief backers were Deane Johnson, the California lawyer who had married Anne and wanted to protect his wife's interests, and Peter Flanigan, the Nixon aide who wanted to protect the interests of his sister, who was Murray's wife. Murray resented MacDonald's "interference," and there was more quarreling and blame-laying.

At this point, Murray announced that he had received commitments for financing ranging from three to ten million dollars. It was rumored that this money was to come from a group headed by Dan Lufkin and Louis Marx, the toy manufacturer. Lufkin was a senior partner in the highly successful brokerage firm of Donaldson, Lufkin & Jenrette and was, in addition to a friend of Murray's, a sort-of relative. His aunt, Mrs. Elgood Lufkin, was the former Marie Murray, whose first husband, John Vincent McDonnell, had been Murray McDonnell's uncle. In fact, Murray had received no commitments for financing from anyone. As soon as the Lufkin-Marx group had looked into, and seen, the shape that the company was in, they left without any offer of money whatever.

Harry Lindh's estimate of the back-office problem was an understatement. It was worse than dreadful. It was totally out of control. Throughout the final months of 1969 the firm continued to lose money, and as, concurrently, the stock market continued to decline in early 1970, McDonnell's losses continued. The $15 million that the firm had been worth in June, 1969, had completely evaporated by the early spring of 1970, and the company was now $3 million in the red. It owed customers another $8.5 million. Waiting for someone to administer the *coup de grâce* became a day-to-day affair, and finally, on the afternoon of March 12, 1970, Murray McDonnell announced that McDonnell & Company was going out of business. Employees emptied the contents of their desks into shopping bags. There was the usual anger, the usual secretaries' tears. A big company does not end with a bang, but with a whimper. McDonnell & Company was declared bankrupt the next morning. It was Friday the thirteenth.

The McDonnells lost whatever stake they had had in the company, which was considerable. To some people, it seemed that they were a case of shirtsleeves-to-shirtsleeves in less than two generations, and, in a way, they were. Actually, however, the family was not really ready for the poorhouse. Most of the McDonnells had, at this point, other resources to fall back on. Still, there was some serious belt-tightening to be done. One of Murray McDonnell's sisters confided to friends that she might, in a discreet way, take in boarders to help pay for the upkeep on her big Park Avenue apartment. Another sister, Charlotte, announced that she was taking a job at Saks Fifth Avenue as a fashion consultant, and her husband began taking jobs modeling men's fashions. (Still, a few months later, Charlotte was able to buy a new thoroughbred horse for her Southampton stable.) Anna Murray McDonnell announced that she would have to sell her big Southampton house. Fortunately, she had a ready buyer with ready cash—her granddaughter, Charlotte Ford. Anne Ford Johnson's divorce settlement from Henry Ford has never been announced, but it is assumed to be comfortably in seven figures. Brother Bish McDonnell is happy that he was able to extract himself from the company before all the troubles began. Anna Murray McDonnell is still able to keep up her big, antique-filled apartment at 660 Park Avenue. "And," she told friends not long after the holocaust, "no matter what has happened, nothing will ever persuade me to get rid of my butler, Paul." Paul still stands regally behind his mistress's chair while dinner is being served, announcing the courses as they appear, in French.

Chapter 25

AFTERMATH

In 1960, Murray McDonnell, then thirty-seven, had appeared the picture of cheery confidence in his company's spanking-new offices at 120 Broadway, their walls covered with expensive modern art, which, he said, many of his customers accused him of having had finger-painted by his children. He proudly pointed to the fact that the stocks recommended by his research department had performed 93.4 percent better than the Dow Jones Industrial Averages. Ten years later, he seemed not a broken man but older, quieter, a little sadder, the victim, he feels, of circumstances. Within his family, he is regarded not as a pariah, but with a curious and difficult mixture of bitterness and love; incompetence is a hard shortcoming to forgive. "Explain Murray to me," one of his sisters asked their mother. "He is my son," Mrs. McDonnell said simply.

Murray's brother-in-law, Peter Flanigan, is close to President Nixon in Washington and has been called a Mr. Fix-it for businessmen interested in high administration favors, and may have helped Murray's situation somewhat. But the punishment—barred for life from ever being a principal in a member firm of the New York Stock Exchange—was harsh enough, and Murray McDonnell has become *persona non grata* with the Securities and Exchange Commission. On April 13, 1970, another unlucky day, the SEC filed an action against Murray and his company in the United States District Court of the Southern District of New York, charging that from, on, or about November, 1968, to the then present time, McDonnell & Company and Murray had been, and were still, offering for sale, and selling, shares of the common stock of the company, and the promissory notes of the company, to over eighty McDonnell & Company employees for approximately $2.9 million. No registration statement, as required by the SEC, had been filed. As a result of this, Murray McDonnell was accused of "having directly and indirectly violated, are violating, and are about to violate Sections 5-A and 5-C of Securities Act 15, U.S.C. 77-Ea and 77-Ec." The complaint alleged that Murray had offered and sold stock and promissory notes of his company "by means of untrue statements of material facts and omissions to state material facts necessary in order to make the statements made."

The complaint went on to say that Murray had not stated the true condition of the McDonnell back-office operations, nor the true state of its books and records, and that McDonnell & Company had failed to comply with the financial requirements imposed upon the company, and other member firms, under Rule 325 of the New York Stock Exchange. It charged that Murray had concealed the large operating losses of the company, particularly for the period of September through December, 1968. On April 19, 1970, Murray McDonnell consented to the judgment against him: never again to sell stock in his company, and life banishment from any post in a member firm. He was, however, permitted to continue as a registered securities salesman on his own. He has managed to take a number of his old accounts with him, including those of the Catholic Church, and still manages to earn a large annual income from commissions.

There are, of course, the countless other lawsuits to be faced as a result of the company's demise, all arising out of the same charge: fraud and deception. Many of these cases may drag on for years, but at least one other judgment has been handed down against Murray, obtained in Illinois by George Mark, who had been one of the officers in Murray's firm, whom Murray had solicited to buy stock without the proper prospectus being filed with the SEC.

When a firm such as McDonnell & Company goes bankrupt, the Stock Exchange steps in. In order to see that customers of such a company do not lose money, or lose as little as possible, the New York Stock Exchange several years ago established a special trust fund, contributed to by all member firms. The fund is used to pay off customers who have had accounts with firms that have lost money, or have been unable to return their customers' securities. In the case of McDonnell & Company, the Stock Exchange had to pay off more than $8.5 million.

It is also, ironically, possible that a number of people profited greatly from the demise of McDonnell & Company. Because of the hopeless confusion in the back office, the sloppy record-keeping, and the nonfunctioning computer system, it was not easy to tell which customers had been paid off and which had not. A McDonnell customer might claim, for example, that he owned securities which the company had not sent him when, in fact, they had been sent to him. Such claims were often impossible to check. Or the customer might write for his securities, wait for an interval without receiving them, and then write again. If, in the interim between the two letters, the securities were mailed, new securities in the same amounts might, under the chaotic McDonnell system, be mailed out a second time. The customer might not choose to admit that he had been paid off twice, and there is no way of telling how many people were paid in duplicate or even in triplicate. When the lion dies, the jackals descend.

There are more than twenty million Americans of Irish descent in the United States today—six times the present population of Ireland—out of 47.5 million Roman Catholics, and as opposed to roughly six million Jews. They have succeeded, it might seem, by sheer force of numbers. But one of the great secrets of the success —and the failure—of the Irish in America is based on that mysterious ingredient known as charm. It was his charm that brought Alfred E. Smith very close to the White House, and helped bring John F. Kennedy, the first Irish Catholic President, all the way into it. Charm may also have helped destroy Kennedy, who insisted on riding bareheaded in an open car through the streets of Dallas (it would make a better impression). Charm for years made Grover Whalen the official "greeter" for New York City, and charm and an instinctive ability to please people gave John Ringling North the Greatest Show on Earth. There is charm in the voice of Morton Downey, and it was charm that made everyone want to shake the hand that shook the hand of John L. Sullivan.

Charm has sent the Irish in America sailing into High Society, and made a preoccupation with the upper classes a characteristic even of those who didn't quite go sailing in—as was the case with both John O'Hara and Scott Fitzgerald, whose fiction nearly always dealt with the ways of the very rich. Charm was at the heart of the appeal of fictional Irish, from Scarlett O'Hara to Kitty Foyle. It has been said that Ireland is a nation of poets, dreamers, and orators, and the Irish have certainly carried on this tradition in this country in the arts, letters, the theater, and politics. They have given us Lotta Crabtree, George M. Cohan, Victor Herbert, Laurette Taylor, Maureen O'Sullivan, Maureen O'Hara, Maureen Stapleton, Frank Fay, Patricia Collinge, James Cagney, Ray Bolger, Geraldine Fitzgerald, Barry Sullivan, Pat O'Brien,

Eugene O'Neill, John Drew, and all the Barrymores. They have given us lively entertainers and columnists—Ed and Pegeen Fitzgerald, Jack O'Brien, Pete Hamill, Frank Coniff, Bob Considine, Joseph X. Dever, Jimmy Breslin, and Joe Flaherty of the *Village Voice*. They have given us a string of Sullivans—Frank Sullivan, Mark Sullivan, Louis Sullivan, and Annie Sullivan, who gave "ears" to Helen Keller. There is even charm in Ed Sullivan's Celtic gloom. It was a kind of Celtic mysticism that led Bishop James Pike, born a Catholic but an Episcopalian convert, to wander into the desert to his death. It was his charm that led President Franklin D. Roosevelt to appoint Basil O'Connor to head up his March of Dimes. If a Jew, Raoul Fleischmann, published *The New Yorker*, and a Protestant, Harold Ross, edited it, it was an Irishman, appropriately—John Peter Toohey—who named it.

John Quinn, who was Thomas Fortune Ryan's lawyer and also one of the twentieth century's most important collectors of manuscripts and paintings, was Irish himself, but he affected a disdain for the race. Quinn once wrote, "Ireland consists of drunkards, murderers, thieves, humbugs, ex-policemen, Unionists—and honest men." He went on a draw up a chart of national stereotypes:

The French:	Cowardly, untrustworthy, and light-minded
The Spanish:	Lazy, cruel, guitar players, and untrustworthy
The Germans:	Fat, and very untrustworthy
The Americans:	Unprincipled, rushing, untrustworthy, and very nasty
The Japanese:	Imitative
The Irish:	All of the above, with the addition of not being funny any more

Mr. Quinn did not add charm to his list of Irish traits.

"Everything about the Irish is attractive," says Charlotte Mc-Donnell Harris. "They're beautiful-looking, witty, gay, and very brave." Mrs. Harris points out that Ireland was the first British colony, and the first to break the backbone of British colonial rule on the eastern side of the Atlantic. When Britain gave independence to Southern Ireland in 1922, after four years of terrorism and guerrilla warfare, Britain started down the long road of imperial withdrawal that would wind through India, Palestine, Kenya, and Cyprus. The Irish charm and willingness to do battle have made them excellent politicians, excellent salesmen. Murray McDonnell was a good salesman, and yet, in a way, his charm and salesmanship contributed to his downfall and disgrace because, if one is a salesman, one must have something sound to sell. Meanwhile, the family points out, Murray has taken his punishment like a man.

With charm, good looks, social poise, and sales ability has been linked another Irish trait—the dark and gloomy side of the Celtic nature. Perhaps this combination of characteristics has contributed to a problem that runs like a recurrent theme through Irish life—alcohol. Like the dashing and heavy-drinking Scott Fitzgerald and John O'Hara themselves, the Irish have provided—particularly in the 1920's and 1930's, when drinking was regarded as something of a social accomplishment—a number of dashing and hard-drinking figures who might have stepped right out of the pages of Fitzgerald or O'Hara novels. There was Judge Morgan J. O'Brien's son, Kenneth, who cut a striking social swathe in New York in the gilded, madcap era of Prohibition. Extraordinarily handsome, he had been a great social leader at Yale, in all the best clubs and honor societies. He is said to have been the prototype of a character in O'Hara's *Butterfield 8*, the splendid-looking judge's son who is sent to Yale for social polish, and then to Fordham Law School to gain local political know-how. Kenneth

O'Brien made a brilliant marriage—to Clarence Mackay's daughter, Katherine—and joined his father's law firm. But he drank too much, and was not too successful as a lawyer. Through his father's influence, he was appointed a justice of the New York State Supreme Court, though the legal profession and the Bar Association were critical of the appointment. He was a fair judge, but his drinking and high living led to his eventual divorce and early death.

A contemporary of Morgan J. O'Brien's, with the latter's same style, assurance, and social suavity (it was O'Brien who opened up Southampton to the Catholics), was James A. O'Gorman. A successful lawyer like O'Brien, O'Gorman was the first Irish Catholic to be elected to the United States Senate. It was in the days when state legislators still elected Senators, and the Democrats had at first backed William Sheehan, who was known as "Blue-Eyed Billy," and who had the support of Tammany Hall under Charles F. Murphy. But the Tammany Democrats were anathema to the wing of the Democrats of which Franklin D. Roosevelt, then a State Senator, was a leader. O'Gorman was then chosen as a compromise candidate to end the split, and this gave FDR his first state-wide prominence.

James O'Gorman's son, James A. O'Gorman, Jr., was every bit as handsome and popular as Kenneth O'Brien, but he, too, had a drinking problem. He became a lawyer too, but, perhaps because he was overshadowed by his father, he never matched his father's achievements.

George MacDonald was another imposing patriarchal figure. Born on a farm in western Pennsylvania, he had gone to Venezuela to seek his fortune, and found it, like Doheny and Buckley, in oil. He came back to New York and made another fortune in utilities. He had the appearance and the bearing of the actor C. Aubrey Smith, who specialized in playing roles of titled nobility in films. He had been made a Papal Marquis, and liked to be called Marquis MacDonald, and the Marquis was a glorious sight in his red Papal Chamberlain uniform at ceremonies in St. Patrick's Cathedral, or in his white tie and tails flashing with his assorted ribbons, medals, and decorations at the Knights of Malta banquets, where he was a Grand Master. His name decorated the boards of all sorts of corporations, and he loved clubs, belonging to the Metropolitan, the Turf and Field, the New York Yacht, the Piping Rock, the Creek, and the Pilgrims. At one point, he kept five private cigar vaults in five separate New York clubs.

His son, Byrnes MacDonald, was another glamorous young man in the twenties and thirties. At Princeton, he played polo and, because his father thought dormitory life would be too harsh for him, he rented a large private house near the Princeton campus where he lived with a manservant during his undergraduate years. Byrnes MacDonald's father had brought his son up to be a gentleman of leisure, and so Byrnes never worked at all. He devoted his life to society, travel, his clubs—he belonged to even more than his father—and partying.

Yale—perhaps because it was considered to wield more power on Wall Street than Harvard or Princeton—was usually the favorite college among F.I.F. families who did not send their sons to Catholic universities. An urbane and stylish and party-loving Yale dropout was Maurice B. ("Lefty") Flynn, whose father had become a wealthy New York insurance broker. At Yale, Lefty Flynn had been enormously popular—a varsity football player, a talented musician, in all the best clubs—and a wild and gilded youth of the glittering Cole Porter days. Halfway through college, he eloped with an actress, went to Hollywood, partied extensively, got a divorce, married another actress, and then became a movie actor, mostly in Westerns, married several more times, and finally settled down with Norah Langhorne, one of the famous Langhorne sisters of Virginia, one of whom became Lady Astor. Lefty and Norah Flynn became one of Hollywood's most glamorous, popular, party-going couples.

Another famous Yale Irishman was Tom Shevlin, who was an

All-American end in the early 1900's. The son of a Minnesota lumber tycoon, he was every bit as colorful and popular in the raccoon-coated Stutz-Bearcatted era of New Haven as Lefty Flynn, and his father supplied him with unlimited funds for automobiles, clothes, entertainment, and whiskey. After college, however, Tom Shevlin settled down with the family lumber business and worked successfully at it, though he died young. His children became prominent as social figures in New York and Palm Beach, and one of his daughters-in-law received a great deal of publicity when it was reported that she had been the secret "first wife" of John F. Kennedy—an allegation that was denied by the Kennedys, and has never been proven.

Even in proper, WASPish Boston, the Irish charm and good looks have gradually helped the Irish Catholics make social inroads. Until quite recently, Irish names hardly ever appeared on the boards of Boston's most prestigious banks, corporations, museums, and hospitals, and there were virtually no Irish Catholic members of the elite Vincent and Somerset clubs. If an Irish name appeared on the letterhead of a prominent Boston law firm, it was assumed to be there only for the purpose of dealing with Boston's Irish politicians. Recently, however, the situation has been changing, though it is still considered "better" in Boston if an Irishman is from somewhere else. If, for instance, he has come to Boston from New York or California, via a correct New England prep school and Yale, he will have a better chance of being accepted socially—and rising in business—than a boy who was born in Dorchester and went to Boston College.

Throughout the story of the Irish in America runs the theme of money—money and, with it, social acceptance. If anything, money has been more a preoccupation with the Irish than it has been with the Jews, who tended, when they made money, to spend it more on philanthropy and cultural endeavors than on high living, great houses, and fast cars. Second only to the Church, and keeping the Faith, has been the importance of making money to American Irish families. J. Patrick Lannan, the multimillionaire industrialist, has recalled how, as a child, his Irish father drummed into him the necessity of making money, getting ahead, making more money. Whenever old man Lannan was approached by one of his children for money, he would wail, "Sure, an' it's a beggar's ass I'll be scratching when I'm ninety!"

Scott Fitzgerald himself liked to point out that on one side of his family, the Fitzgeralds, was aristocracy; the other side was peasant. "I have a streak of peasant vulgarity that I like to cultivate," he said (and in his celebrated drinking bouts he certainly managed to achieve his aim). His mother, Fitzgerald used to say, was "a rich peasant," Milly McQuillan. She kept telling him, "All this family stuff is a lot of bull. All you have to know is where the money is coming from." And John O'Hara, through all of whose novels the money theme runs strong, remained embittered that his father, a prosperous doctor, died without leaving enough money for his son to go to Yale. O'Hara had to go out and get a job instead. O'Hara complained so bitterly, and so often, about this deprivation in his life that, many years later when O'Hara was in his forties, a friend commented, "Let's take up a collection to send John to Yale."

Chapter 26

"ROBERT THE ROUÉ"

Probably the circumstances that distress the founding fathers of the First Irish Families—if they are indeed watching their voluminous broods from their Catholic heaven—would involve the many instances of divorce, mixed marriage, and subsequent lapses from the Church that have occurred among members of the later generations. Of the fourteen children of James Francis McDonnell, four have been divorced, although only one—Anne Ford—has remarried, and to a divorced man. (Her brother, Gerard McDonnell, divorced his wife, and then remarried her a week later.) Today, even the site of the great Ford wedding is gone—washed out to sea in a great Northeaster storm. In 1956, Jeanne Murray and Alfred Gwynne Vanderbilt were divorced after eleven years of marriage and two children, and Vanderbilt married another Jean—Jean Harvey, related to the Chicago Cudahys. Jeanne Vanderbilt, though she has been "romantically linked" in the press with a number of men, from

Joseph L. Mankiewicz to Pete Rozelle, has never remarried. Her brother, Jake Murray, has been married three times, divorced twice (his second wife died), and has left the Church.

Others have had marriages of which the older generation would most certainly have disapproved. The two "perfect convent girls," the Ford sisters, have both entered into unions which cannot have pleased the Sisters of the Sacred Heart of Mary who taught them: Anne to an Italian stockbroker, Giancarlo Uzielli, whose mother was a Jewish Rothschild; Charlotte to the Greek shipping tycoon Stavros Niarchos after his divorce from his second wife, Eugenie (whose sister Tina had divorced another shipping tycoon, Aristotle Onassis, five years earlier). The Niarchos yacht *Creole*, if not the largest in the world, is certainly the most lavishly decorated, with a three-million-dollar art collection purchased from the late Edward G. Robinson which includes several Van Goghs, Renoirs, a Gauguin, and a Rouault. The Niarchoses, who were married hastily by a judge in Juarez, Mexico, have since been divorced, after one child, and Charlotte Ford, after resuming her maiden name for a while, has remarried. Niarchos, meanwhile, has married his second wife's sister, Tina, after her divorce from her second husband, the Marquis of Blandford. What—if he is looking down from above—can Great-Grandpa Murray be thinking of such proceedings? He who would not even permit his children to date a Protestant. And what would he have thought when one of his grandsons, H. Lester Cuddihy, Jr., married his sister's governess, Gabrielle? Gabrielle, however, received her mother-in-law's usual gift of a mink coat, just as all the other girls in the family did.

Perhaps the most unusual F.I.F. marriage of all occurred in 1972 when another of Thomas E. Murray's great-grandchildren, Jeanne Murray Vanderbilt's daughter Heidi, was married to young Jones Harris, the son of the producer Jed Harris (né Jacob Horowitz) and Ruth Gordon, the actress. A year earlier, Heidi

Vanderbilt's brother, Alfred G. Vanderbilt, Jr., married a girl named Alison Platten. He is the first Vanderbilt to be a rock musician, and plays the electric bass guitar with a group called the Fine Wine, which he helped found. The couple were married in the Presbyterian Church.

"We are all victims of the Ecumenical Council," says Charlotte McDonnell Harris, referring to the Church's recent, more relaxed stand on divorce and marriage to non-Catholics. "We were brought up to think that divorce was unthinkable, that marriage was for all eternity. There were some people who could manage to get their marriages annulled in Rome, but it took years and cost a fortune. Now it can be done quickly and inexpensively in a matter of weeks. It's very difficult, when all your life you've been taught that something is a sin and then, all at once, you're told that it isn't." Another in the family says, "It used to be all so simple—simple and beautiful. A thing was either black or white, right or wrong, a sin or not a sin. It used to be lovely. If you lost something, you prayed to St. Jude, and you were sure that you would find it again. Before the girls' basketball game at Sacred Heart, you prayed for your team to win, and you prayed again at timeouts. You took no chances. If God saw every sparrow, wouldn't he also see a set shot from midcourt? It made no difference that members of our rival team at Blessed Sacrament were praying for their team too. For every sin or shortcoming, there was punishment, a moral. If a girl did not bathe every day and wash her hands before meals, she would get leprosy. First her fingers would rot, then her toes, then her nose. One by one, the parts of your body turned yellow, smelled horribly, and then dropped off. If a boy cursed and used profanity, he would get cancer of the tongue. If he repented, his last words before his tongue was cut out would be 'Jesus, Mary, Joseph.' The mystery and magic of the Church have been taken away by this modernization, the Latin gone from the liturgy. The Church has changed a lot in the last ten years, and in my opinion the change has not been for the good." The Church still will not condone remarriage after a divorce, and so those who wish to remarry must leave the Church—or accept the fact that they are living in sin.

Not all the younger members of the First Irish Families have drifted away from the Church, of course. When Auntie Marie Murray celebrated her eightieth birthday at the Windham Mountain Club not long ago, more than a hundred of her grandchildren were in attendance, and Mrs. Murray was proud to point out that every single one of them was attending a Catholic school. Another of Grandpa Thomas E. Murray's granddaughters, Mary Jane Cuddihy MacGuire, remains a staunch and devout Catholic "right down the line," despite her husband's early death. Mary Jane MacGuire not only adheres strictly to her religion, but she has inherited an Irish temper, and is something of a firebrand. In New York a few years ago she attended a theater which was presenting a revue called *Beyond the Fringe*. One of the skits included a pantomime of three figures standing with arms raised, one actor wearing a halo, which she deemed to be a parody and mockery of the Crucifixion. She telephoned the producer and threatened to set fire to the theater if the skit was not dropped. When this didn't work, she telephoned the Chancery office and lodged a caustic formal complaint. Eventually, she succeeded in getting to Father Laurence McGinley, the president of Fordham, who threatened to send down the whole Fordham basketball team to break up the place if the sketch was not stopped. It was stopped.

Several years ago, in an economy move, the City of New York announced that it would discontinue the traditional practice of painting a green line down the center of Fifth Avenue for the annual Saint Patrick's Day parade. This news made Mary Jane MacGuire indignant; it seemed a slight to the Irish. Her daughter Bea was also irked by the city's move and, with a group of her teenage Irish Catholic friends, the girls decided that they would paint the green stripe down Fifth Avenue *themselves*. Mary Jane Mac-Guire helped the girls mix the green paint in her Park Avenue kitchen.

The girls went out on the night before the parade with their paint cans and brushes, started to paint, and were promptly arrested for malicious mischief. They were herded into a paddy wagon and marched into New York's Women's House of Detention, proudly singing "The Wearin' of the Green." The arresting officer turned out to be an Irish Protestant. The judge was black. But Mary Jane MacGuire had engaged a Jewish lawyer, and the girls were soon released and the charges dropped.

The most glamorous and in many ways the most bizarre of all Thomas E. Murray's grandchildren was Mary Jane Cuddihy's younger brother Bob. Of all her brothers, Mary Jane loved Bob the most—loved him, even though she was often critical of him. Tall, slender, and dazzlingly handsome, he possessed a wild Irish sense of humor and fun, and an even wilder Irish temper. He loved girls, sports, parties, adventure, and in the late 1930's and 1940's he was the personification of Flaming Youth and, at the same time, frequently the despair of his family. Still, the warmth and glow of his charm were of such intensity that it was impossible not to forgive his pranks. Everybody loved Bob Cuddihy, and he flashed across the lives of his friends and family like a playful star. His cousin Jake Murray made Bob the hero of his novel, *The Devil Walks on Water*—a turbulent, fast-moving, unpredictable, and overwhelming character named Briney Mitchel. But the family has always felt that the novel never really did Bob justice.

Bob Cuddihy seemed to have been born in the eye of a hurricane, and, in fact, his name first hit the newspapers in 1937 when he was rescued by a Rhode Island state trooper and a fire chief after drifting for an hour in a leaky rowboat in choppy seas off Narragansett Bay. He was then a freshman at Portsmouth Priory, and had grown tired of playing with the rowboat on shore and so had just let himself drift off on his own. That night he was the center of attention among his fellow students with the tales of his adventure. A year later, his name was in the papers again. Thirteen-year-old Bob Cuddihy and a young classmate had disappeared from Portsmouth during the 1938 hurricane. The youths were gone for days, and were feared dead. During the search, a young man who looked very much like the missing Cuddihy boy turned up at the Hancock Pharmacy at Seventy-second Street and Madison Avenue in New York, not far from his family's house, and ordered an ice cream soda. "Aren't you the boy they're looking for?" the druggist asked him. "No, that's my brother," the young man replied.

It turned out that the two boys had been on an extended junket up and down the East Coast, walking for miles over washed-out roads and through flooded cities, having the time of their lives. They had hitchhiked to Providence, Boston, up into Maine, had tried to get to Canada, had come back to New York, and had, in all, covered more than a thousand miles in their travels. They were finally found asleep on a bench in the Baldwin Long Island Railroad station. They hadn't liked the school, they explained, and had figured that in the middle of a hurricane was the perfect time to run away.

Bob Cuddihy didn't like schools of any variety, and, in all, he was enrolled in—and escaped from—some thirteen different schools, including Portsmouth, Canterbury, Cranwell, Lawrence Smith, Georgetown—every Catholic school his parents could find. Cranwell, his mother used to note, was the only school that ever paid her the tuition back. At one point, he even ended up in a school for retarded children. A priest whom the family had consulted about the situation had mistaken the nature of the problem, and recommended the school. "What kind of a school *is* this, anyway?" he asked his parents on the telephone after a day or so. "There's one guy here who does nothing but bang on a drum all day long." His parents, however, decided to keep him there. After all, they reasoned, at least it was a school. He did not stay long.

The last school tried was Loyola in Montreal. From Loyola he ran away and enlisted in the Canadian Army. He was only fourteen, but, because he looked older than his years, he was taken in. Army life bored him, and so he deserted. The Canadian Army tried to court-martial him for desertion, but, when they discovered that he was under-age, there was nothing they could do. In his car in Southampton he would drive across lawns, between trees and hedges, to take short cuts to his cousins' houses, where he would park outside windows, toot his horn, and gather up all the children to take them to Corwith's Pharmacy for sodas and ice cream. If Corwith's happened to be closed, he would bang on the door so loudly that one would suppose a prescription was needed for a dying man. Once the door opened a crack, Bob would insert a foot and then argue and wheedle so attractively that eventually the manager would relent and let the group troop in. Once his sister Mary Jane discovered that she needed dinner rolls before a party at her house in Rye. Gristede's was closed. "Don't worry, I'll open Gristede's for you," he said cheerfully, and did. There was a song of the period called "Robert the Roué from Reading, P.A.," and that became Bob's nickname. Later, it was shortened to "The Roo." Some of his friends also called him "Fearless Freddie."

Robert the Roué disliked work as much as he disliked school, though a succession of jobs was tried. Nothing stuck and, at one point, his mother took him to Children's Court—to scare him, more than anything else. Gaily he telephoned his girl friend before departing for court, "Don't worry—this is just a put-up job. I'll see you tonight." Nonetheless, for a while a parole officer called at his house each morning to escort him to his place of employment. When his father tried cutting off his spending money, he promptly sued his father for nonsupport. While his parents spent the weekdays in their New York house, Bob and his raft of friends took over the Southampton place, where they passed most of their time partying and running up bills at local shops and liquor stores. His sister remonstrated with him. "Look," she said, "you're suing Daddy for nonsupport. But you've got him supporting you *and* all your friends." For spending money, he took etchings off the walls of the Seventy-third Street house and sold them. How did he manage to get away with such behavior? Because of his great good looks and bursting charm.

Naturally, he loved night life and was a popular figure at such bright spots as Armando's and the old El Morocco. Once he confided to a reporter that he had vowed never again to taste anything stronger than ginger ale, and yet, a few nights later, he was at El Morocco with his friends drinking champagne.

In 1945, when he was barely twenty-one, he announced his marriage to a beautiful socialite-actress named Betsy Ryan—Scotch-Irish Protestant, and no kin of the other Ryans. He had met Betsy at a party at Armando's, and Nancy Randolph, society editor of the *Daily News*, learned of the secret even before Bob's dismayed parents. Earlier that year his cousin Jeanne had eloped with Alfred Vanderbilt, and, the following year, both the Vanderbilts and the Bob Cuddihys were dropped from the *Social Register*.

The marriage was, as might have been expected, tempestuous, stormy, though party-filled, with many nights at night clubs. Once, after a party, when Bob Cuddihy was stopped for speeding and was asked to show his license and registration, the policeman threatening to take away both, Betsy hit the patrolman over the head with the heel of her high-heeled slipper. There were quarrels, separations, reconciliations. Bob Cuddihy became jealous of the attentions paid to Betsy by Marion Hargrove, the writer. Finally, in 1951, from his fourteen-room house in Southampton, Bob Cuddihy announced that he and Betsy were getting a divorce. They had been married just six years, and there were five small children. "She's left me several times before," Bob told a reporter at El Morocco, "and now she's left for good." He added wearily, "I'm sorry to have taken so much of your time. I wish I could say that at least I'd known you before spilling my troubles to you. I wish I could say we'd even met once. In fact," he sighed, "I wish I could say I even read your column."

Seven months later, Betsy Cuddihy married a Southampton real-estate man named Lawrence Godbee, who had four children of his own by a previous marriage. At the time, she surrendered custody of her own children to Bob Cuddihy. The children adored their father, and spent several years living alone with him. There was always excitement of one form or another. Once the garage burned down, and, when he had collected the insurance money, Bob Cuddihy asked the children if it wouldn't be more fun to have a swimming pool than a new garage. The children agreed, and so the money was used to build the pool. Then, in 1956, Bob Cuddihy announced his marriage to a Knoxville, Tennessee, girl named Mary Smiley, a coolly blonde and beautiful television and fashion model—and another Protestant—whom the family promptly nicknamed "the unsmiling Miss Smiley." Unsmiling or not, the new Mrs. Cuddihy took her husband's children under her wing.

Not quite nine months later, at quarter of eight on a summer evening, Bob Cuddihy was driving his car—fast, as usual—along the Dune Road in Westhampton Beach. He was traveling east and ahead lay the Surf 'n' Sand Restaurant when his car went out of control. It skidded, sidewiped a telephone pole, skidded again, turned over, and burst into flames. In the crash, the driver was thrown fifteen feet from the car. At first he seemed unhurt, cheerful and nonchalant as ever. But he was taken to Riverhead Hospital, where he died four hours later of internal injuries. Robert the Roué was dead at the age of thirty-two.

One of the first to hear the news was his sister Mary Jane. Their mother was spending the summer on the Jersey shore, where she was recovering from a heart attack. Mary Jane decided that she must break the news to her mother as gently and as gradually as possible, lest she suffer another attack. She telephoned her and said, "Mother, there's been an accident, and Bob's badly hurt. He may not live." Immediately her mother asked, "Has he seen a priest?" Mary Jane—who at that point did not know the answer to the question—replied, "Yes." "Did he receive the Last Rites?" Mary Jane replied again, "Yes. He's back in the Church." Her mother sighed, relieved at least of that anxiety.

Next Mary Jane telephoned Riverhead Hospital and asked, "Did my brother see a priest?" Yes, she was told, a priest had visited him, and she was given the priest's name. She then got the priest on the telephone—"a dumb Irish priest," she says—and asked him if he had administered the Last Rites. "No," the priest told her. "I looked in on him, but he didn't seem sick enough. I didn't do anything." "You fool," she said, "would it interest you to know that he's dead?" She slammed down the phone.

She had lied to her mother. But she decided that she would have to let the lie stand. After all, she could not bear to have her mother go through the rest of her life believing, as she would have to believe if she knew the truth, that her son was in hell, and forever.

The trouble was, of course, that a Catholic who is known publicly to be living outside the Church, and who has not been received back, cannot be buried in consecrated ground. Mary Jane telephoned the pastor at St. Thomas More Church in New York, Monsignor Philip J. Furlong, and explained the situation to him, asking him whether, out of consideration for her ailing mother, her brother could not have a Catholic burial. No, Monsignor Furlong replied, he could not; it was absolutely out of the question. The next morning, since there was no time to be lost, Mary Jane Cuddihy MacGuire herded her brother's five small children into her car and drove to New York, and to Monsignor

Furlong's office, where she sat the children down before the priest. She began asking the children questions. "Who took you to Mass every Sunday?" They replied, "Our daddy did." "Who taught you your catechism?" They replied, "Our daddy did." She continued with the questions, and each time the response was the same. She asked, "Where is your daddy now?" They answered, "Our daddy is in heaven." Suddenly the priest rose from his chair, eyes brimming, and excused himself. He came back a few minutes later and said, "I've just talked to the Chancery, to Cardinal Spellman. It's all right."

And so Bob Cuddihy was buried a Catholic, and the secret of the lie lived on, locked in Mary Jane's heart.

Bob Cuddihy's death touched off a terrible court battle for custody of the children. Their mother, Betsy, now Mrs. Godbee, wanted them back. Bob's widow swore that his dying words to her had been "I'm dying, Mary—please take care of the kids." Mary Smiley Cuddihy's lawyers contended that Betsy Godbee was an unfit mother, that she was an alcoholic. Bob's brother confirmed this. Betsy's lawyers contended that she had reformed and no longer drank, and there was confused testimony as to whether she had ever been an alcoholic or whether she had suffered, instead, from a form of epilepsy. A nurse, Stella Gray of Southampton, testifying in Bob's widow's behalf, said, on the contrary, that Betsy had often given the children liquor "for their colds," and that she had once crashed her car into a tree and emerged from the accident "so drunk she couldn't walk a straight line." On another occasion, the nurse stated, Betsy had spent over two hours in the Southampton house, raging drunk and smashing windows. In the end, however, the court awarded the children to Betsy, who, after all, was their natural mother. At one point while all this was going on, two of Bob Cuddihy's brothers were walking on the road at Westhampton, not far from where the accident had occurred, when one of them spotted a matchbook cover fluttering in the wind. He picked it up and saw that it advertised the Federal Pacific Electric Corporation of Long Island of Long Island City, their brother's last employer. He had been the firm's district sales manager. The matchbook cover appeared weathered at the edges. "I've kept the matchbook cover, and put it in a frame," John Murray Cuddihy says. "Very black Irish of me I suppose, but I keep it as a reminder of what happened to Bob."

That was in the summer of 1957. A year or so later, Mary Smiley Cuddihy was married again, to a man named Arthur M. Murray, Jr., a Catholic and in the *Social Register*, but no relation to any of the other Murrays, nor to the Arthur Murray Dance Studio family.

In the fall of 1961, Betsy Cuddihy Godbee was driving her ten-year-old Packard convertible along Deerfield Road in Water Mill. Failing to negotiate a sharp left curve, her car left the road, crashed through a rail fence and into two large oak trees. The impact of the crash was so severe that her body was thrown completely through the windshield of her car. She died two and half hours later in Southampton Hospital without regaining consciousness. Now Bob Cuddihy's children—Robbie, Edith, Sean, Christopher, and a little girl named Michael Elizabeth—were orphans.

So the children, now aged seven to fifteen, were plunged into another custody fight, one which turned Cuddihys against Cuddihys. One of Bob's brothers, Thomas M. Cuddihy, had been named executor of Betsy Godbee's estate, and at the time of her death assumed custody of his nieces and nephews. But there were those in the family who questioned Tom Cuddihy's qualifications to stand *in loco parentis*, including the children's two grandmothers, Mrs. Lester Cuddihy and Mrs. Leonard Ryan.

The grandmothers—who, after all, as older ladies could not have been exactly overjoyed at the sudden prospect of five small children to care for—did at length agree to let Tom have custody, but only on one condition: the grandmothers were to have regular visitation privileges, in order to be able to check on how things were going. Then Tom Cuddihy did an astonishing thing. Without consulting or advising anyone, and in defiance of a court order, he shipped all five children off to England. The two older children were enrolled in Kilquahanity House, Castle Douglas, Scotland, and the three younger ones were placed in the controversial Summerhill School in Leiston, England. Summerhill, now defunct, was known as a school run by the children themselves; study was optional, and the child was his own boss. It was known as "the most revolutionary school in Great Britain," where students were given "absolute freedom"—academically, theologically, and sexually.

Immediately Mrs. Lester Cuddihy filed an action against her son, demanding that his guardianship rights be revoked. She complained that not only could she not visit her grandchildren, as ordered by the court, but she could not even communicate with them. Of his mother's suit against him, Tom Cuddihy commented matter-of-factly at the time, "Well, the only thing I know is that all of the kids are happy at the moment—we correspond back and forth and I hope to get over there by Christmas." He had put the children in schools abroad, he said, because, "all things considered, the educational opportunities there are better both on my budget and because of the limited amount of money available to the children."

Other Cuddihys joined the foray. John Murray Cuddihy wrote a lengthy letter to the judge who was hearing the case, denouncing his own brother as "erratic and unreliable."

The battle dragged on for months and, meanwhile, the children, protected from all the family discord surrounding their future by the width of the Atlantic Ocean, began to enjoy the new surroundings in which their Uncle Tom had placed them. They had indeed been banged around a lot, and, after all of that, the sunny greenness of the British Isles must have seemed extraordinarily peaceful. Their letters home were happy and hopeful, even though one of the younger ones, Sean, achieved the unusual distinction of being the only child ever expelled from permissive Summerhill; he was placed in another English school. They did not *want* to come back to New York. And so, in the end, the grandmothers relented. Both women were getting older, and Mrs. Cuddihy was ailing. It became, in the end, a question of: if Tom Cuddihy, who wanted to be their guardian, was not permitted to be, who else was there who was willing or able to assume the job? The children, though they made occasional visits home, remained in Britain, where they became thoroughly Anglicized. Relations between Tom Cuddihy and the rest of his family have, meanwhile, remained somewhat cool. Today, Tom's brothers and sisters do not know where Tom lives.

On July 31, 1970, the *New York Times* published an announcement of the marriage of Robert the Roué's oldest son, Robert A. Cuddihy, Jr., to a Scottish girl named Elizabeth Bryden, from the village of Lockerbie, near Kilquahanity in Dumfriesshire where Robbie had gone to school. The bridegroom was at the time a student at the University of Edinburgh, and the couple were married in the Protestant Church of Scotland. Robbie had come back to the United States for a while and attended Portsmouth Priory, which pleased his grandmother. But his heart was in the Highlands, and he returned to graduate from Scotland's Napier College. Like his great-grandfather, old Grandpa R. J. Cuddihy, he had become a publisher, having bought a firm called Islander Publications, whose fortnightly newspaper, the *Islander*, Robbie Cuddihy himself published from the island of Arran. He had also become active in the Labour Party, and edited the Red Paper on Education, a critique of the British educational system.

The *Times* announcement was unusual in that it printed a photograph of the couple's wedding invitation, which was, as the *Times* put it with its usual understatement, "a move away from strictures of etiquette." Printed in sepia on poster-weight paper, the invitation was eight inches wide and sixteen inches long, and it displayed a photograph of the bride and groom—Robbie looking very British with a walking stick, high collar, and big Windsor-knotted tie with a regimental stripe—posed, smiling and happy, on the steps of the church prior to the ceremony. What would Emily Post have thought? Clearly, Robbie Cuddihy is the uncommon product of an uncommon father, an uncommon uncle, and an uncommon family.

Our story ends on a note of grace.

Many years after her brother Bob's violent death, Mary Jane Cuddihy MacGuire was at a New York cocktail party. There she fell into conversation with a young Catholic priest and, during the course of it, let drop the fact that her maiden name had been Cuddihy. The priest was thoughtful for a moment, and then asked her, "Did your family ever have a summer place in the Hamptons?" Yes, she replied, they all had had places there for years.

"Did you have a relative named Robert Cuddihy?" he asked her.

"Yes, he was my brother," she replied.

"You know," the priest said, "I rented a little place out there for the summer of 1957, on the Dune Road at Westhampton Beach. One night there was an automobile accident not far from my house. I heard the crash, and went out to see if there was anything I could do to help. The young man said he was a Catholic. It wasn't till the next day that I learned from the newspaper that his name was Robert Cuddihy. He didn't look to me to be in too bad shape, but, just in case, I administered the Last Rites to him."

And so the lie, which she had believed for so many years to have been a lie, turned out, in the end, not to have been a lie at all. Before his death, Bob Cuddihy had been received back into the Church.

"I think it was St. Augustine who said that God always writes straight, but in crooked lines," Mary Jane MacGuire says. "We

298

may not always understand His ways, or His reasons, or His aims or plan for us at the time, but in the end it all becomes clear—clear as a bell. It's one of the reasons why my faith is so strong, so indestructible. My faith has carried me through my husband's death, Bob's death, the death of one of my own babies, and the fact that one of my other children is retarded. When my baby died, I didn't go to a psychiatrist, I went to a priest. I need a church whenever I know I'm wrong. I'd die if I didn't have my faith and the Church. I could be King of England, and I'd die if I couldn't have the Sacrament. That's all. I'd just die."

Petition addressed to the descendants of

Thomas E. Murray

File No. 6561 - 1929

THE PEOPLE OF THE STATE OF NEW YORK
BY THE GRACE OF GOD, FREE AND INDEPENDENT:

TO: Daniel Bradley Murray, Katherine Murray McQuail, Anna
Murray McDonnell, Julia Murray Cuddihy, Marie Murray Lufkin,
Jeanne Durand Murray, Therese M. Cummings, Rosamond Murray
Byers, Joan Murray Boucher, Marcia Murray Cavanagh, Judith Mur-
ray Donovan, Thomas E. Murray, Jr., Marie Murray Harris, James
Brady Murray, Rev. D. Bradley Murray, S.J., Anne Murray O'Neil,
Jane Murray Sheridan, Francis Brady Murray, Joseph G. Murray,
S.J., Peter Murray, Margot Murray, Jeanne Murray Vanderbilt,
Patricia Murray Roche, John Francis Murray, Catherine Murray
McManus, Constance Anne Murray (Sister Saint Joseph), Mary
Elizabeth M. Coniff, Thomas Edward Murray, II, Herbert Lester
Cuddihy, Jr., Jane Cuddihy MacGuire, John Murray Cuddihy, Robert

Anthony Cuddihy, Thomas Murray Cuddihy, Michael Cuddihy, Ann Marie Cuddihy, John Vincent McDonnell Lufkin, Thomas E. Murray McDonnell Lufkin, Marie Murray Lufkin, Catherine McDonnell Sullivan, James F. McDonnell, Jr., Anne McDonnell Ford, Charlotte McDonnell Harris, Thomas E. Murray McDonnell, Charles Edward McDonnell, Gerard McDonnell, Genevieve McDonnell Bissell, Sheila McDonnell Cooley, Mary McDonnell, Barbara McDonnell Hennessy, Sean McDonnell, Margaret Mary McDonnell, Morgan McDonnell, Walter Cummings, III, Keith Cummings, Mark Cummings, Buckley M. Byers, Jr., Joseph M. Byers, Joan Bradley Boucher, Jerome H. P. Boucher, Jr., David Farrell Boucher, Frank Burns Cavanagh, Marina Murray Cavanagh, Carol Cavanagh, Edward J. Donovan, III, Rita Marie Murray, Maureen Anne Murray, Thomas E. Murray, III, Daniel Bradley Murray, George H. Murray, Marie Murray Harris, Anne Murray Harris, Basil Harris, III, Margaret Mary Harris, Thomas Murray Harris, Katherine Lewis Harris, Robert Harris, James B. Murray, Jr., Matthew Murray, Christopher Murray, Robert Murray, Stephen Murray, Andrew Murray, Paul B. Murray, Jr., Joseph G. Murray, Anne M. Murray, John Thomas Murray, Marie Barbara Murray, Stephen Joseph O'Neil, Peter Anthony O'Neil, Thomas I. Sheridan, III, Jane Frances Sheridan, Marie Murray Sheridan, Herbert Lester Cuddihy, III, Henri Andre Cuddihy, Judith Ann MacGuire, Beatrice Ann MacGuire, Julia Murray MacGuire, James Joseph MacGuire, Myles Phillip MacGuire, Thomas Murray Cuddihy, Jr., Jacqueline Adele Cuddihy, Patricia Murray Cuddihy, Robert A. Cuddihy, Jr., Elizabeth Cuddihy, Sean Cuddihy, Michael Cuddihy, Christopher Cuddihy, Diana Marie Lufkin, David Warren Lufkin, Bradley Moulton Lufkin, Marie Murray Lufkin, Suzanne Marie Lufkin, Heidi de Lourdes Vanderbilt, Alfred Gwynne Vanderbilt, Jr., Deidre Murray Roche, Robin Durand Roche, Hilary Somers Roche, Melinda Gray Murray, John Francis Murray, III, Thomas Bradley Murray, Helen Sayre Murray, Anthony Francis Conniff, Michael Andrew Conniff, James F. McDonnell, III, George McDonnell, Reece McDonnell, Louise Fayra McDonnell, Patricia Anne McDonnell, Michael Flanigan McDonnell, Meegan Aimee McDonnell, Stephen McDonnell, Charlotte Ford, Anne Ford, Edsel Ford, Richard L. Harris, Jr., Meegan Harris, Laura Harris, Charles E. McDonnell, Jr., Mary Kathryn McDonnell, John F. Hennessy, III, Raymond P. Sullivan, III, Maureen Anne Sullivan, Sheila Anne Sullivan, Kevin Paul Sullivan, Karen Sullivan, Sheila Cooley, Leslie Anne Cooley, Richard Pierce Cooley, Jr., Anne McDonnell, Morgan McDonnell, Jr., James Ford McDonnell, Dirk Peter McDonnell,

SEND GREETING:

WHEREAS, Joseph Bradley Murray, Thomas E. Murray and Paul B. Murray, who reside respectively at the Pierre Hotel, Fifth Avenue and 61st Street, 686 Park Avenue, both in the Borough of Manhattan, New York City, and Red Ground Road, Old Westbury, Nassau County, State of New York, have presented their account as Trustees of the Last Will and Testament of Thomas E. Murray, deceased, lately residing at 783 St. Marks Avenue, Borough of Brooklyn, County of Kings, City and State of New York, and a petition praying that their account as surviving Trustees of the trusts created by the terms of paragraphs SECOND, THIRD, FOURTH, FIFTH, SIXTH, SEVENTH and EIGHTH of the Last Will and Testament of Thomas E. Murray, deceased, may be judicially settled, that payments by them of income for the account of any minor made to his or her parent or to the infant himself or herself, as shown by the accounts filed herein, be approved, that payments made out of principal and income to the beneficiaries, as shown by the said accounts, be approved, that the said Trustees be authorized and empowered to file in this Court restrictions on the power of appointment now in their possession or which may hereafter be delivered to them, that they may be granted permission to resign as Trustees of such separate trusts as they may designate upon the termination of these proceedings, and upon the filing by said Trustees of an instrument in writing selecting their successors, pursuant to the provisions of paragraph EIGHTH of the said Last Will and Testament, and that they be allowed such single commissions as they may be lawfully

303

entitled to receive on the principal of the various trusts embraced herein, and that the persons above named may be cited to show cause why such settlement and the relief above set forth should not be had.

NOW, THEREFORE, you and each of you are hereby cited to show cause before our Surrogate's Court of the County of Kings, to be held in the Court Room at the Hall of Records, in the County of Kings, on the 30 day of April 1956, at 9:30 o'clock in the forenoon, why such settlement and the relief above set forth should not be had.

IN TESTIMONY WHEREOF, we have caused the Seal of our said Surrogate's Court to be hereto affixed.

WITNESS, HON. MAXIMILIAN MOSS, Surrogate of our said County, at the Borough of Brooklyn, in the said County, the 24th day of February 1956.

ALBERT M. LEAVITT
Clerk of the Surrogate's Court.

INDEX

Grace Steamship Line, 192, 232
Graham, Sir James, 13
Grand Knights of the Holy Sepulchre, 243
Grant, Ulysses S., Jr., 137
Gray, Stella, 294
"Great Elm," Sharon, Conn., Buckley estate, 212, 217, 219, 220
Greeley, Father Andrew M., 250
Greenwich, Conn., 261–262
Griffin, Adm. R. S., 113
Grosse Île, Quebec, 41
Grosse Pointe, Mich., 258
Guerin, Alice Cuddihy (Mrs. Thomas Guerin), 71
Guild of the Infant Saviour, 247
Gwyn, Quintin Jermy, 245

Hamill, Pete, 278
Hamilton, Alexander, 28
"Harbor Hill," Long Island, Mackay estate, 140–141, 196
Harding, Warren G., 66, 111, 112, 119, 126; death, 117–118; election, 109; Fall and Doheny as friends, 109; investigation of his conduct, 118, 123; in oil lands case, 113, 115–116
Harding, Mrs. Warren G., 117, 147
Hargrove, Marion, 291
Harper's Bazaar, 220
Harriman, E. H., 155
Harris, Basil, 229
Harris, Mrs. Basil, 248
Harris, Basil, Jr., 233
Harris, Charlotte McDonnell, 7, 96, 97, 184, 233, 272, 279, 285
Harris, Heidi Vanderbilt (Mrs. Jones Harris), 285
Harris, Jed, 285
Harris, Jones, 285

Hartigan, Monsignor, 239
Harvard Business School, 262
Harvard University, 43, 92, 235, 239
Hawthorne, Rose, 68
Hayden, Stone & Company, 175
Hays, Will, 182, 184
Hazard, Robert, 19
Hearst, George, 143
Hearst, William Randolph, 143
Helmsley, Harry, 249
Hennessy, Barbara McDonnell (Mrs. John F. Hennessy, Jr.), 98, 233
Henri, Robert, 226
Henri d'Orléans, 245
Herbert, Victor, 277
Hertz, John D., 179
Hill, James J., 155
Hill, Lord George, 28
Hitz, William, 132
Hoehling, Adolph A., 124
Hogan, Frank J.: in Doheny's trials, 122, 124–126, 131–132; in Fall's trial, 128–131
Hoguet, Robert Louis, 229
Hoguet, Mrs. Robert Louis, 91, 229
Hoguet family, 238
Holy Cross University, 238–239
Homestake mine, 143
Hoover, Herbert, 66
Hope Diamond, 145–146, 148
Hopkins, Mark, 135
Hughes, Charles Evans, 65, 164
Humphrey, George, 205
Huntington, Collis P., 135
Huntington, U.S.S., 110, 111
Hyde, H. B., 153
Hyde, James Hazen, 153–155

"Inisfada," Manhasset, Long Island, Brady estate, 192–194, 196–197

Murray, John F. (Jack, son of Thomas E. Murray), 45, 48, 49, 59, 88–90

Murray, John F., Jr. (Jake), 239, 285; *The Devil Walks on Water*, 250, 288

Murray, Joseph Bradley, 46, 48, 49, 87–90, 92, 95, 226; family, 88; marriage, 22, 58–60

Murray, Marie, *see* Lufkin, Marie Murray

Murray, Patricia, 94

Murray, Philip A., 229

Murray, Rosamund (Mrs. Buckley Byers), 96, 98–99

Murray, Theresa Farrell (Mrs. Joseph Bradley Murray), 88, 231; marriage, 22, 58–60

Murray, Thomas E., 22, 35–39, 49, 52–54, 58, 71, 148, 190, 199, 232, 250, 285; Catholic beliefs and practices, 36–38; death, 53; early career, 23–25; family, 35, 37–39, 46–49, 54, 75, 287; fortune, size of, 53; house, 783 St. Marks Avenue, Brooklyn, 36; inventions, 24–25, 35, 36, 38–39, 45, 54, 87; marriage, 25, 35; Papal honors, 36, 244; petition on his trust fund, 6, 301–304; Southampton house, 45; will, 90

Murray, Thomas E., Jr., 46–48, 89–94, 97–100, 200–207, 223–224, 229, 239, 243, 250; on Atomic Energy Commission, 202–206; atomic energy control, ideas on, 203–207; *Nuclear Policy for War and Peace*, 206–207; Papal honors, 91, 244; patents, 201; quarrel with his brother Jack, 89–90

Murray, Thomas E., II, 233

Murray, Mrs. Thomas E., Jr., 48, 231

Murray family, 5–6, 39, 58, 85, 87, 90–91, 103, 149, 175, 182, 184, 186, 200, 224, 228, 238, 241, 247; intellectual life, 250–251; at Southampton, 46–49, 51, 52, 93

Murray Hill Hotel, New York, 77

Murray Manufacturing Company, 36, 99

Nantasket, Mass., 185

National Cigarette Company, 152

National Review, 218, 219

National Security Council, 204

Navy Department, U.S., oil lands leased, 110–111, 113, 133

New Orleans, 150

Newport, R. I., 40–41, 236–237

Newsweek, 72

New York (City): churches, fashionable, 248; Irish immigrants in, 16–20, 41; Police Department, Lexow Committee investigation, 34–35

New York (State): Assembly, 31; Senate, 31–35

New York Archdiocese, 5, 249, 262, 266

New York Athletic Club, 232, 270

New York *Daily News*, 100, 207

New Yorker, The, 73, 141, 278

New York *Evening Post*, 63

New York *Journal*, 96

New York *Mirror*, 96

New York Stock Exchange, *see* Stock Exchange, New York

New York *Sun*, 17

318

Ryan, Ida Barry (Mrs. Thomas Fortune Ryan), 150, 153, 157

Ryan, Irene McKenna (Mrs. Allan A. Ryan), 172

Ryan, Janet Newbold (Mrs. Allan A. Ryan, Jr.), 172

Ryan, John Barry, 169, 171, 172, 232

Ryan, John Barry, Jr., 173

Ryan, John Barry, III, 173

Ryan, Joseph, Jr., 173

Ryan, Joseph P., 229

Ryan, Mrs. Leonard, 295–297

Ryan, Margaret Kahn (Mrs. John Barry Ryan, Jr.), 173

Ryan, Margaret Moorhead Rea (Mrs. Thomas Fortune Ryan II), 173

Ryan, Mary T. Nicoll (Mrs. Thomas Fortune Ryan), 157–158, 169

Ryan, Mayme Cook Masters (Mrs. Thomas Fortune Ryan II), 173

Ryan, Miriam, 170

Ryan, Nan Morgan (Mrs. John Barry Ryan), 172

Ryan, Nannie Moore (Mrs. Joseph Ryan, Jr.), 173

Ryan, Philip, 149

Ryan, Priscilla St. George (Mrs. Allan A. Ryan, Jr.), 172

Ryan, Theodore, 172

Ryan, Thomas Fortune, 150–158, 163, 165, 172, 178; and Allan, his son, 158, 165, 168; converted to Catholicism, 150–151; and Equitable Life Assurance Society, 153–156; second marriage, 157–158; in tobacco industry, 152; will and estate, 169–170

Ryan, Thomas Fortune, II, 173

Ryan family, 149–150, 171–174, 232

Rye, N.Y., 46

Sachs, Dr. Julius, 236

Sachs Collegiate Institute, 236

Sacred Heart, Order of, 84; nuns, 240; schools, 239–241

Sacred Heart Convent, Tarrytown, N.Y., 85

St. George's School, 237

St. Jude Children's Hospital, Memphis, Tenn., 245

St. Louis, 150

St. Michael's College, Toronto, 239

St. Patrick's Cathedral, New York, 84, 96, 174, 248

St. Paul, 150, 223

St. Paul's School, 235

St. Vincent's Hospital, New York, 248

Saltaire, Fire Island, 232

Sanford, John, 79

San Francisco, 135–137, 142–143, 150, 224

Saturday Evening Post, 65, 117

Scandinavian Catholics, 223

Schenck, Joseph M., 181–182

Schiff, Jacob H., 154–155, 173

Schiff family, 59, 103

Schwab, Charles M., 59, 174; Allan Ryan and, 158, 163, 169, 171

Securities and Exchange Commission, 180–181, 275

Senate Committee on Public Lands and Surveys, 118

Sharon, William, 135

Sharon, Conn., 212

Sheehan, William, 280

Sheen, Monsignor Fulton J., 96–98, 258

319

322

73 74 75 76 77 10 9 8 7 6 5 4 3 2 1